The Many Faces of Socioeconomic Change

Critical Frontiers of Theory, Research, and Policy in International Development Studies

Series Editors

Andrew Fischer, Naomi Hossain, Briony Jones, Alfredo Saad Filho, Benjamin Selwyn, and Fiona Tregenna

The contemporary world is characterized by massive wealth alongside widespread poverty, inequality, and environmental destruction – all bound up through class, race, and gender dynamics of inequality and oppression.

Critical Frontiers in International Development Studies, the official book series of the Development Studies Association of the UK, was established to contribute to critical thinking about local, national, and global processes of structural transformation. The series publishes cutting-edge monographs that promote critical development studies as an interdisciplinary and applied field, and shape the theory, practice, and teaching of international development for a new generation of scholars, students, and practitioners. As the series evolves, we wish to publish a diverse and inclusive range of authors whose work engages in critical, multidisciplinary, decolonial, and methodologically plural development studies.

The Development Studies Association (DSA) is delighted that Oxford University Press has re-issued John Toye's final book, *The Many Faces of Socio-economic Development*, as part of the DSA-OUP book series. Entitled *Critical Frontiers of Theory, Research, and Policy in International Development Studies*, John's book is a perfect fit, offering a critical reading of the full range of ideas about development that have emerged over the past three centuries and which continue to shape development thinking and practice today. In addition, John was DSA President from 1994-1996 and a continuous source of support and advice to Adam Swallow at OUP as it sought to capture and publish the best development research. Given the DSA's commitment to advancing the field of development studies and to challenging multiple inequalities, we are particularly pleased that *The Many Faces of Socio-economic Development* will be re-issued as a paperback and as an open access publication. Our thanks to the DSA and one of John's former institutions, Oxford University, for the financial support that has made this possible. We hope it will be widely read and help to inspire current and future generations of development scholars and practitioners.

Andrew Fischer, Naomi Hossain, Briony Jones, Alfredo Saad Filho, Benjamin Selwyn, and Fiona Tregenna (DSA-OUP Book Series Editors)
Adam Swallow (OUP Economics Editor)
Sam Hickey (DSA President, 2020-2023)

The Many Faces of Socioeconomic Change

John Toye

OXFORD
UNIVERSITY PRESS

OXFORD
UNIVERSITY PRESS

Great Clarendon Street, Oxford, OX2 6DP,
United Kingdom

Oxford University Press is a department of the University of Oxford.
It furthers the University's objective of excellence in research, scholarship,
and education by publishing worldwide. Oxford is a registered trade mark of
Oxford University Press in the UK and in certain other countries

Published in the United States of America by Oxford University Press
198 Madison Avenue, New York, NY 10016, United States of America

British Library Cataloguing in Publication Data
Data available

Library of Congress Cataloging in Publication Data
Data available

ISBN 978-0-19-872334-9 (Hbk.)
ISBN 978-0-19-288201-1 (Pbk.)

To Janet in celebration of fifty years of our marriage,
with love and gratitude.

Foreword

This ambitious work covers over three centuries of development and thinking about development. It is impressive in its scale – in coverage of thought and time and of theory and contexts. *Many Faces* provides brilliant sketches of the ideas of a huge range of thinkers. Stimulating, provocative and enjoyable, it is an excellent reflection of the breadth, depth, and erudition of John Toye himself.

John, who sadly died in 2021, was a scholar, historian, and development analyst who invariably assumed the role of Adam Smith's 'impartial spectator' in exploring and evaluating development issues. He was an economist, but not in the narrow, technical, ahistorical form that dominates contemporary economics. John was immersed in ideas, not just methods, about how to understand the opportunities for human flourishing. These qualities are all apparent in *The Many Faces*.

The world has changed massively and at an accelerating rate over the last three centuries. The focus of the book is on the views of the major analysts of development rather than the actual processes of transformation that occurred. The vast changes in the role of the state, the structure of the economy, ideas about individuals and collectives, the class composition of society, trade and globalization, education and technology, and incomes and poverty, over these centuries form a quiet background to the evolving analysis.

It soon becomes clear from John's account that the insights and arguments of the early thinkers – Adam Smith, Ferguson, Petty, Herder, Montesquieu, Condorcet, Guizot – remain amazingly relevant. Their thinking is so frequently echoed in later writings. For example, many of the early authors observed and predicted that capitalist development would result in rising inequality – look at the work of contemporary scholars (Atkinson, Milanovic, Piketty, and so many others) to see these debates continuing. Others noted that capitalism was associated with the creation of artificial wants such that there would never be enough goods or services to reach an equilibrium in which all were satisfied: reflecting the present-day dilemmas of unsustainable levels of consumption and resource use.

Contemporary debates (and deep anxieties) about identity and conflict are also in evidence. In the late 18th century, Herder noted that there was not one culture but many, and that each was to be valued – presaging some of the views of Amartya Sen in *Identity and Violence*. Montesquieu argued that the development of commerce would reduce conflict ('doux commerce'), a controversial perspective which is still contested. (As we write Russia's post-1990 engagement with capitalist commerce seems anything but 'doux' as it applies its oil and gas-created wealth to invading Ukraine and threatening nuclear warfare). The 19th century debates the book explores, concerning the objectives of development–utility maximization, human rights – presage contemporary discussions on the relative importance of incomes, happiness, and capabilities as overriding objectives.

The title of John's book (*The Many Faces of Socioeconomic Change*) can be taken in two very different directions. On the one hand, as the manifold ways in which the concept of 'development' can be interpreted – as a normative project, or as an analysis of the dynamics of societal change, or as a set of interventions in which societies are consciously developed, usually by elites and often by outsiders. Alternatively, the many faces may reflect the different trajectories that countries have taken, as illustrated in chapter four of this volume, presenting fascinating vignettes on the differing trajectories of Japan, China, Russia, and India. This book provides rich insights on both interpretations.

Historically most of those writing about development provide optimistic analyses – envisaging the possibilities, even likelihood, of progress, and often valiantly claiming that they know how to achieve it. Rostow went furthest in this view, perhaps, arguing around 1960 that a dozen or more countries could achieve self-sustaining growth by 1970. Yet, perhaps befitting the role of an 'impartial spectator', Toye himself is more downbeat in his conclusion. In the final chapter he suggests that neo-liberalism may be 'the last grand narrative of development', as those who analyze development focus on micro-level studies and randomized control trials. We should not take this conclusion as definitive, but rather as indicative: a challenge to future generations of thinkers. As the book shows so powerfully, brilliant and creative thinkers have been responsible for successive grand narratives of development that have waxed and waned and returned over the centuries. It seems highly unlikely that this will or should stop now.

Frances Stewart, Professor Emeritus of Development Economics, University of Oxford and DSA President 1990-1992

David Hulme, Professor of Development Studies, University of Manchester and DSA President 2014-2017

Preface

Anyone who has spent an adult lifetime lecturing to university students, as I have, has probably shared my experience of bafflement when meeting again former students who quote back to me things that they recall from my lectures and has wondered: Did I really say that? I wonder why? What could I have meant? Is it true? Yet my aphorisms, whatever they were, had made a lasting impression on at least one hearer.

We are very impressionable in our student days, and I recall mine with greater clarity than I do my time as a lecturer. One incident remains vividly in my memory. When I was first studying the economics of development, I attended a class given by the young Bill Warren, a Glaswegian and a neo-Marxist, on the activities of trades unions in Africa. Warren gave an interesting and well-informed account of their structure, behaviour, and impact on the labour market. The Head of the Department was sitting in on the class, presumably as part of some sort of quality control exercise, and at the end of the class complained in the hearing of everyone in the room: 'Bill, you are supposed to be teaching the young people economics, but what you are teaching them is sociology!'

My first reaction to this reprimand was one of indignation on behalf of the young lecturer whom the Head of Department had crassly humiliated in front of his students. My next thought was of the absurdity of insisting on analysing development by means of an economic logic that is devoid of social content. How could an economics that has nothing to say about the operations of the trade unions produce a credible analysis of the labour market in Africa, or anywhere else?

In the past fifty years, the separation of economics and non-economic disciplines has worsened, for reasons that I have discussed elsewhere. The growing intellectual distance has been camouflaged by the move by economists onto subject matter previously treated by other social science specialists—historians, sociologists, and political analysts. The emergence of the economics of politics is by no means a move towards convergence of disciplines or disciplinary cooperation: it is an assertion of the relevance of the economists' toolkit of parsimonious modelling, data collection, and econometrics to subjects previously analysed by other methods, now condemned as 'primitive' and 'soft'.

A recent example of the expansion of economic methods into novel subject areas is the analysis of civil wars in developing countries. The method was used to formulate a simple algebraic model of the costs and benefits of rebellion for potential rebels. This confers a false air of precision on fuzzy concepts. Numerical proxies are then regressed on the outbreak of civil wars. The regression statistics are satisfactory, so a new universal proposition is announced: civil wars result from greed, not grievance.

This is a false dichotomy. Material conditions clearly have a role in starting or prolonging conflicts, but individualistic theories validated by fragile empirical proxies sweep specificity and contingency out of sight and generate explanations that are reductionist and misleading.

Specific rebellion scenarios must be understood in their social context. These are often struggles over distribution and to that extent involved the motive of greed, but in Southern Nigeria, for example, there was also a motive of grievance—the gross and self-serving corruption of public officials. Traditional mechanisms for ensuring accountability were available to legitimate remedies for the grievances of the marginalized. The formation of youth militias and vigilante groups is a recognized community response for pursuing accountability and rectifying grievance. To treat rebellion as the outcome of a cost/benefit calculation is an oversimplification. To ask whether a rebellion's cause is either greed or grievance is to set up a false dichotomy: most rebellions will be driven by both.

The greed or grievance controversy illustrates a broader point. An attempt to focus narrowly on economic concepts in theorizing involves stripping away and discarding sociological variables, especially when they are difficult to measure. This residue is often referred to as 'the sociological tangle', but it provides the social context in which economic models produce their results. Development is too large a subject to be reduced to economic development. Economics without sociology is only half of the story; most the great writers on the subject realized that they needed to analyse socioeconomic development.

Acknowledgements

The original idea for this book came from Sophie Ahmed when she was a commissioning editor at Polity Press. I wrote the first two draft chapters quickly enough, but my responsibilities as Director of the Institute of Development Studies at the University of Sussex precluded further work on the draft. I thank Sophie for her understanding in releasing me from my contract.

The experience of co-directing the E.S.R.C.-funded Global Poverty Research Group strengthened my interest in the interface between economics and sociology in the history of development theory. I would like to pay a special tribute to David Hulme, who co-directed the Group, and to thank its members who contributed to the special issue of the *Journal of Development Studies* (Volume 42, Number 7, December 2006).

I owe a great debt to Adam Swallow, the Economics Editor at Oxford University Press, for agreeing that I should make a fresh start in the writing of the book; for his kindness and patience when I suffered various forms of ill health that made me miss deadlines; and for his astute editorial comments when the draft text was finally submitted. For the past few months, I have been fortunate in having the services of two good research assistants, Ola Akintola in Oxford and Peerapat Chokesuwattanaskul in Cambridge, and I wish to thank them warmly for their help in completing the manuscript. Finally, I must express my gratitude to those friends and colleagues who have offered me encouragement and support, and various forms of practical assistance. Without implying that they would agree with the contents of this book I mention Tony Atkinson, Ha-Joon Chang, Valpy Fitzgerald, Richard Kozul-Wright, Finn Tarp, and Richard Toye.

I have been extremely fortunate in receiving the assistance of an excellent production team at Oxford University Press. I would like to thank Katie Bishop, Lisa Eaton, and Charles Lauder very sincerely for all their efforts on my behalf during the publishing process for this book. They have made every allowance for my physical limitations and diminished capacities. I greatly appreciate their care and consideration.

John Toye

Pinehurst, Cambridge
December 2016

Contents

1

Introduction to ideas of development

Among the delusions which at different periods have possessed themselves of the minds of large masses of the human race, perhaps the most curious—certainly the least creditable—is the modern soi-disant science of political economy, based on the idea that an advantageous code of social action may be determined irrespectively of the influence of social affection.

—John Ruskin, *Unto This Last*

The aim of this book

This book provides a survey of different ways in which the economic, socio-cultural, and political aspects of human progress have been studied since the time of Adam Smith. Inevitably, over such a long time span, it has been necessary to concentrate on highlighting the most significant contributions, rather than attempting an exhaustive treatment. The aim has been to bring into focus an outline of the of the main long-term changes in the way that socioeconomic development has been envisaged.

The argument presented is that the idea of socioeconomic development emerged with the creation of grand evolutionary sequences of social progress that were the products of Enlightenment and mid-Victorian thinkers. By the middle of the twentieth century, when interest in the accelerating development gave the topic a new impetus, its scope narrowed to a set of economically based strategies to accelerate economic development. After 1960, however, faith in such strategies began to wane, in the face of indifferent results and a general faltering of confidence in economists' claims to be scientific experts. In the twenty-first century, development research is being pursued using an array of fragmented and disconnected methods. It has become a tool kit from which practitioners select techniques that they regard as most reliable and useful.

At present, the question of the methodology of social science is again in a state of turmoil. The recent financial and economic crisis has fed and intensified the sense of disarray. The role that economists played in the huge concatenation of folly that produced the Great Recession of 2008 onwards is now under the spotlight of public scrutiny. Why did the overwhelming majority of economists fail to anticipate the crisis? Why did they not warn the public of the dangers ahead? Why were the very few who did warn of the risks ahead reviled by their professional colleagues as 'Luddites'?

These questions have broadened out into a more widely ranging debate about the current state of the discipline of economics. Have recent events unmasked economics as a pseudo-science? Is it a body of thought that is fatally flawed as a guide to public policy? The distinguished economic commentator Martin Wolf wrote that 'even two months before the crisis broke, the chairman of the [US] Federal Reserve [Board] had next to no idea what was about to hit him, his institution and the global economy' (Wolf 2014). Wolf's description of Ben Bernanke as 'almost clueless' invites questions about how well current economics training fits public officials for dealing with the real world.

This question is of major concern to many students and would-be students of economics. As a result of these anxieties, many of them are turning away from the subject, but some are campaigning for a new economics curriculum. They say, justifiably, that they do not want to be fed with shoddy or misleading material, especially at a time of rising university tuition fees. They are demanding that the economics curriculum be rewritten so that it is better suited to the world that we live in, and in which they will be seeking employment. The Institute for New Economic Thinking has a team of twenty economists in Oxford University who have set about that task and are producing a new online textbook being tried out in in different universities around the world.

It would be a gross exaggeration to say that the whole subject needs to be rewritten. The baby must not be thrown out with the bath water. The appropriate negative aim is to purge the curriculum of some key fundamental assumptions that have framed the discipline of economics: the axiom that people actually do behave rationally, that markets are perfectly efficient and that economies tend to self-stabilize and converge on equilibrium outcomes, and that these equilibrium outcomes are socially optimal. The positive aim is to create a new economics that is more realistic and more empirically grounded. This involves a better appreciation of the complexity of human motivation and of the potentially dysfunctional aspects of macroeconomic dynamics.

Without delving further into this debate, one salient feature of the students' campaign for reform deserves notice. It is their call for better teaching of economic history and the history of economic thought. It might be thought to be paradoxical to try to move forward by studying the past, but at present the past of the discipline is taught in a very selective way, if at all. University departments of economic history have been closed down or merged into larger centres of social studies; and the history of economic thought has made way in the economics curriculum for more technical and more fashionable material.

Even the *Financial Times* put its weight behind the campaign to reform the economics curriculum so that it would better reflect the problems of the real world. Two of its reform suggestions were to embrace economic history and its catalogue of manias and crashes and to pay more attention to unorthodox economic thinkers. The examples cited were Joseph Schumpeter, Friedrich Hayek, and—yes—Karl Marx. In fact, in the sixty-five study groups that have sprung up in thirty countries, the names of Maynard Keynes and Hyman Minsky also feature. In this book about ideas of socioeconomic development, Marx, Keynes, and Schumpeter are among the *dramatis personae*, along with a supporting cast of less well-known unorthodox economic thinkers.

When does the story begin?

Are you sitting comfortably? Then I shall begin. Yet before I can do that, I must know where to begin. Then I run into the problem that confronts all historians, which is the arbitrary nature of all beginnings. History is a seamless web. Historians can cut it up and give names to different 'periods', but since all beginnings have their own beginnings, historians have to find a way to break into this infinite regress.

I argue that the idea of development dates from the middle of the eighteenth century and is a product of the Scottish Enlightenment, but I also recognize the arbitrary aspect of this proposition. In the England of the mid-seventeenth century, the term 'improvement' came into frequent use in discussions of public policy, meaning gradual, but cumulative betterment of socioeconomic conditions (Slack 2014). It is necessary to explain why this does not mark the start of the story.

'Improvement' derived from land improvement and schemes to raise the productivity of land, such as clearing land for cultivation, land drainage, and cutting river channels to speed water transport of agricultural inputs and outputs. These were all worthwhile activities, usually undertaken by local landowners acting individually or collectively, but they were piecemeal and uncoordinated and often small in scale. The draining of the Fens from the 1630s was an exception, but the project was too large to succeed with the available technology (windmills) and the Fens were flooded again by the turn of the century.

Beyond the agricultural sector, men variously referred to as 'projectors', 'gentlemen adventurers', and 'undertakers' were investing in and operating new projects in manufacturing and foreign trade, some successfully, and some disastrously. They were carrying through important but relatively small-scale changes for private profit that would benefit at best only a tiny percentage of the population. The terminology of 'projecting', 'undertaking', and 'improvement' was never envisaged as applicable at the level of entire societies.

Although improvement was thought of as gradually cumulative, it never amounted to a concept of linear social progress. The historical writers of the time had not purged their narratives of myths and popular legends. They served up inaccurate chronologies of curious anecdotes often without any interpretation. When an interpretative framework was provided, it was typically the Christian narrative starting from the expulsion from the Garden of Eden and leading to the Last Judgement, which was a narrative of decline and decay. In this Christian framework, new discoveries could be explained only as manifestations of God's Providence (Slack 2014: 36–43).

Until a different valuation could be found for discoveries, the idea of development could not emerge. It came after the quarrel of the ancients and the moderns that surfaced in France in the 1690s and sputtered on there and elsewhere until1750. Originally, it was a debate about literary styles and whether writers should aim to follow classical models, but it broadened out into a division between defenders of authority in politics and religion and advocates of scientific enquiry, even if it ended up challenging the authority of Christianity and the political regime. The moderns' view won the day. Their clinching argument was that the Greek and Roman classical world had no knowledge of printing, firearms, or the nautical compass, three inventions that gave the modern world superiority in communication, the exercise of power, and long distance travel. It was precisely these three capabilities that allowed the idea of development to take hold.

Although the activities and thinking of the improvers and projectors of seventeenth-century England do not amount to a beginning to the history of the idea of development, they did lay some groundwork for it. Advocates of improvement such as John Graunt, Gregory King, William Petty, and Charles Davenant were pioneers of 'political arithmetic'. This was the collection and study of numerical information about population, land, and incomes. Their aim was numerical reasoning on matters relating to government policy. This practice, too, would feed into the idea of development.

The origin of 'development'

In 1762, Adam Smith noted the arrival into English usage of a new word borrowed from the French, the word 'develop'. In a lecture on rhetoric, he commented:

This word however has within these few years been most unaccountably thrust out of common use by a French word of not half the strength or significance, to wit Develope. This word tho of the same signification with unfold can never convey the idea so strongly to an English reader. (Bryce 1983: 3)

Smith's objection to the replacement of 'unfold' by 'develop' was not related to any difference in meaning of the two words, but to a difference in their power to communicate that meaning. Notwithstanding Smith's blast, 'develop' had acquired an important metaphorical meaning. People began to speak of the developing faculties of the human mind and then, in an active sense, of developing the faculties of the human mind. At the same time the noun 'development' was also imported from French. The word was thus rapidly connected with the central idea of the age—the advance of reason. Mental self-cultivation and the individual pursuit of enlightenment were widely celebrated aspirations of the time.

Apart from the growing popularity of 'to develop', a new vocabulary was emerging in the eighteenth century to facilitate discussion of the idea of what today we call 'development'. Two of the key English words in this new vocabulary were 'society' and 'progress', both of which acquired additional extended meanings around this time. To a literal meaning, an abstract one was added. In its literal sense, 'society' referred to acts of companionship and socializing within face-to-face communities, and voluntary association with people who were familiar. The new, extended, and abstract meaning, with the indefinite article in front, *a society*, was a collective noun that simply meant people who have a way of life in common, regardless of whether they have ever met each other. Participation in common customs and institutions, and being ruled by the same laws, was enough to constitute a society, without necessarily involving a direct network of personal social relations. The consciousness of a collective entity sustained, at least in part, by impersonal social relations was an intellectual landmark of great significance.

The new idea that the philosophers of the Enlightenment wanted to explore was that of the 'progress' of societies. The word 'progress', like 'society' itself, started with a literal meaning. It meant a journey or a procession, for example, of a group of pilgrims, or of a prince with his royal retainers moving from place to place. Around the middle of the eighteenth century, the word acquired an additional abstract sense of the movement from worse to better in the condition of a social group or nation. Progress came to signify a generalized linear improvement in the conditions of life. It represented the summing up of all the specific improvements in all the manifold piecemeal endeavours of a society as the achievement of something better than had existed in the past. This general and linear aspect of the idea of progress reinforced the earlier idea that improvement was gradual and cumulative. Now it was seen also as continuous, feeding on itself.

Philosophers wanted to express their perception that European societies had experienced an all-round gain in the course of the previous century, and had generally reached levels of living that had hardly been known before. Science had made immense strides. In medicine, Harvey had established the circulation of the blood. In physics and astronomy, Newton had laid out scientific laws that could be separated from the realm of magic and the occult. In exploring the world, European navigators had found more, but not quite all, of the unknown coasts of the world, thanks to the navigational and cartographic skills of seamen like James Cook. Drawing up 'the great map of mankind', in Edmund Burke's phrase, travellers were discovering the number and nature of the different types of human society. Commerce had flourished and furnished many new items of luxury consumption. Although not free of wars, people had not experienced wars of the same ferocity and destructiveness as the religious and dynastic struggles of the seventeenth century. Artists had produced outstanding achievements in architecture, music, literature, art, and design. All of this gradually consolidated a shared outlook that was both complacent about the present and optimistic about the future.

The new awareness of society in the abstract was not immediately accompanied by a strong sense of opposition between society and the individual. It is true that the individual began to be seen increasingly as the bearer of a unique and separated personal existence apart from society, and that books like Rousseau's *Confessions*, which dramatically enhanced this perspective, could find a ready audience. Nevertheless, this heightened individualism did not seem deeply problematic to most literati. The majority held that enhanced individualism was in harmony with social progress. As Alexander Pope put it, in what might have been the motto of eighteenth-century social thinkers, 'self-love and social are the same'.

Above all, the marketplace began to be perceived as a manifestation of that harmony. Although limited benevolence was acknowledged as a cardinal feature of human nature, individual self-seeking was perceived as socially functional, leading people to provide for the needs of others, and in ever more complex and luxurious ways. This was a further recognition of the possibility that societies could be integrated by impersonal relationships, in this case the links of the marketplace in the wider sense of an extended economic system.

'Civilization' or 'development'?

G. F. Herder's *Ideas on the Philosophy of the History of Mankind* (1784–91) stimulated a new appreciation of nationalism. Herder contested the assumption that there existed one single culture, the culture of Europe. Cultures, he asserted, existed in the plural, and all were equal in value. The culture of Europe was in no way superior to that of non-Europeans, and, optimistically, he denied that it was destined to dominate the entire globe. 'The very thought of a superior European culture is a blatant insult to the majesty of nature', he declared.

This benign interpretation of nationalism prevailed initially. However, suspicions about European ambitions of cultural domination were fed by another new word that came into prominence during the nineteenth century, 'civilization'. It had several distinct senses. One is as an ideal; another is as a process of attaining that ideal through movement to higher levels of social improvement. Civilization is the social *summum bonum*, but also the target to which societies aspire, and thirdly the process by which they approach the target. In the nineteenth century, much discourse that we would recognize as being about development was carried on in the language of civilization. Indeed, Gilbert Rist has speculated that:

> There might well have been hesitation about the right generic term for the many different practices designed to increase human well-being...'Civilization' in the transitive sense of a process—widely used until the end of the First World War— could have been brought back into currency.   (Rist 1997: 25)

It was not brought back, and instead, development became the common currency.

The reason civilization fell out of favour was because it became too controversial. A third sense of civilization is as the end result of a process of civilization—a state of achieved social improvement, as measured by greater wealth, urbanization, rule of law, and social cooperation. Claims that Europe had reached a state of civilization, while other countries were still sunk in barbarism, formed the rhetorical basis to legitimate Europe's self-appointed mission to civilize the rest of the world—including by extending colonial rule. This was a contested and resented claim. Many non-European societies regarded themselves as already civilized, and stigmatized European invaders as 'barbaric'. The normative dissonance thereby created rendered civilization an increasingly useless term for the pursuit of objective social science.

In 1935 the economist Ida Greaves made the point forcefully:

> The assumption that people who manage their production without using machines are savage, and therefore stupid; or that a belief in magic is indicative of superstitious fear while deference to a supernatural religion is a mark of civilization, may be agreeable convictions to some people, but there is no scientific index of correlation between economic and intellectual progress...The term civilization, or civilized, has acquired too many extraneous connotations to be of significance in this specific connection [of economic organization].   (Greaves 1968: 40)

Organic and constructive development

The greater currency of development exposed the different senses in which it, too, was understood. Like civilization, development can indicate an ideal end state to be striven for, a process of movement towards the ideal, or an achieved state of socioeconomic improvement. The first sense is clearly normative, the second is clearly positive, and the third is both normative and positive. Much confusion can be and has been caused by failure to keep the three meanings distinct and by blurring the distinction between the normative and the positive modes of usage.

The first positive accounts of socioeconomic development as a process had strong associations with the early theories of biological evolution. Erasmus Darwin's poem *The Temple of Nature* illustrates the closeness between the two: it was originally titled *The Origin of Society*. The literal root in 'unfolding' made the word development serviceable for use as an organic metaphor. Organic development occurs because the mature form of a biological entity is already contained in its first and simplest form, and because the conditions required for its successful growth are present. Organic development is therefore essentially passive, dependent on external conditions (the availability of light, heat, shelter, nutrients, etc.) for its mature form to be realized. This happens according to a pre-existing plan. The notion of a code or a programme which controls a natural process from start to finish adds predetermination to passivity as qualities of organic development.

In the nineteenth century the idea of development was sometimes applied to nations in this organic sense. 'Nations proceed in a course of Development, their later manifestations being potentially present in the earliest elements', is a quotation from 1861 recorded by Raymond Williams (1976: 103). In this quotation, national development is understood as a teleological evolution, with the 'earliest elements' determining the form of the 'later manifestations'. Today, one might use the analogy of DNA, the genetic material that programmes subsequent bodily growth. This is one way of understanding socioeconomic development, but by no means the only one, or the most plausible one.

Biological evolution can also be understood as a nonteleological process. Existing species may die out and new species may emerge without such events being a response to either a prior purpose or an overall cosmic goal. Extinction or survival may reflect only worse or better adaptation to the natural habitat. If that is so, 'the survival of the fittest' becomes a tautology or truism: the fittest to survive do survive under the conditions that they face, regardless of their fitness in other respects, including their powers of adaptation if conditions should change. This nonteleological version of evolution can be described as 'mechanical', because it consists of the winnowing of randomly varying life forms as a result of changing ecological conditions.

Nonteleological evolution can also be applied as a metaphor to the vicissitudes of human societies, but with differing messages. Since Charles Darwin believed that progress was in the nature of things, many that applied his arguments to human society simply assumed that they were describing the progressive improvement of mankind. By contrast, the 'Social Darwinists' supplied a darker interpretation, based on the supposition that civilized societies had partially escaped from the forces of evolution by adopting social practices (such as laws of primogeniture, poor laws, medical treatments) that encouraged eugenic degeneration of their population. That put them at a disadvantage in the struggle with less 'civilized' societies. Social Darwinism is thus a transitional theory that mixes nonteleological evolution with the consequences of human will and action.

Karl Marx stands at this theoretical crossroads. He elaborates an evolutionary theory of socioeconomic development that is essentially progressive, since one socioeconomic formation gives way to another that is more advanced. Yet a social group that is not a class, the intelligentsia, is mandated to move society to its inevitable next stage. Marx himself devotes all his personal energies to pushing it forward and recruiting others to do so as well. His critics find this combination of evolution and agency inconsistent and contradictory. Its significance is that it exemplifies the Victorian transition from an organic conception of development to a constructive conception.

In the constructive conception of development, the nature of causation is strictly instrumental. In engineering, the metal object that is forged depends only on the type of hammers used to shape it and the number, angle, and force of the blows delivered. Constructive development involves creating instruments for the purposive shaping of societies, and the channelling of economic and social processes to produce intended outcomes. It is correctly described as 'social engineering', but it is practised on entire societies. The term first came into use at the end of the nineteenth century and looked forward to the application of social scientific knowledge of societies to the manipulation of large-scale social change.

Governments had for a long time been trying to modify the behaviour of their subjects or citizens by various means—using laws, their enforcement, economic pressures, and political propaganda. The quality of social engineering depends on such influences as whether the government that attempts it is authoritarian or democratic, the scale and comprehensiveness of the attempted transformation, and whether the social science on which it is based is a reliable basis for action. The term social engineering often carries a negative connotation. This arose because in the twentieth century it often involved authoritarian governments experimenting on large populations without adequate knowledge or concern for the consequences of their experiments.

Social engineering requires social engineers. They necessarily form a political elite, but what kind of elite should it be? One answer was that it should be an elite of talent, and not a hereditary elite. In 1825, Henri, Comte de Saint-Simon argued: 'The ambition of scientists, artists and industrialists to participate in the administration of national interests is not dangerous to the community. It is advantageous rather, since they can only succeed in their ambition through solid achievements.' For most of the nineteenth century, however, older landed elites managed to hold onto political power by allying with new industrial wealth.

In the twentieth century, engineers rose to leading political positions in the Soviet Union and China. In 1986, 89 per cent of Soviet Politburo members had an engineering background and the majority of the leadership of the Chinese Communist Party were professional engineers.

In Western democratic countries, calls for a sociology that would be the leading social science had not been answered, and economists increasingly took on the role of influential policy advisors to governments. Their subject had bolstered its claims to be a science, rather than a branch of moral philosophy. It underwent a significant increase in sophistication. William Jevons, Carl Menger, Leon Walras, and Alfred Marshall all played a part in replacing the old political economy of John Stuart Mill and Karl Marx with a new 'economics' that claimed to be a science. Central to the transformation was the introduction of differential calculus into economic theory, which permitted the mathematical representation of marginal changes of its key variables. This provided economics with the mathematical calculus that gave it a patina of credibility analogous to that of natural science.

As any science becomes more sophisticated, it also becomes less intelligible to the ordinary intelligent person. The scope is increased for the growth of a mystique of expertise, in which advice becomes oracular and must be accepted on trust by the nonexperts. In its application to development, economics has enjoyed over the past hundred years an initial period of public trust followed by one of a gradual loss of confidence. While the prestige of the experts remained high, trust was forthcoming. When the experts began to quarrel on major issues, public confidence in the validity of the science started to evaporate. The trajectory of development economics is not surprising, given the multifaceted and intractable nature of the task of engineering the socioeconomic development of entire societies. It is reasonable to suppose that a range of intellectual disciplines, and not just economics, must be required for the accomplishment of such a task.

Development economics loses credibility

When the end of empire put development on the international political agenda at the end of the Second World War, little in the way of prior thinking or practical experience was ready to hand. The views of former colonial officials were disregarded as tainted by racist and discriminatory attitudes. The most original attempt to transform an entire society was the Bolshevik creation of the Soviet Union, which was flawed in many ways, nontransparent, and involved in a Cold War with the hegemonic power, the United States. Sir John Hicks defined development economics as 'a practical subject that draws on any theory relevant to it (including sociological theory)' (Hicks 1965: 3–4). With such a theoretically heterogenous subject, some basic *gestalt* must direct the modelling process.

The early development models had very restricted materials as their *gestalt*. Foremost were the modernization experiences of Eastern Europe (Rosenstein-Rodan 1943; Mandelbaum 1945; Kalecki 1954; Gerschenkron 1962). The influence of émigré economists from Eastern Europe on the early forms of development economics was a major legacy of the Second World War. An equally important legacy was the high prestige of government planning of wartime industrial production and the invention of new methods of operational research. This created confidence in the idea that a policy science of development could emerge in peacetime. The final element of the war legacy was the building of new international institutions—the United Nations, the IMF, and the World Bank—that could become the organizational drivers of a global development campaign.

These three features of the wartime and post-war scenes were ephemeral. The influence of the émigré East European economists had evaporated by the 1960s; the allure of national economic plans had also faded by then (except perhaps in the UK); and the promise of the UN had been quickly neutralized by the Cold War. By the era of decolonization while the goal of socioeconomic development became ever more popular, the capacity of economists to delineate practical strategies to reach it became more doubtful and more doubted. In the 1970s these doubts erupted into fierce controversies and contests. The return of conservative parties to power in the West unleashed the forces of globalization and established new norms of economic policy in the 1980s. These new norms were a frontal attack on a supposed syndrome of protectionism that lumped together import controls, overvalued exchange rates, and inflation. The remedies included in programmes of structural adjustment went far beyond the degree of liberalization that had brought East Asian economies rapid success. The neo-liberal agenda was succeeded by a neo-conservative one.

The neo-conservative narrative of development, with its composite syndrome of protectionism and its steam-hammer remedies, will likely be the last grand narrative of development. History has moved on and in the direction of a research method that disdains grand narratives in favour of a myriad of narrowly focused policy questions. Development economics, a practical subject, can benefit from drawing on medical evaluation methods and students should be trained in their use. However, students need and actively desire to be educated as well as trained. This book aims to educate them about the grand narratives of socioeconomic development that are now part of the history of social science.

References

Bryce, J., C., ed. (1983). *Adam Smith, Lectures on Rhetoric and Belles Lettres*. Oxford: Clarendon Press.

Gerschenkron, A. (1962). *Economic Backwardness in Historical Perspective: A Book of Essays*. Cambridge, MA: Belknap Press of Harvard University Press.

Greaves, I. C. (1968). *Modern production among backward peoples*. New York: Augustus M. Kelley. (Originally published 1935, London: Allen and Unwin.)

Hicks, J. R. (1965). *Capital and Growth*. Oxford: Oxford University Press.

Kalecki, M. (1954). El problema del financiamento del desarrollo economico. *Ell Trimestre Economico* 21(4), 381–401.

Mandelbaum, K. (1945). *The Industrialisation of Backward Areas*. Oxford: Blackwell.

Rist, G. (1997). *The History of Development: From Western Origins to Global Faith*. London: Zed Books.

Rosenstein-Rodan, P. N. (1943). Problems of industrialisation of eastern and south-eastern Europe. *Economic Journal* 53(210/211), 202–11.

Slack, P. (2014). *The Invention of Improvement: Information and Material Progress in Seventeenth-Century England*. Oxford: Oxford University Press.

Williams, R. (1976). *Key Words*. London: Fontana Paperbacks.

Wolf, M. (2014). *The Shifts and the Shocks, What We've Learned—and Have Still to Learn—From the Financial Crisis*. London: Allen Lane.

2

Evolutionary social progress, 1762–1848

I remember when we were all reading Adam Smith. <u>There</u> is a book, now. I took in all the new ideas at one time—human perfectibility, now. But some say, history moves in circles; and that may be very well argued; I have argued it, myself.

—Mr Brooke in *Middlemarch*

The idea of evolution, far from being a modern discovery, is as old as ancient Greek philosophy. Embryonic forms of a theory of evolution are to be found in the works of Empedocles and of the Latin authors Lucretius and Epicurus. Heraclitus produced another strand of evolutionary thinking based on the teleological principle, i.e. the idea that movement towards an end state is implicit in the purpose for which something exists. These early descriptions of evolutionary sequences are, however, often combined with the idea of endless repetition of these sequences over time.

By the eighteenth century, the main residue of classical thinking in European philosophy was the profoundly anti-evolutionary idea, derived from Aristotle, of the great chain of being (Lovejoy 1936). According to this, all forms of life were ranged along a chain of infinite gradations from simple to complex. This implied that life forms were of relatively recent origin (consistent with biblical stories of Creation) and were unchanged and unchanging. A few daring spirits were starting to doubt this. The Comte de Buffon set out to prove that the earth must be much older than the 4,004 years that was the conventional Christian dating of Creation. James Hutton's supported de Buffon's view. Erasmus Darwin went a step further, coupling the idea of an earth 'millions of ages' old with the claim that living things had changed and evolved during this huge time span. In a number of ways, Erasmus Darwin anticipated the evolutionary theory of his grandson Charles (King-Hele 1999, 363). Prominent philosophers of the German Enlightenment, such as Goethe, Kant, and Herder, also contributed to the theme of gradual evolution of the earth and its life forms.

These evolutionary speculations were not bolstered with much in the way of geological, archaeological, or paleontological evidence. That only began to be accumulated in the following century. So it is rather remarkable that in the middle of the eighteenth century, some Enlightenment thinkers had already propounded an evolutionary account of the development of human society. Their context in reality was that by 1760 the society and economy of Great Britain had already begun to diverge significantly from the agriculture-based societies in continental Europe. According to Wrigley (2004), by that date the economy was larger and more advanced than previous economic histories, focused around the Industrial Revolution, had implied. The question of the origins of this new and dynamic commercial society plainly invited some analysis.

The economic divergence of Great Britain may explain why the Enlightenment was not a unified movement of ideas, but one that varied significantly both in its regional manifestations in Europe and over time (Himmelfarb 2006). The Scottish Enlightenment, for example, had a different tone and took a different course from the Enlightenment in France. In both countries, no doubt, the philosophers of the day shared a similar point of departure. They all venerated science and reason. They all abhorred superstition, and looked back to classical times (mistakenly) as being free from the constraints of religion.

In France, their views often exhibited a strident anti-clericalism that openly challenged the authority of the wealthy and powerful Catholic Church. In Scotland, by contrast, the savants were much less inclined to publicize their religious beliefs, or lack of them, and to confront openly the authority of the Kirk. The classic example of prudent caution about religious beliefs was David Hume, who wrote his *Dialogues Concerning Natural Religion* (expressing scepticism of the traditional arguments for the existence of God) in the 1750s, but who on the advice of friends did not publish it during his lifetime. It appeared posthumously in 1779, and the publisher remained anonymous (Bell 1990/1779: 2). The Scottish attitude contrasted with that of the English historian Edward Gibbon, who in his *Decline and Fall of the Roman Empire*, indulged in overt anti-clerical mockery (Siedentop 2014).

Another marked difference was that the French philosophers deliberately provoked dissatisfaction with the social inequalities and political exclusiveness of the old regime in France. It was rare for a Scottish thinker to take a similar line, although John Millar, author of *The Origin of the Distinction of Ranks*, did. He favoured the abolition of slavery and supported the principles of the French Revolution. By contrast, most of the Scottish philosophers took a positive view of their burgeoning 'commercial society', illustrated by the neoclassical elegance of Edinburgh's New Town, where David Hume made his home in retirement. They wanted to explore the basis of commercial society in moral sentiment and sought to understand how it had emerged from earlier forms of society.

Travellers' tales from America

By the end of the seventeenth century John Locke's *Treatise on Government* had already argued that men gained the right to own land when they nixed their labour with the soil, but that this right to property was exercised differently according to societies' use of money and their opportunities to trade. Without money and commerce, he believed, the distribution of landed property would be more equal, regulated only by the consumption needs of the families who were farming. In the presence of money and commerce, an incentive for more extensive cultivation would be at work and lead to a more unequal distribution of landed property. He identified 'the middle of the in-land parts of America' as the place where farmers would have 'no hopes of Commerce with other Parts of the World'. He ended by asserting 'thus in the beginning all the world was America, and more so than that is now; for no such thing as money was anywhere known' (Laslett 1964: 319).

In Locke's time, the accepted accounts of human society 'in the beginning' came from the Book of Genesis, and its stories of God's creation of the world, and of Adam and Eve in the Garden of Eden. By the middle of the eighteenth century, alternative accounts began to appear from the pens of both Scottish and French philosophers. What had sparked their appearance? One important stimulus was the reports of explorers, and particularly of people who had travelled in America. Today, when explorers go for the first time to places where man has never been before, there is no life, so that all that they can do is to collect scientific samples of inert matter. The US landing of men on the moon in 1969 produced chemical and engineering discoveries, but did nothing whatever to advance anthropology or sociology. In the eighteenth century, by contrast, voyagers to places previously unknown to Europeans discovered new forms of human society. Reports of previously unknown societies gave a powerful stimulus to fresh thinking about the origin and evolution of society itself.

Among the travellers in America were two Frenchmen, who on their return to Europe published influential reports of their travels. One was Jean-Francois Lafitau's *Moeurs des Sauvages Ameriquains, comparées aux moeurs de premiers temps* (1724). The other was by Father Francois-Xavier de Charlevoix. These were widely read by the literary savants of the time (Forbes 1966: 81–96; Meek 1976). They gave detailed descriptions of the way of life of the Americans, that is to say, of the indigenous, or native, Americans. What they had to report was nothing short of astonishing to the philosophers. The travellers believed that

15

they had discovered in America people who were more primitive than any that were previously known.

The way of life of the indigenous North Americans showed no evidence of the sophisticated and extensive agriculture-based society that the Spanish *conquistadores* had encountered, when they had conquered the empires of the Aztecs in Mexico and the Incas in Peru. More surprising still, the indigenous North Americans had no knowledge of the domestication of animals. They survived almost exclusively by hunting (with bows and arrows) bison (a type of wild ox also called the North American buffalo), and by fishing and gathering nuts and fruits—although they did also cultivate maize in small gardens. The aspect of native American society that most impressed the philosophers as primitive was not its beliefs nor its customs nor its culture. It was its means of material existence, which the philosophers termed its 'mode of subsistence'.

How to make sense of this discovery? One question in particular came into many minds. Did the newly discovered natives across the ocean represent an image of what European society had been like in previous ages? If one put the Bible to one side, as the eighteenth-century philosophers tended to do, the other main source of available historical information was the classical litera-ture of Greece and Rome. This was interrogated for classical parallels to life on the plains of North America. From the pages of Thucydides, Caesar, and Tacitus, the descriptions of the Tartars and the Scythians came closest of all the ancient European tribes to travellers' descriptions of native Americans. This, incidentally, led onto speculation that the ancestors of the native Americans had arrived there by crossing the Bering Straits—a plausible theory, no doubt, but one which archaeologists and anthropologists still have insufficient evidence to confirm.

The philosophers pioneered a new method of thinking about the material foundations of society. It was based on combining descriptions from contem-porary travellers' accounts of America and descriptions from classical histor-ians as a single pool of panel data. Mixing evidence drawn from the present and the past in this way seemed to them to open up the possibility of a comparative study of human societies across both space and time. It was an imaginative leap, based on assumptions that were later challenged, that uni-fied the fields of human geography and ancient history with the aim of understanding the evolution of societies.

This intellectual leap produced the earliest attempt to construct a model of economic and social development. One important component of the model already existed in Montesquieu's *L'Esprit des Lois*, although the model itself did not. That component was a typology of modes of subsistence. In Book XVIII, Montesquieu had identified four modes of subsistence. They were engaging in trade and navigation, the cultivation of the earth, the keeping of flocks and herds, and, finally, hunting. These four material modes of living appear again and again in the social thought of Montesquieu's eighteenth-century successors, and feature centrally in the model of socioeconomic progress that Adam Smith used as the context for his lectures at the University of Glasgow on jurisprudence.

Smith was a philosopher with an intellectual range as broad as any person of his day. He wrote on the science of astronomy, on physics, on moral philosophy, and on rhetoric before publishing his great contribution to political economy, *The Wealth of Nations* in 1776. The four-stage model of social progress was expounded well before that book, in a course of lectures that he gave at the University of Glasgow in 1762–3. These remained unknown for over a century and only came to light much later in the form of two sets of lecture notes that students had written. They were most recently published as *Lectures on Jurisprudence* (Meek et al. 1978).

Adam Smith's model of socioeconomic progress

Montesquieu had discussed climate, religion, and forms of government, as well as the mode of subsistence, as influences shaping legal systems. Smith gave the mode of subsistence the central causal role in the moulding of society. Subsistence provided society with its economic foundation, which affected all its institutions, including its civil and criminal laws, and the character of its cultural life. (Here we see in embryo Marx's later distinction between an economic base and a social and political superstructure.) Smith's central analytic innovation is the placing of Montesquieu's four modes of subsistence in a chronological sequence that represents the evolution of social progress. The ordering of the sequence was inspired by John Locke's insight that America was 'a Pattern of the first Ages in Asia and Europe' (Laslett 1964: 357). The travellers' tales of native Americans were taken as a true mirror of the very first stage of society, including Europe's own distant past.

All the earliest societies were said to be organized around hunting, fishing, and the collection of such edible nuts and fruit as were naturally provided, in the way reported of the native population of North America. This idea could easily have been regarded as blasphemous. The Book of Genesis (chapter 4, verse 2) says explicitly of the sons of Adam that 'Abel was a keeper of sheep' and that Cain was 'a tiller of the ground'. According to the Bible, Cain and Abel were not hunters, gatherers, or fishermen. The philosophers, however, fudged this difficulty by conceding the point, while asserting that in the beginning the world *was* America, *but only after the Flood*—a wholly unconvincing compromise with biblical orthodoxy.

17

The second epoch in the model was based on the domestication of animals and the management of flocks and herds. These pastoral societies were supposed to be at first nomadic, like those of the Tartars and the Scythians. Later they were said to become sedentary, as the nomads found land suitable for permanent pasturage.

In the third age or stage of the model, the sedentary pastoralists began to cultivate what had previously been their permanent pasture, living off the harvests they could raise. Finally, when all the land available for agriculture was being exploited, the modern age arrived, in which people's subsistence was primarily derived from the pursuits of trade and commerce.

In the model, these four epochs follow one another in time, and the sequence is progressive, in the sense that each one brings human institutions and culture to a higher level of development than the one that existed in the previous period. The superiority of each stage over those that preceded it was not only a matter of increased wealth and income. It comprehended also the greater size, complexity, and sophistication of the society's institutions, its legal system, its government, its religious establishment, and its greater mastery of the skills of artisan craftsmanship and the fine arts. (As regards the latter, the outstanding illustration of commercial society was the technical sophistication, aesthetic qualities, and marketing innovations of Josiah Wedgwood's pottery.)

In their recognition of commercial society as the culmination of social improvement, the Scottish philosophers remained firmly in the tradition of Montesquieu. He had singled out commerce, *le doux commerce,* as he called it, as a powerful force for advancing civilization. Apart from the creation of new types of contract and financial instrument to facilitate foreign trade, and the opportunity to acquire new knowledge and skills from other cultures, he thought that the practice of commerce would humanize politics, improving the quality of government. He thought that a flourishing commerce would deter monarchs from entering capriciously into bloody quarrels with their neighbours. By creating a mutual interest in preserving peace, commerce would limit the impulses that had previously led to princely aggression. This in turn would lighten the burden of taxation and hasten the accumulation of national wealth. At the same time citizens who devoted themselves to mercantile activities would acquire greater gentility of manners, and avoid extreme and destructive passions (Hirschman 1977: 60–3). From the creation and growth of the economic interests of both sovereigns and citizens, he believed that one could reliably predict the emergence of a more rationally governed society.

In his Glasgow lectures, Smith uses the four-stage theory of progress to explain the growth and evolution of different types of law, contract, and regulation. He uses the same theory to expound the emergence of property relations, social hierarchy, and different forms of government. Changes in both jurisprudence and politics are related back causally to his quite precise scheme of successive modes of subsistence. He maintained that 'in a certain view of things all the arts, the sciences, law and government, even wisdom and virtue itself tend all to this one thing, the providing meat, drink, rayment, and lodging for men'.

Although Adam Smith was the originator of the four-stage model, he was not its only exponent. Many writers of the Scottish Enlightenment, such as Smith's associates Sir John Dalrymple and Lord Kames, made use of it. The model also appears in Adam Ferguson's *Essay on the History of Civil Society* (1767), John Millar's *The Origin of the Distinction of Ranks* (1771), and William Robertson's *History of America* (1777). Each treated it somewhat differently, but these differences are much less important than the fact that it served as a major theme of the work of the most advanced social thinkers of the time in Scotland.

The idea of the noble savage

The French *lumières*, by contrast, had little enthusiasm for Smith's four-stage model. It can be found in the published work of Turgot and Helvétius. It did not, however, merit an article in Denis Diderot's *Encyclopédie*, where it appears only as a contextual influence on the way that some of the other articles were written. Most conspicuously, it found no favour with Jean-Jacques Rousseau, who challenged the assumption that the move away from the savage state constituted progress. He held that a man in the savage state had the noblest character—one of simplicity, innocence, and integrity of feeling, in contrast to the elaborate manners of eighteenth-century French society, which were artificial and false.

Rousseau's radical rejection of the model in the name of the authenticity of the primitive foreshadowed the romanticism that would increasingly colour European thought in the next decades. His dissent pointed up the lack of a psychological and spiritual dimension in the Enlightenment's view of social development. Surely, Rousseau's dissent implicitly asked, there is a deep superficiality and complacency in accepting the polished and refined face of the new commercial society as the apogee of human development? That question still seemed eccentric in the eighteenth century when the mainstream expectation, indeed hope, was that involvement in economic activity and wealth accumulation would precisely 'repress certain human drives and proclivities and ... fashion a less multifaceted, less unpredictable, and more "one-dimensional" human personality' (Hirschman 1977: 132). Nonetheless, Rousseau's doubts foreshadowed the later accusation that the social philosophy of the Enlightenment was suffused with bourgeois optimism.

Problems with Smith's account of progress

In addition, the imaginative leap underlying Smith's model also came in for criticism. Dugald Stewart, one of Adam Smith first biographers, criticized the underlying method of speculative or conjectural history. He pointed out that the method proceeded by assuming the uniformity of human nature, and then by imagining how a person of such a nature would react in a given set of material circumstances. This picture would, he suggested, not necessarily correspond with what had actually happened.

However, it should be said in their defence that the Scottish philosophers were not deliberately ignoring established facts, but merely using conjecture to make good the absence of established facts. The first domestication of animals, the invention of agriculture, and the very beginnings of towns and commerce occurred in the Neolithic period of 10,000 to 3000 BC. This is the era of prehistory, and prehistory by definition is the era when there are no written historical facts. The science of identifying seeds and bones that now permits better understanding of prehistory did not then exist. Speculation was the only game in town.

What the eighteenth-century imagination had produced was a schematic sequence of unfolding or evolving progress, a rational account of the stages that apparently must have taken place in order for societies to get from hunting and gathering to the way of life that the eighteenth century knew and experienced. Perhaps it was not surprising that Enlightenment philosophers made their 'must have been' a process of the accumulation of social knowledge. However, as such, the four-stage theory was especially vulnerable to two critical questions. If the model were to remain a central focus of discourses on development they had to be resolved, but in fact the theory was not robust enough to provide any resolution.

One criticism concerned the succession of stages. Was it really true that the modes of subsistence followed one after the other, and did not coexist in the same society? Was not the typical European society of the day a mixture of commercial, agricultural, and pastoral? Typologies are all very well, but do societies never come in mixed genres? Was this mixing just the result of overlooking the overlaps of untidy transitions between epochs, or was the theory an oversimplification?

Today, the application of modern scientific methods, such as radiocarbon dating, accelerator mass spectrometry, and gene and chromosome analysis, to the remains of seeds and bones provides us with a very different and more complex picture of development in the prehistoric era. What these modern methods have not overturned is the proposition that initially all people were hunter-gatherers, thereby contradicting the Genesis stories. What is disputed is a subsequent succession of pastoralist and agricultural stages. Where food production emerged, the processes of seed and animal domestication seem to have gone hand in hand, and neither process was linked to whether people were nomadic or sedentary (Diamond 2005: 100, Table 5.1). Some nomadic people were cultivators of crops and some sedentary peoples, like the aborigines of Australia, never became food producers at all.

Secondly, the four-stage model did not explain clearly how the supposed transitions between epochs take place. It lacked convincing dynamics. The Scottish philosophers were impressed by the fit between the mode of subsistence and the arts and institutions of society. They were not clear on how the change from one good fit to another good fit came about. Adam Smith appealed to the pressure of population increase as the spur of innovation. 'As their numbers increased, [people] would be necessitated to contrive some other method whereby to support themselves', he speculated. Was it really just a matter of necessity being the mother of invention in the mode of subsistence—hunger provoking a discovery that led to the diffusion of a crucial innovation?

Adam Smith argued that 'the contrivance they [i.e. the hungry hunters] would most naturally think of would be to tame some of those wild animals that they caught'. His model of social learning implicitly assumes that there existed equal opportunities for this kind of learning and innovation. He assumed that animals that humans could domesticate are found everywhere and that the sole problem is for the humans to realize that the animals can be tamed, and to work out a method of doing so. Modern research tells us that this was not so. Animals that could be domesticated and plants that could be cultivated were not, in fact, distributed equally across the surface of the globe. The initial distribution favoured Europe and Asia, where domestication of wheat, peas, olives, rice, millet, sheep, goats, pigs, and silkworms had taken place by 7500 BC. This early start compared with America, where people had domesticated corn, beans, squash, potato, manioc, sunflower, turkey, and llama only as late as 2500 BC (Diamond 2005). The nature and pace of development in different parts of the world was constrained by marked variations in their original natural endowments, and not just by the speed of social learning. The successful development of commercial society that Europeans tended to attribute to their own enterprise and ingenuity had other, and less self-flattering, causes.

Burke and Condorcet on revolution in France

The outbreak of the French Revolution was the event that finally shattered facile optimism about social progress. Edmund Burke's *Reflections on the Revolution in France* (1790) most dramatically marked the rupture. Burke had

21

previously supported liberal causes, sympathizing with the revolt of the American colonists and prosecuting Warren Hastings and the East India Company for their depredations in India. However, he bridled at the militant anti-Catholicism of the French *philosophes*, which reached its political culmination in November 1789, when the French National Assembly nationalized the property of the Catholic Church. Burke thought he detected a conspiracy of the enlightened to demolish venerable institutions and to replace them with new ones fashioned according to theoretical reasoning. He predicted with perspicacity and prescience how vulnerable such a newfangled political order would be to the forces of fanaticism, zealotry, terror, and war.

Burke laid out a vision of terrifying pessimism, of a revolution of great ferocity spreading from France to England and to the rest of continental Europe. Heralded by beguiling ideas like the rights of man and slogans like 'liberty, equality and fraternity', it would unleash 'the swinish multitude' (Burke's words), provoke violence and chaos, breed new forms of tyranny, and pull down such social progress as the eighteenth century had achieved. Yet Burke's *Reflections* overstated and overdramatized the failures of the *philosophes* and the travails of Europe. Although the French *philosophes* were highly critical of the *Ancien Régime* in France, they were not by temperament revolutionaries, nor did they (with one notable exception) participate in the French Revolution. They did favour—often in a rather vague way—various reforms, but most would have preferred to see them carried through by an enlightened despot. Voltaire paid court to Frederick II of Prussia, as did Diderot to Catherine the Great of Russia. An appeal to the people was not on their agenda, because such a small proportion of the population was deemed capable of being educated and there was a pervasive fear among the *philosophes*, too, of the rabble going on the rampage.

The Marquis de Condorcet was the exception, the only *philosophe* who engaged with the Revolution, and his engagement cost him his life. Building on the ideas of his patron Turgot, he argued, in his *Esquisse d'un tableau historique des progres de l'esprit humain* (1794), that a correct understanding of past experience allowed one to foresee the future trajectory of the human mind with confidence. Further, because the past had represented the slow accumulation of knowledge and civilization at the expense of superstition and despotism, the future would see further progress in the same direction. In fact, he went on to forecast, with just as much prescience as Burke, the abolition of slavery, the end of colonialism, and the elimination of other socially imposed forms of inequality. Against Burke's dark foreboding, Condorcet saw bright light at the end of history's tunnel. On his assumptions, it was reasonable to expect that the golden age lay in the future, rather than in the past. However, apart from Condorcet, the expectation of ever-continuing social improvement was itself a victim of the French revolutionary upheaval.

Guizot, liberalism, and the rise of the bourgeoisie

As the Worship of the Supreme Being succeeded the Festival of Reason, the Terror claimed further victims. After her lawyer husband had gone to the guillotine in 1794, the mother of François Guizot escaped with him, aged seven, to Geneva. There the young François was educated among fellow Protestants in classical and modern languages, philosophy, and history. Despite the wartime disruption of links between Britain and France, communications between Geneva and Britain remained open. Thus, Guizot was able to absorb the work of the social thinkers of the Scottish Enlightenment. After returning to Paris, he was appointed in 1812, at the early age of twenty-five, to be Professor of Modern History at the Sorbonne.

He became active politically as a constitutional royalist when Louis XVIII was restored to the throne in France in 1815. Guizot had a clear liberal agenda, the accountability of royal ministers to an elected chamber of deputies, and the decentralization of power, by the setting up of elected local governments. His political programme was based on his historical studies. The most significant of these was his *Histoire Générale de la Civilisation en Europe*, given as a series of public lectures in 1828. Having previously translated Gibbon's *Decline and Fall of the Roman Empire* into French, he felt able to survey the whole period of European history from the collapse of the Roman Empire to the outbreak of the French Revolution.

His historical method had a distinctly Scottish flavour to it. He insisted that it was not enough to write history as the story of different political institutions, and how they affected the societies where they existed. Rather, it was necessary first to study the composition of society, the condition of the various social ranks as determined by property ownership, and the relations between classes. These factors, he argued, shaped the nature of political institutions, before those institutions act reciprocally on the society. His *Histoire Générale* emphasized the interdependence between the state of society and politics. He applied the sociological method, which he had learned from the Scots, to the mediaeval and modern history of Europe.

In a significant way, however, Guizot went further than those who had influenced him. Unlike them, he did not limit himself to tracing a process of social development. Heeding Rousseau, he recognized the importance of the question of the development of the individual. What if society developed, but it did so in ways that were repugnant to the sensibilities of individuals, as in Rousseau's claim that French society was highly developed, yet artificial and false? Guizot's definition of civilization included both social development and the development of the individual. For him, the process of civilization was a twin development, the development of material life and the development of *une mentalité*, a mental outlook. These two sets of facts, he argued, have 'so intimate and necessary a relation between them, that if they are not simultaneously produced, they are not withstanding inseparable, and sooner or later one brings the other' (Siedentop 1997/1846: 19). In Europe, he asserted, Christianity had produced the new intellectual and moral outlook of individualism, and that outlook was intimately bound up with Europe's social and political development.

The centrepiece of his analysis of European social and political development was, however, not concerned with the role of the Church and religion, but with the history of the relations between the feudal lords and the towns. His account focuses on the economic revival of the towns in the early Middle Ages, and their resistance (which economic revival made increasingly effect-ive) to the periodic depredations of the feudal lords and their clients. In his Seventh Lecture, he discussed what he repeatedly refers to as the 'insurrections of the towns', in the course of a 'contest of classes', leading to the concession of charters that promised the inhabitants of the town freedom of movement and the freedom to buy and sell (Siedentop 1997/1846: 119–36). These were the eleventh-century beginnings, localized and unselfconscious, of a *bour-geoisie* that took another six centuries to become a formidable class.

The political thrust of this analysis was that the monarchy of the *Ancien Régime* had supported, and had itself drawn strength from the rising bourgeois class. In the era of Louis XIV, the subduing of the old feudal aristocracy by the monarchy, in alliance with a more socially extensive and coherent *bourgeoisie*, had led to an overcentralized polity that could be captured too easily by revolutionaries and counter-revolutionaries alike. That is why he campaigned for political decentralization.

Guizot's political opportunity came after the 1830 July revolution. As the first minister of King Louis Philippe between 1840 and 1848, his later career made a mockery of his earlier liberal principles. Not only did he do little to decentralize power, but he also put central power at the service of the *grande bourgeoisie*, an assortment of bankers, promoters, industrialists, and lawyers. When someone complained to him that the property qualification for voting in France was too high, he replied: 'then why don't you get richer?' Guizot's fall, after the revolution of 1848, was generally unlamented. Later, he became remembered more for his political obtuseness than for his earlier path-breaking analysis of European history. Yet that analysis forms the missing link between Adam Smith's four-stage model and the reformulation of it, with a new and very different political message, by Karl Marx.

Marx's revision of the Scottish Enlightenment model

Politically, by the middle of the 1840s, Guizot and Marx were at opposite ends of the political spectrum. The former was at the height of his power, while the latter, having been expelled from the Rhineland for offences against Prussian press censorship, was a refugee revolutionist in Paris. Marx, the rebellious infant, used his new freedom in France to ridicule publicly the bad grammar of a Proclamation issued by Frederick William IV of Prussia. The Prussians called on the French government to expel Marx from France, and it was Guizot, as Minister of the Interior, who signed the expulsion order (Fernbach 1973; Wheen 1999: 90). Marx scurried away to Brussels.

However, if Guizot the minister treated Marx shabbily, to Guizot the historian Marx already owed a very significant intellectual debt. While still in the Rhineland in 1843–4, Marx had read the works of the French historians, including those of the young Guizot. It was in these books that he found the idea that allowed him to extract himself from the philosophical dilemmas of post-Hegelian German idealism, and break out onto the terrain of economic and social reality. It was this: that class struggle was the key to understanding both social development and social psychology. Marx moved on from the Scottish philosophers' evolutionary account of prehistory to an evolutionary account of history in the very long run that was of his own making. He generalized Guizot's account of the emergence of the *bourgeoisie*, from one phase in European history to a universal truth, as applicable to the world as to Europe, and as applicable to the future as to the past.

The fact that Guizot had allied himself with the *grande bourgeoisie*, and was fully engaged in the politics of class struggle reinforced Marx's vision of the broader and continuing relevance of Guizot's historical analysis of class struggle. In the first paragraph of *The Communist Manifesto*, Marx pointed to Guizot as one of the European leaders who in 1848 was haunted by the spectre of a coming social revolution. At the same time, Marx acknowledged his intellectual debt to Guizot the historian. Not normally a modest man, Marx admitted:

> No credit is due to me for discovering the existence of classes in modern society or the struggle between them. Long before me bourgeois historians had described the historical development of this class struggle. What I did that was new was to prove: 1) that the existence of classes is only bound up with particular historical phases in the development of production, 2) that class struggle necessarily leads to the dictatorship of the proletariat, 3) that this dictatorship itself only constitutes the transition to the abolition of all classes and to a classless society. (Marx to Weydemeyer, 5 March 1852, in *Marx–Engels Selected Correspondence*, 1965: 69)

Like the Scottish philosophers and historians, Marx embraced a materialist conception of history, but unlike them he claimed that it was the phases in the development of the mode of production that mattered most, not the mode of subsistence. For him, the legal relations and political forms originating in the material conditions of life, the 'social relations of production', correspond to stages in the development of the material forces of *production* and the legal framework for the exploitation of labour that is required to unleash these productive forces.

Marx then tackled the question that the Scottish philosophers had failed to resolve, the dynamics of social change. He argued that the material forces of production and the social relations of production do not remain appropriate to each other indefinitely. At first the social relations are helpful to the emergence of new productive forces, but there comes a time when the developing productive forces come into conflict with the existing social relations of production, that is to say, the framework of property relations within which they have hitherto operated. As Marx put it, 'from forms of development of the productive forces, these relations turn into their fetters... then begins an era of social revolution'.

Was this an adequate solution to the problem of social dynamics? Some think not, arguing that this explanation involves a chicken-and-egg problem. Which comes first? Does technical change induce changes in the social relations of production, or is it vice versa (Eagleton 2012: 38–40)? This is to set up a false dichotomy. Changes in technology and changes in economic institutions occur in parallel, not in sequence. Marx is saying that sometimes they are congruent, but sometimes they are not. The guild system may support artisanal handicrafts, but may impede the emergence of large-scale manufacturing. Corn laws protect existing landlords, but restrict the food supply for an industrial labour force.

Incongruence between technical and social relations of production generates class struggle, and eventually a revolution to bring about the replacement of a dominant social class by its successor. Revolution therefore was more than an outbreak of mass violence leading to the replacement of political leaders. Each framework of property relations is the basis for the dominance of one social class. The epochs of history until Marx's time, he thought, could be defined in terms of a progression of dominant social classes and the type of property relations that established and underpinned their dominance. In broad outline, said Marx, 'the Asiatic, ancient, feudal and modern bourgeois modes of production may be designated as epochs marking progress in the economic development of society'. Each mode of production has distinct legal and social relations that legitimize the different forms of the exploitation of labour needed for production—from outright slavery to the much more subtle exploitation of the wage contract. The succession of modes of production constitutes the progressive sequence of the four stages of history that precede the classless society.

Thus, for Marx, in understanding the dynamics of social development, the modes of subsistence must be replaced by the modes of production as the key driver of the eras of human progress. By discovering the class struggle as the motor of social change, he predicted that commercial society, so esteemed by

Adam Smith, would collapse under the weight of its own contradictions. And the dictatorship of the proletariat would accomplish the final transition from bourgeois society to the classless society of socialism or communism.

Marx regarded himself as the Darwin of socioeconomic development (Postan 1971: 159–63). It is an apt comparison because, like Darwin in the biological sphere, he had found a vague theory of evolution already in existence. Yet in social science, as in biology, it was one that lacked a credible driving force. Darwin identified the driving force in biology as the process of natural selection. Marx identified the driving force of socioeconomic development as the conflict between the forces and the social relations of production, erupting at that moment as the struggle of the proletariat to supplant the bourgeoisie. As Darwin did to biology, so Marx did to social science: both men made evolution the dominant theory of the age.

References

Bell, J. M., ed. (1990). *David Hume: Dialogues Concerning Natural Religion 1779*. London: Penguin Books.

Burke, E. (2003/1790). *Reflections on the Revolution in France*. New Haven, CT: Yale University Press.

Caritat, J.-A.-N., Marquis de Condorcet (1988/1794). *Esquisse d'un tableau historique des progres de l'esprit humain*. Paris: G. F. Flammarion.

Diamond, J. (2005/1997). *Guns, Germs and Steel: A Short History of Everything for the Last 13,000 Years*. London: Vintage Books.

Eagleton, T. (2012). *Why Marx was Right*. New Haven, CT: Yale University Press.

Fernbach, D., ed. (1973). *Karl Marx: Surveys from Exile*. London: Allen Lane at the Penguin Press.

Forbes, D., ed. (1966). *Adam Ferguson: An Essay on the History of Civil Society 1767*. Edinburgh: Edinburgh University Press.

Himmelfarb, G. (2006). *The Roads to Modernity: The British, French and American Enlightenments*. New York: Vintage Books.

Hirschman, A. O. (1977). *The Passions and the Interests: Political Arguments for Capitalism before Its Triumph*. Princeton, NJ: Princeton University Press.

King-Hele, D. (1999). *Erasmus Darwin: A Life of Unequalled Achievement*. London: Giles de La Mare Publishers.

Laslett, P., ed. (1964). *John Locke: Two Treatises of Government*. Cambridge: Cambridge University Press.

Lovejoy, A. O. (1936). *The Great Chain of Being: A Study of the History of an Idea*. Cambridge, MA: Harvard University Press.

Marx, K. (1965). *Marx-Engels Selected Correspondence*. London: Lawrence and Wishart.

Meek, R. L. (1976). *Social Science and the Ignoble Savage*. Cambridge: Cambridge University Press.

Meek, R. L., Raphael, D. D., and Stein, P. G., eds (1978). *Adam Smith: Lectures on Jurisprudence*. Oxford: Clarendon Press.

Postan, M. (1971). *Fact and Relevance: Essays in Historical Method*. Cambridge: Cambridge University Press.

Siedentop, L., ed. (1997). *Francois Guizot: The History of Civilization in Europe*, trans. William Hazlitt (1846). London: Penguin Books.

Siedentop, L. (2014). *Inventing the Individual: The Origins of Western Liberalism*. London: Allen Lane, Penguin Books.

Wheen, F. (1999). *Karl Marx*. London: Fourth Estate.

Wrigley, E. A. (2004). *Poverty, Progress and Population*. Cambridge: Cambridge University Press.

3

Development within the limits of order, 1820–70

The fact is, human reason may carry you a little too far—over the hedge in fact...I have always been in favour of a little theory: we must have Thought; else we shall be landed back in the dark ages.

—Mr Brooke in *Middlemarch*

Marx's famous final comment on the philosophy of Ludwig Feuerbach was: 'the philosophers have only interpreted the world, in various ways; the point is to change it'. His own social and political theories were driven above all by the economic and social realities of his time and place and his reaction to them. For him, the truth of any materialistic philosophy was that theory and practice were fused in unity. For the rest of his life Marx, with Engels, while struggling to complete *Das Kapital*, engaged in revolutionary political activity on a Europe-wide scale.

Yet the idea that, before Marx, 'philosophers have only interpreted the world', and that he was the first to realize that the point was to change it, is surely misleading. His criticism was correctly applied to Feuerbach and some of the German post-Hegelians. It did not apply to many European intellectuals outside that tiny circle—thinkers like Saint-Simon, Comte, Bentham, and John Stuart Mill. Although they were eminent intellectuals rather than eminent philosophers, all of them actively sought new directions of social progress (Himmelfarb 2006: 95). However, they all did so burdened by the belief that the Enlightenment had taken a wrong turning, and that human reason had carried European society 'over the hedge' to a nasty landing in Napoleon's wars of conquest. They feared that the aftermath of the French Revolution and Napoleonic conquest would pose insoluble social and political problems unless the leading intellects of the age could chart a new course for Europe's development.

The French Revolution and the succeeding twenty years of war were cataclysmic events that continued to challenge the thinkers of Europe long after they were over. They were generally recognized as a structural break in the history of Europe, cutting it off from the *Ancien Régime* and opening up the prospect of a new and more problematic age. It was assumed that such progress as had been achieved in the eighteenth century was no longer guaranteed to continue and, as a result, something had to be done to ensure European society against similar revolutionary disasters in the future.

France: The reconciliation of progress with order

In France, Henri, comte de Saint-Simon and his disciple Auguste Comte exercised a powerful influence through their writings on nineteenth-century European thought. Both wrestled with the social and political legacy of the French Revolution, the Terror, and Napoleon's combination of internal reform with external conquest. They pondered what sort of future these events presaged for France and Europe. Saint-Simon saw scientists and artists as the vanguard of the society of the future, but he also acknowledged that in the recent past they had caused political disruption. He endorsed Burke's conspiracy theory of the activities of the French *philosophes*. 'The first popular movement [in France] was secretly stirred up by the scientists and artists ... [they were provoked] to exalt more and more the ambition of the ignorant, and to break the bonds of subordination which contained the wild passions of the have-nots' (Markham 1952: 3).

Nevertheless, he did not endorse the most famous rhetorical passage in the *Reflections*, Burke's great lament that 'the age of chivalry is gone [and that] of sophisters, economists, and calculators has succeeded' (Burke 2003/1790: 65). On the contrary, now that the social order of Europe had to be reorganized, past experience had taught the scientists and artists to leave direct political power in the hands of the property-owning class, while they provided the intellectual leadership for social reorganization. In this way, the repercussions of the French Revolution could be brought to closure.

At the same time as Saint-Simon gave a qualified endorsement to Burke, he gave a qualified endorsement to Condorcet's picture of the continuing progress of the human mind. The scientists and artists were the people who were able to learn from their experience and had the capacity to proceed with innovation. Provided that property owners had the political power to act as the governors of the progress of the human mind, continuing progress could be reconciled with social order.

This reconciliation would, however, require a qualification of Condorcet's views on religion. His outright anti-clericalism was now seen as a major error. His account of the priesthood as peddlers of superstition, deliberate deceivers, and exploiters of mankind had contributed to the revolutionary anarchy and violence of the have-nots. In former times, in the theological age, the Catholic Church had provided the spiritual bonds of European society. Since the subsequent advances of science had dissolved these bonds with disastrous results, the task for the future was to forge a new kind of spiritual bond in order to hold society together. Saint-Simon outlined a New Christianity that would be ecumenical, universal, and would promote a doctrine that would favour the poor: 'the rich, by increasing the well-being of the poor, would improve their own lot'. This doctrine would unite the governing elite for their social task. 'New Christianity is called upon . . . to link together the scientists, artists, and industrialists and to make them the managing directors of the human race' (Markham 1952: 89, 105).

New Christianity had an immediate political purpose. It was to be a middle way between reaction and liberalism. Writers like Joseph de Maistre and the Vicomte de Bonald supported the reactionary policies of the restored Bourbon monarchs Louis XVIII and Charles X, and their programme of restoring the divine right of kings, Catholicism of the Ultramontane tendency, and government censorship. At the other extreme, the liberal reformers like Guizot and Benjamin Constant favoured laissez-faire policies. The reactionaries wanted to restore the *Ancien Régime* in full, as if there had been no revolution, provoking Talleyrand to remark: 'they have learned nothing and forgotten nothing'. The liberals believed that a new form of society had already arrived, so reaction was an impossible political project. They were more concerned that any future revolution should be an *industrial* revolution in France, as it was in England. They did not believe, however, that an ordered society had to be united by sharing a determinate common purpose. The Saint-Simonians' middle way gained fresh political traction after the reactionary policies of Charles X had provoked the revolution of 1830 and the laissez-faire policies of Louis Philippe and Guizot had provoked the revolution of 1848.

Apart from these contemporary political issues, Saint-Simon and his disciples had a wider significance. Their call for a reorganization of European society rested on the assumption that its existing trajectory had to be redirected. It had to be changed from one where industrialists worked in isolation, the rich exploited the poor, and nations were constantly at war. A constructive response was required to create the new positive era. This could come only from an elite group of scientists and artists in alliance with a politically empowered propertied class.

This elite alliance, however, must act as trustees for the interests of the class of unenlightened have-nots, because trusteeship for the poor was the sole basis of the legitimacy of their government. In the three ideas that progress that must be consciously ordered, that a propertied class must ally with a scientific elite, and that this alliance must act as trustees for the interests of the poor, here one may discern the moment when the idea of social progress ceased to be understood as a matter of evolution and was transformed into the idea of a project of conscious and deliberate development (Cowen and Shenton 1996: 27).

The role of Auguste Comte was to expound Saint-Simonian ideas, but to insist that political and moral studies needed to be given a more scientific foundation before the elite could guide public opinion along the right lines, and that doing so was a prerequisite for devising appropriate institutions of government. The call for a more scientific foundation, however, did not mean that the science of society had to adopt the methods of the natural sciences. Comte knew that each natural science had its own scientific method. The students of society still had to devise their own scientific method, and Comte looked forward to the emergence of 'social physics' or 'sociology' (Jones 1998: xix–xx).

The method of the yet-to-emerge sociology would be to produce generalizations from history that would guide political decision-making, a proposal that begged a number of important questions. Sociology would correct the error of the economists, who had argued that the well-being of society was brought about by the operation of individual self-interest. It would put the role of sympathy, benevolence, and cooperation in the positive era on a scientific footing. This intellectual prospectus placed social scientists in a quandary. Were they to engage on free enquiry, following the truth where so ever it led them? Or were they to produce a science that provided the justification for society's common purpose and the spiritual bond that would guarantee social order? Positivism seemed to favour the latter two goals.

Britain: home of the Utilitarian calculus

In Britain, too, Jeremy Bentham was a radical legal reformer who tried to steer a middle way between reaction and revolution. His *Fragment on Government* (1776) was a critical riposte to William Blackstone's *Commentaries on the Laws of England* (1765–9). He saw Blackstone as an apologist for the existing state of English common law as much as he was an expositor of its content. Even when the common law was obscure and arbitrary, Blackstone sought to make it seem rational and just, nurturing a sense of inevitability that the law was as it was. Bentham disagreed with Blackstone's defence of judge-made law, legal fictions, social contract theory, and his appeal to natural law, a theological doctrine that was used to sanctify the legal and penal status quo—and Bentham said so in strong terms. He wanted to see England provided with a written legal code and a reformed prison system (Harrison 1948).

Bentham initially supported the French Revolution. As a result of his correspondence with Mirabeau and other revolutionary leaders, he was made an honorary citizen of France. However, after the Jacobins seized power in 1792, he applied his critical powers to demolish their discourse of natural rights, describing it as 'simple nonsense'. He wrote in *Anarchical Fallacies* (1843): 'this rhetorical nonsense ends in the old strain of mischievous nonsense for immediately a list of these pretended natural rights is given . . . and of these rights, whatever they are, there is not, it seems, any one of which any government can, upon any occasion whatever, abrogate in the smallest particle'. In addition, supporters of natural rights notoriously produced different lists when they were called upon to enumerate the natural rights.

In place of the appeal to natural rights, Bentham advocated a single principle of both individual morality and governmental action. It was so to act as to produce 'the greatest happiness of the greatest number'. He thought that the Unitarian preacher and chemical experimenter, Joseph Priestley, had originally suggested it to him. Bentham elaborated this principle—also known as the principle of utility—by arguing that both pleasure and pain are unitary concepts and polar opposites, and that the consequences of action are subject to exact calculation. This basic principle was expanded into the notion of a hedonic or felicific calculus that was capable of being applied as a decision criterion of both individual and governmental actions (Burns and Hart 1970: 11–50).

The burden of defending the principle of utility to Victorian Britain fell to John Stuart Mill, son of James Mill, who had been Bentham's secretary. The elder Mill indoctrinated the younger at an early age with Bentham's ideas. This precocious education caused J. S. Mill to have a nervous breakdown when he became aware of his own mental reservations about what he had been taught. His later attempts to qualify and refine the utilitarian doctrine in *Utilitarianism* (1863)—to distinguish higher from lower pleasures and produce a derivation for the social feelings of mankind—are rather unconvincing. In the end his defence of the principle tends to raise more doubts. His making the concepts of pleasure and pain as comprehensive as he does merely drains them of meaning. Moreover, the degree to which the consequences of action are knowable and thus calculable in terms of the principle of utility remains another significant difficulty with it.

Given his doubts about the emotional thinness of Bentham's philosophy, Mill was initially attracted to Comte's positivism. He saw Comte as an ally when writing his *System of Logic* (1843). This was a refutation of the intuitionist philosophy of William Whewell, which Mill worried could provide a basis for unreasoned and unexamined theological doctrines and associated reactionary views. However, he also approved of Comte's emphasis on the benefits of a spiritual power being active in societies, as the Catholic Church had been in mediaeval Europe, and agreed with him that 'the moral and intellectual ascendancy, once exercised by priests, must in time, pass into the hands of philosophers and will naturally do so when they become sufficiently unanimous, and in other respects worthy to possess it' (Mill 1924/1873: 179).

However, Mill broke with Comte over his later writings on the Religion of Humanity, of which Comte absurdly declared himself the high priest, and which he seemed to wish to use to control the behaviour of every member of the community. Mill saw this as a truly alarming attempt to erect a practical spiritual despotism, and a 'monumental warning to thinkers on society and politics, of what happens when once men lose sight in their speculations, of the value of Liberty and Individuality' (Mill 1924/1873: 180–1).

Mill's own credentials in relation to the value of liberty and individuality can be questioned. In *On Liberty*, he wrote in defence of the individual's unchecked exercise of both, with the sole restriction that they should not be allowed to curtail the liberty and individuality of others. However, in other writings, on the role of universities in moral education for example, he sometimes gives the impression that he did not value liberty and individuality for their intrinsic merit, but because they would inevitably lead to the establishment and preservation of the rules of conduct most advantageous for mankind—in other words, the universal adoption of the principle of utility that he espoused (Cowling 1963: 115). The idea of a body of secular moral teachers (a moral and intellectual ascendancy of philosophers) who would spread a rational moral consensus does indeed sometimes clash in his writings with his strong pronouncements in favour of liberty. Like Saint-Simon and Comte, Mill never entirely abandoned the idea of the need for a spiritual authority in society, and even changed his mind to recognize the utility of religion (Himmelfarb 2004: 94–120).

Regardless of Mill's own inconsistency on this question, the principle of utility retained a strong grip on British public opinion, especially in relation to government action. It is understandable why this should have been so. The growth of individualism and the accelerating divergence of Britain's economy and society from other agriculture-based societies during the mid-nineteenth century, including spreading secularization, left increasing numbers of the population without the psychological anchor of a settled moral life, but with an arbitrary inheritance of conflicting moral rules. As more issues had to be resolved by government action, the need for a public criterion for settling evaluative disagreements became both more urgent and more difficult to provide. The principle of utility, which apparently embodied the liberal concept of happiness, dominated all others because it was so amorphous and adaptable that it seemed to be the criterion for all contingencies (MacIntyre 1967: 243).

After the 1848 revolutions had failed, the threat of political instability and violence receded. Marx became a refugee in London, dividing his time between trying to complete *Das Kapital* in the British Museum and organizing revolutionary politics in continental Europe. By the time that he was buried in

Highgate Cemetery in 1883, his ideas had made hardly any impact in his country of self-imposed exile, although this was where, according to his own theory, they should have been most apposite. Small manifestations of Marx's political influence did appear in England in the 1880s. One was the Social Democratic Federation (SDF), founded in 1884 by the wealthy stockbroker H. M. Hyndman. Another was the rival Socialist League, founded by William Morris soon afterwards. Despite a couple of unruly demonstrations in London, a distinctively Marxist form of socialist politics never took root there. British socialism took on a defiantly anti-Marxist cast.

The elasticity of the concept of utility allowed it to be used to defend the paternalism involved in the assumption and exercise of trusteeship. The greater happiness secured for the many could be represented as the price to be paid for their lack of freedom to make their own choices. This was the context of Fabian socialism, which advanced 'schemes of [social and political] reform initiated from above by the enlightened few for the welfare of the unenlightened many' (MacIntyre 1967: 238). When the Fabian Society was established in 1884, it drew membership away from the SDF, but became clearly defined as a group of metropolitan middle-class writers and intellectuals who aspired to exercise political influence through their chosen means of advancing socialism—the writing of tracts and pamphlets and the giving of public lectures—and not organizing riots.

Their political objective was the transfer of land and industrial capital to the administration of a fully democratic state, for the general benefit of the community. They were in some respects the heirs of Saint-Simon, Comte, and the positivists, who sought the more efficient and equitable use of resources for the benefit of all and advocated the method of trusteeship as the means to achieve it (Cowen and Shenton 1996: 25–7). Many of the early Fabians were, in fact, positivists or positivist sympathizers and the ideal of scientific or rational administration was common to both positivists and Fabians (Himmelfarb 1992: 358-60). However, in politics they hoped for widening democracy to discipline a state that would gradually take over the ownership of private property.

The Fabians decisively rejected the revolutionary class politics of Marx. The transfer of resources to the control and regulation of a democratic state was to be achieved slowly and gradually, in a process of evolution, not revolution. Going slowly and accepting the inevitable delays, while not losing sight of the goal—the military tactics of the Roman general Fabius Maximus—*that* was the way to reconcile progress with order.

However, Marx and Engels had proclaimed their own political economy as 'scientific socialism', trying to give it a superior epistemological status to that of the 'utopian socialism' or 'sentimental socialism' propagated by others, including the positivists. The early Fabians needed to be able to trump that claim. They found what they needed in the new modern economics of marginal utility, which was after all just a systematic application to economic life of the utility principle. Under the guidance of two of its practitioners, Philip Wicksteed and Francis Ysidro Edgeworth, marginal utility economics had a double value. On the one hand, by showing that unearned Ricardian rent can accrue to all the factors of production, it provided a justification for the gradual transfer of their ownership to a democratic state for the benefit of the community. On the other, it contradicted the Marxian labour theory of value and the doctrine that only capitalists extracted surplus value (Durbin 1984: 41, 50).

In this way, the British Fabians were able to separate their form of socialism from the revival of Marxism as a revolutionary political creed, and from the brief and temporary eruptions of Marxist political activity in London in the 1880s.

Germany: nationalism, manufacturing, and protection

The French Revolution had a profound and irreversible impact on Germany. After 1792 France declared war, Germany was invaded and occupied, then subjected to a major political reorganization. Smaller political units were abolished or merged into larger ones and their legal, judicial, and administrative systems were reformed. After its defeat at Jena in 1806, Prussia underwent the Stein–Hardenburg reforms, abolishing feudal status, inaugurating local government in towns, reforming the army, and greatly improving education provision. In the economic sphere, the restrictive practices of the guilds were removed, as were internal barriers to trade. Prussia's economic potential was further improved at the Congress of Vienna, which granted it the new territories of Rhineland and Westphalia as a bulwark against future French invasion.

In the aftermath, the problem of reconciling order and progress was seen as less acute than it was seen in France or Britain. There had been little popular resistance to the Napoleonic occupation and the changes it imposed; the post-1815 rulers saw little reason to reverse them, as in general they had improved the efficiency of public administration and economic life. Germany had experienced no great political awakening. Germany's liberals were a diverse collection of educated middle-class professionals who could not unite on a common programme of reform, and posed no substantial threat to order. Moreover, Prince Metternich maintained a system of political repression in the adjacent Hapsburg Empire that acted as a warning to its German neighbours to do likewise.

In intellectual terms, Friedrich Hegel, the foremost philosopher of the post-occupation years, did have his own views on the reconciliation of order and progress. They were nested in a much larger metaphysical scheme designed to explain the Providence of God in human history (Hegel 1953/1837). Hegel's starting point was a distinction between development in nature from development in human life. In nature, he argued, development is a matter of 'quiet unfolding' by which the potential of a germ realizes itself. By contrast, in human life, the Spirit must realize its potential by developing in the arena of human consciousness and human will, which will necessarily be an arena of clashes and conflict. In world history, the Spirit is at constant war with itself and in a state of alienation.

Nested inside this schematic account of the working of God's Providence is Hegel's theory of the dialectic—the stages of history through which the Spirit successively transforms itself in a secular process of thesis, antithesis, and synthesis, until it arrives at the end of history—the realization of the concept of freedom. Hegel saw the French Revolution as a world historical event, in which though the potential for a moral transformation was present, it was only partially achieved. The religious and political dogmas of the old regime had been swept away, but the French *philosophes'* pursuit of an absolute freedom contained no scope for moral creation. In *The Philosophy of Right*, therefore, he argued for the individual rights to respect and recognition to be reconciled with an idea of a common good embodied in the state (Smith 1989). Like Comte, Hegel believed that societies required a shared ideal of common good, but unlike Comte he did not see the need for a body of savants and scientists independent of the temporal power. Rather, he regarded that as the role of the state, and for this he has been accused of glorifying the Prussian state of his day.

Hegel also argued that nature did not always permit the Spirit to work out its self-realization in history. In some parts of the earth, the zones of extreme climate, nature was too powerful for man to be able to assert his spiritual freedom, and the mind was unable to progress. 'The frost which grips the inhabitants of Lappland and the fiery heat of Africa are forces of too powerful a nature for man to resist... in regions such as these, dire necessity can never be escaped or overcome... the torrid or frigid zones, as such, are not the theatre on which world history is enacted' (quoted in Cowen and Shenton 1996: 126).

At the time that Hegel was writing, the German territories were still primarily agricultural in character, but early signs of a social and economic transformation were appearing. A feudal organization of society was beginning to give way to a more class-based one; the population was expanding fairly rapidly; and communications were being improved steadily as canals and railways were built and roads and river navigation improved. Trade was also facilitated as the *Zollverein* or customs union was established among eighteen territories in 1834. Despite the strengthening of Prussia's economic position, social unrest and political instability were always threatening and German unification, even of a 'small Germany', was still a long way off.

It was rather remarkable then that Friedrich List, a German journalist and economist, in his 1841 treatise later translated as *The National System of Political Economy*, pronounced that the economy had to be analysed from the viewpoint of the nation. That the state had a role to play in the economy was his big message, and the role for the state that he prescribed was to enlarge the productive powers of the nation. This required the promotion of manufacturing, since manufacturing would in turn enhance technical progress, art, infrastructure, political freedom, urbanization, and the nation's military capability. For late starters on the path of development, like Germany, the promotion of manufacturing would be inconsistent with Adam Smith's recommendation of universal free trade. List agreed with Smith that that would be the appropriate trade policy if the whole world were already united in one cosmopolitan political union. However, that was certainly not yet the case. In a world that was still composed of nations, the appropriate policy was for each nation to protect its manufacturing industry.

Smith's four-stage model had pictured slow evolutionary progress, similar to what was occurring in Germany in the 1830s. In contrast, List had spent time in America where he had seen change take place at a much accelerated pace, something that he attributed to Alexander Hamilton's policies designed to promote manufacturing. List did not believe that import duties on manufactured imports were invariably beneficial for the domestic industry concerned. He advocated taking a close look at the particular industrial context in judging whether protection was appropriate at all, and a close consideration of any rates in excess of moderate revenue duties.

List did, however, believe that manufacturing generated greater benefits than Smith had permitted for in *The Wealth of Nations*. Smith had argued that manufacturing allowed greater scope than farming for the specialization and division of labour, thereby increasing average labour productivity in manufacturing industry and reducing the unit cost of its products. List pointed out that what was crucial to the superiority of manufacturing was not just the division of labour but also the union of labour in carrying out many specialized tasks jointly. He criticized Smith for confining his analysis to the economics of individual industries and ignoring the positive externalities that each industry provided for others, such as the training of labour and the results of industrial research—both important benefits of joint and associated labour activities.

For List, the direct and indirect benefits of the growth of manufacturing were such that, once agriculture had developed sufficiently, the secret of development was to transfer labour to manufacturing:

Under a normal development of the productive powers of the State, the greater part of the increase of the agricultural population (as soon as it has attained a certain degree of culture) should transfer itself to manufacturing industry, and the excess of the agricultural products should partly serve for supplying the manufacturing population with provisions and raw materials, and partly for procuring for the agriculturalists the manufactured goods, machines, and utensils which they require for their own consumption, and for the increase of their own production.

(List 1977/1885: 155)

List thought the 'agricultural and industrial productive power will increase reciprocally, and indeed "ad infinitum"'.

Just as Hegel did, List held a crude theory of environmental determinism, according to which the world is divided into temperate and extreme climatic (frigid and tropical) zones. Living in temperate zones is more conducive to the supply of physical and mental effort than living in extreme climatic zones. This difference determined the prospects for economic development in each zone. While nations in the temperate zone were favourably placed to succeed in manufacturing, those in extreme climatic zones were not. (Charles Dickens agreed, and in *Bleak House* made a joke of Mr Quale's project of teaching African natives 'to turn piano-forte legs and establish an export trade'.)

List argued that manufacturing confers additional advantages on those temperate nations able to undertake it successfully. These included a merchant marine and naval power, so they are enabled to acquire colonies. The trade policy for a nation's trade with colonies, however, should be free trade, that is, the free exchange of manufactured goods for agricultural products and raw materials. List's recommended trade regime for colonies is best described as free trade imperialism, a trade that would allow the economies of the colonies to grow, but not as fast as those of the mother countries.

Thus, tropical countries would inevitably become dependent on nations in the temperate zone, but this dependence would be somewhat mitigated as more of the latter acquired colonies and competition in the export of manufactures would intensify. A free trade regime would also support the colonial power in its civilizing mission of 'economical education' and the transfer of political institutions. List here refers to a form of trusteeship for weak and inferior countries (Cowen and Shenton 1996: 164–5).

Unlike Condorcet, List saw no end to colonialism, and encouraged European nations and the United States to develop their own colonies in order to break the virtual monopoly then enjoyed by Great Britain. He wrote: 'this exchange between the countries of the temperate zone and the countries of the torrid zone is based on natural causes, and will be so for all time. Hence India has given up her manufacturing power with her independence to England; hence all Asiatic countries of the torrid zone will pass gradually under the dominion of the manufacturing commercial nations of the temperate zone' (List 1977/1885: 270). In his view, there was nothing wrong with colonialism and its noncompetitive pattern of free trade; for him, the real problem was that Germany did not yet have its place in the sun.

List assumed that tropical countries were at a lower level of civilization, and that colonization would allow them not only to improve their wealth, but also to raise their level of civilization. His belief in the civilizing mission of colonialism was widespread among European writers of the nineteenth century.

Karl Marx savagely criticized List for hypocrisy in wanting to protect German industry from competition, while exposing tropical countries industries to its full force (Cowen and Shenton 1996: 165–8). Yet he shared List's view of colonizers' civilizing mission. He wrote, for example, in the *New York Daily Tribune* of England's double mission in India: 'one destructive, the other regenerating—the annihilation of the old Asiatic society and the laying of the foundations of Western society in Asia'. He disagreed with List only in preferring the British as colonizers of India (Fernbach 1973: 319–25).

When Indian nationalists first began to discuss the appropriate trajectory for their country's development, once the British had gone, some turned to the ideas of Friedrich List. *The National System of Political Economy* was not translated into English until as late as 1885. In 1889, Mahadev G. Ranade endorsed the use of tariff protection for infant industries as the route to India's economic development (Arndt 1987: 18). However, without apparently knowing it, Ranade was advocating the application to India of a policy that List had proposed only for Germany, the United States, and a few other countries. Ranade overlooked or deliberately ignored what List had written about the impossibility of tropical countries like India building manufacturing industry (Boianovsky 2013).

Conclusion

Throughout the nineteenth century, as industrialization gradually spread out from Britain to France, the Low Countries, Germany, and beyond, it brought with it a political conundrum. The growth of industry relied on a large and disciplined workforce, drawn together in expanding urban areas. Yet, given the appalling living and working conditions in most industrial towns, the spirit of revolutionary politics was far from being extinguished in the hovels of the labouring class, which was increasingly viewed as dangerous and unpredictable. This was the spectre that *The Communist Manifesto* rightly declared haunted the undemocratic governing elites of Europe at mid-century—popular resistance, not necessarily any more democratic, that would wreck the grand schemes and projects that could improve living conditions as well as enrich their backers.

Small wonder that the intellectuals of Europe, some of them well before Marx and Engels, formulated ideas of directed development that would reconcile the requirements of progress with public order. Small wonder that they wanted to gain political legitimacy by posing as trustees for the interests of the downtrodden masses. Their diverse designs of socialism, however, were never as utopian as Marx and Engels later charged. In Western Europe at least, they somehow guided national governments through the changes that they needed to make in order to steer clear of revolution politics.

In the 1950s Oxford University offered only a single lecture on Marx. It was given by Isaiah Berlin, and its title was 'Why Marx was Wrong'. In 2009, Terry Eagleton responded with *Why Marx was Right*, a lively riposte although actually arguing why some of Marx's critics were wrong, as many of them certainly were, rather than why Marx was right. Though Marx was far from wholly wrong, he was certainly wrong in some important respects.

For example, his attribution of utopianism to others could apply also to some of his own doctrines. His failure to appreciate the stirring power of nationalism, even as Italy and then the small version of Germany were politically unified, could be interpreted as a retreat into a fantasy of class-driven politics. So could his failure to foresee the consequent intensification of national rivalries, including the new nations' competitive drive for their own colonies at the end of the century. These rivalries were to drive Europe into a wasteland of war and depression for the first half of the following century and confound a neat world of class divisions. When political revolutions finally did take place, they were much more the result of dislocation and defeat in war than they were of class consciousness and class struggles.

In the next chapter, we examine another proposition of Marx and Engels. It is the claim that economic forces unleashed in Europe would spread to the rest of the world in a way that would allow the European bourgeois class to create the entire world in its own image. Would this happen? Could this happen? Or was this judgement another Marxist utopian view?

References

Arndt, H. (1987). *Economic Development: The History of an Idea*. Chicago: University of Chicago Press.

Blackstone, W. (1765–9). *Commentaries upon the Laws of England*. Oxford: Clarendon Press.

Boianovsky, M. (2013). Friedrich List and the economic fate of tropical countries. *History of Political Economy* 45(4), 647–91.

Burke, E. (2003/1790). *Reflections on the Revolution in France*. New Haven, CT: Yale University Press.

Burns, J. H., and Hart, H. L. A., eds (1970). *The Collected Works of Jeremy Bentham: An Introduction to the Principles of Morals and Legislation*. London: Athlone Press.

Cowen, M. P., and Shenton, R. W. (1996). *Doctrines of Development*. London: Routledge.

Cowling, M. (1963). *Mill and Liberalism*. Cambridge: Cambridge University Press.

Durbin, E. (1984). Fabian socialism and economic science, in B. Pimlott, ed., *Fabian Essays in Socialist Thought*. London: Heinemann for Fairleigh Dickinson University Press.

Fernbach, D., ed. (1973). *Karl Marx: Surveys from Exile*. London: Allen Lane at the Penguin Press.

Harrison, W., ed. (1948). *Jeremy Bentham: A Fragment on Government and an Introduction to the Principles of Morals and Legislation*. Oxford: Basil Blackwell.

Hegel, G. W. F. (1953/1837). *Reason in History: A General Introduction to the Philosophy of History*. Indianapolis, IN: Bobbs-Merrill.

Himmelfarb, G. (1992). *Poverty and Compassion: The Moral Imagination of the Late Victorians*. New York: Vintage Paperback.

Himmelfarb, G. (2004). *The Moral Imagination: From Edmund Burke to Lionel Trilling*. London: Souvenir Press.

Himmelfarb, G. (2006). *The Roads to Modernity: The British, French and American Enlightenments*. New York: Alfred A. Knopf.

Jones, H. S., ed. (1998). *Comte: Early Political Writings*. Cambridge: Cambridge University Press.

List, F. (1977/1885). *The National System of Political Economy*. Fairfield, VA: Augustus M. Kelley.

MacIntyre, A. (1967). *A Short History of Ethics*. London: Routledge and Kegan Paul.

Markham, F. M. H., ed. (1952). *Henri Comte de Saint-Simon (1760–1825): Selected Writings*. Oxford: Basil Blackwell.

Mill, J. S. (1924/1873). *Autobiography*. London: Oxford University Press.

Pimlott, B., ed. (1984). *Fabian Essays in Socialist Thought*. London: Heinemann for Fairleigh Dickinson University Press.

Smith, S. B. (1989). *Hegel's Critique of Liberalism: Rights in Context*. Chicago: University of Chicago Press.

4

Development by imitation, 1839–1947

Learn to think imperially.

—Joseph Chamberlain

Marx and Engels on Chinese walls

In the *Manifesto of the Communist Party* (1848), Marx and Engels widened their focus from the class dynamics of individual societies to the entire world scene, and the relationship between bourgeois and non-bourgeois societies. They wrote:

> The bourgeoisie, by the rapid improvement of all instruments of production, by the immensely facilitated means of communication, draws all, even the most barbarian, nations into civilization. The cheap prices of its commodities are the heavy artillery with which it batters down all Chinese walls, with which it forces the barbarians' obstinate hatred of foreigners to capitulate. It compels all nations, on pain of extinction, to adopt the bourgeois mode of production; it compels them to introduce what it calls civilization into their midst, i.e. to become bourgeois themselves. In one word, it creates a world after its own image.   (Fernbach 1973: 71)

Once Great Britain had definitely diverged from the historic path of a European agriculture-based society, it was obvious that any country that aspired to do likewise would have to follow a more or less similar path. It would have to adopt similar forms of technical innovation and create similar types of economic institutions. Marx and Engels' statement asserted that the process of development outside the heartlands of capitalism would be a process of development by imitation. However, they held an extreme version of this thesis. They thought that development would be not just similar but universally the same, with the effect of eliminating all existing national differences. This was because their ignorance of the history of Asia led them to believe that the continent was passive, stagnating, and lacking any history of its own. This was a typical Eurocentric perspective of their period.

The quotation gives a more detailed sketch of the nature of a universal sequence of imitation. Its starting point is the xenophobia of non-bourgeois societies, a xenophobia that had led some of them to cut themselves off almost completely from the rest of the world. It asserts that the threat of extinction in the face of economic competition forces them, despite their 'obstinate hatred of foreigners' to imitate the form of the very society that they hate—what the bourgeoisie venerates as 'civilization'. The bourgeoisie creates the world after its own image as a result of provoking, as a defensive reaction in xenophobic countries, an imitative form of development. So runs the argument.

This chapter explores two questions. The first is whether development by imitation is a useful concept for understanding selected countries' experiences of socioeconomic development. The second is whether the development experiences of those countries that have been and felt threatened by Western societies were similar or different, and, if different, why were they different?

Our point of departure is to note that in the passage quoted earlier from *The Communist Manifesto* Marx and Engels overlooked a very important intermediate step in the argument that cheap commodities batter down Chinese walls. That step was that countries with an obstinate hatred of foreigners first of all must become open to trade. The authors of the *Manifesto* seem to be oblivious of the fact that they were writing at the high tide of British gunboat diplomacy in international relations, and that the exercise of superior naval power was the lever that initially opened up countries closed to trade.

Marx did make good on the omission in a newspaper article, 'Revolution in China and in Europe', for *The New York Daily Tribune*. Commenting on the origins of the Taiping rebellion in China, he wrote in 1853:

> the occasion for this outbreak has unquestionably been afforded by the English cannon forcing upon China that soporific drug called opium. Before the British arms the authority of the Manchu dynasty fell to pieces; the superstitious faith in the eternity of the Celestial Empire broke down; the barbarous and hermetic isolation from the civilized world was infringed; and an opening was made for that intercourse which has since proceeded so rapidly. (Fernbach 1973: 325)

The reference here is to the Chinese government's burning of illegal British opium shipments in Canton harbour in 1839 and the subsequent First Opium War with Britain. Armed with the Congreve rocket launcher, a fleet of sixteen British warships quickly overwhelmed the antiquated Chinese defences, killing 20,000 Chinese people for the loss of 69 men. In August 1842, the Chinese were forced to sign the Treaty of Nanking, which opened five major Chinese ports to trade, ceded the island of Hong Kong to the UK in perpetuity, and provided for the payment of a war indemnity to Britain.

Japan's transformation

The significance of China's humiliation in the First Opium War was not lost on the Americans. In 1849 Captain James Glynn of the US Navy sailed to Nagasaki to demand that the emperor of Tokugawa Japan, which was almost completely closed to foreign trade, negotiate a trade treaty with the United States. On his return, he recommended to the US Congress that the administration's demand for trade negotiations be backed with a show of naval force. This paved the way for the naval expeditions of Commodore Matthew Perry in 1853 and 1854. They produced the Convention of Kanagawa (1854) according to which Japan accepted virtually all of the American demands.

We should note that, once again, it was not the cheap prices of US commodities that acted as the heavy artillery to batter down the Japanese walls. It was the Paixhans shell guns mounted on Perry's ships. The military dimension to this encounter made a profound impression on the Japanese and shaped their development trajectory.

Further treaties of 1858 and 1867 extended to European powers, including to the UK, France, Russia, and the Netherlands, the concessions that the USA had extracted. With no navy and with an archaic military system, the Tokugawa Shogun was unable to resist, despite the damage that the trade concessions did to the Japanese economy. When the Shogun was overthrown in November 1867, the successor regime of the Emperor Meiji resolved to try to recover Japanese independence by adopting sweeping institutional reforms that would establish institutions that imitated those of the Western Powers.

The Japanese form of feudalism was summarily abolished and replaced with equality before the law, rights of private property and the free movement of labour, a modern system of taxation, compulsory primary education, and universal military service. The lower ranks of the former samurai (warrior) class carried through this institutional reconstruction, financed by some of the large merchant houses, like Mitsui and Sumitomo.

The leading intellectual of the Meiji revolution was Yukichi Fukuzawa (1835–1901). He had learned Dutch as a young man in order to be able to study European cannon designs and gunnery, but when he visited Kanagawa in 1859 he discovered that all the European merchants there were speaking English, and not Dutch. He joined the first Japanese diplomatic mission to the USA and stayed for a month in San Francisco (1860), where he bought a *Webster's Dictionary*, from which he taught himself English.

Subsequently he travelled to Western Europe as a translator for the first Japanese diplomatic mission to England, France, the Netherlands, Prussia, and Russia (1862). Using the information gathered on these travels, he published his most famous work, *Things Western* in ten volumes (1867–70). These volumes explained Western institutions and culture in an accessible style to the

Japanese public. They became instant bestsellers. His many other publications included an English-Japanese dictionary, a global geography for children written in multiple volumes of verse, a treatise on the importance of education, and works of moral philosophy—as well as several military manuals. Altogether he sold an astonishing ten million copies of his works.

The nature of Fukuzawa's influence was various. Many Japanese will have seen him simply as an important source of information about the West. Fewer will have absorbed the modern values of individual self-reliance and equality of opportunity that he personally espoused. Either way, he has been recognized as one of the founders of modern Japan.

The motivation for the post-1867 institutional transformation was not welfare-promoting, but was essentially military. The peasantry derived little benefit from it. The switch to fixed money taxes, including the famous Meiji land tax, forced many small peasants to sell their land, and the proportion of tenanted agricultural land rose sharply during the Meiji period. High rents meant that tenants remained close to a subsistence standard of living.

The prominent role played by the state in subsequent economic developments had less to do with any commitment to the state as an instrument of economic development than with finding employment for a large class of military men who had just been rendered functionless—the former samurai. They were recruited to work in an authoritarian bureaucracy, to give them a form of livelihood as the value of their state compensation for giving up their feudal rights was eroded.

Although in the first instance, the military motivation was a defensive response to Western naval incursion, Japan did not long remain on the defensive, but soon imitated Western aggression. Imitation of the West extended to aspiring to acquire a colonial empire of her own, from which to extract trading preferences as well as the natural resources that she lacked. After achieving victory in the Sino-Japanese war (1894–5), the large reparations obtained from China paid for the expansion of the Japanese army and navy, as well as more investment in modern infrastructure. With larger forces Japan was able to defeat Russia in 1905, which brought her Southern Sakhalin, and to annex Korea in 1910. In 1911, Japan was powerful enough to abrogate the last of the hated trading concessions that the Western powers had wrung from her at the end of the Tokugawa era.

Japan's combination of modernization and militarism indicates that Marx's theory of development by imitation is far from a straightforward one. On reflection, it is clear that the hypothesized process involves a central social psychological difficulty. In logic, the theory requires people in non-Western countries to internalize a set of attitudes that they have previously abhorred. Marx and Engels claimed that the Western bourgeoisie 'compels [foreigners] to introduce what it calls civilization into their midst'. However, this claim disregards the distinction between two different aspects of 'civilization', the external and the internal. The former includes science, technology, engineering, architecture, political and economic institutions, and so on. The latter includes religious beliefs, family relations, social customs, and a shared public culture. The problem with the idea of development by imitation is that, while the external aspects can be and have been adopted with relative ease, the internal aspects cannot be, and are not, generally adopted at the same time. Imitation is only partial and does not extend to changing the national psyche and culture.

In a sense, then, development by imitation, or mimetic nationalism as it is sometimes called, is something of an oxymoron. Nationalism implies the retention of these internal aspects while at the same time imitating the many external aspects of an alien civilization. This can produce strange results. Michio Morishima has noted: 'a remarkably idiosyncratic ethos prevails in Japanese society' and that therefore 'Japanese capitalism has to a considerable extent deviated from the typical free enterprise system' (Morishima 1982: viii). The mimetic nationalist reaction therefore will tend to produce different varieties of capitalism, rather than a ubiquitous mirror image of the capitalism of the West. Morishima suggested that the question of how and why the possessors of non-Western internal attitudes gain control over the external techniques produced by the West should be asked not only of Japan, but also of the experiences of China, Russia, and India. We now follow that line of enquiry.

Two women start down China's long road

Much of the Japanese social ethos was derived from Chinese culture, and awareness of China's humiliation at the hands of the British in the Second Opium War (1856–60) was a spur to Japan's transformation in the Meiji era. China was the home of the original 'self-strengthening movement'. Feng Guifen (1809–74) advocated a strategy of building up China's military potential by adopting Western technology and using it to defeat the Western 'barbarians'. His use of the term 'barbarians' indicates plainly enough that China regarded itself as the centre of world civilization, although Marx for his part had written of China's 'barbarous and hermetic isolation' from the civilized world. These contradictory claims about the true locus of civilization underline the important point that each nationality retains its own internal world view, even when embarking on the strategy of development by imitation.

The person who guided the Manchu Imperial dynasty through these troubled waters was known as Yi. She was a young concubine of the Emperor Xianfeng who, faced with the Second Opium War (1856–60) and the burning of the Summer Palace, refused any accommodation with the West. He went into self-imposed exile, while his younger half-brother, Prince Gong, made peace. When Xianfeng died in 1861, Yi took the title Empress Dowager Cixi, and with the support of Dowager Empress Zhen, ruled China on behalf of her son, the new Emperor Tongzhi. Accepting British help, she brought the Taiping rebellion to a close and instituted an uncorrupt customs service to tap the revenue from growing foreign trade (Chang 2014: 63–7).

However, Cixi faced united opposition on the issue of embarking on a range of new large engineering projects, such as building railways, the telegraph, mining, ironworks, shipping, and textiles. Disturbance of traditional burial grounds, thereby provoking the wrath of Heaven, was the conclusive argument for her veto. Nevertheless, the court supported her in building a modern army, an arms industry, and naval steamships, and willy-nilly some mining and manufacturing enterprises made their appearance. At the same time, Cixi began sending diplomatic missions to the West to find out more about these unknown lands.

Constrained by court intrigues against her, Cixi was forced to lie low until regaining power in 1875. Spurred by fears of Japan, she expanded naval spending, opened more ports to foreign trade and now ordered the installation of the telegraph. Mining enterprises were authorized, electricity was introduced, and a modern currency was adopted. Eventually, in 1889, the Beijing-Wuhan railway was built (Chang 2014: 123–8).

Cixi always had to approach modernization very slowly, circumspectly, and selectively. Court intrigues and disunity thus meant that her revolution from above was much more hesitant and dilatory than Japan's, and much more inhibited by the restraints of China's traditional culture. This was to cost China dear in terms of military defeat and invasion by Japan over the next sixty years.

In China, the revolution would instead come from below. Sun Yat-sen was a revolutionary leader and an intellectual who articulated three principles of transformation. They were nationalism, democracy, and the principle of the people's livelihood. This last was a belated recognition that Western dominance did not rest exclusively on its military might, or the creation of certain political institutions, but had an economic basis under conditions that encouraged people to create new forms of livelihood. People in the West enjoyed opportunities to deploy their talents in the economic field; land and natural resources could be fully exploited; and impediments to trade were few. China, Sun argued, must provide the same economic opportunities to its own people.

While Sun Yat-sen's third principle was an important extension to the strategy of development by imitation, in that it moved the objective from military strength to popular welfare, his book *The International Development of*

China (1922) had a focus on technocratic methods. Sun advocated the large-scale expansion of modern infrastructure and the means of production with the use of state capital and capital borrowed from abroad. The way for China to recover the rights that had been ceded to foreigners was to 'employ state power to promote industry, use machinery in production, and give employment to the workers of the nation'.

The emphasis on the welfare of workers did not, however, derive from Marx's ideas. Sun criticized Marxists for failure to realize that China's fundamental problem was poverty and not the unequal distribution of wealth. His book persuaded Heinz Arndt that Sun Yat-sen was 'almost certainly the first to advocate economic development in something like the modern sense and use of the term' (Arndt 1987: 16–17).

Despite the successful overthrow of the Qing dynasty in 1911 and Sun's short periods as President of China, he was never able to unify the country, subdue the various warlords who controlled different parts of it, and actually exercise state power. Then, before Sun's ideas on development could take root, the fate of nationalism in China became entangled with the trajectory of the Bolshevik revolution in Russia.

Marxism–Leninism: Russia's own hybrid

Under its later emperors Russia was exposed to similar external military threats to those that affected Japan and China. Imperial Russia suffered defeats in the Crimean War (1853–6) at the hands of the British, French, and Ottoman empires; in the Russo-Japanese war (1904–5) by Japan; and in the First World War (1914–17) by Germany.

Each of these defeats triggered attempts at reforms that imitated conditions in the West. In the 1860s, various forms of serfdom were abolished. In 1906, the Duma, a consultative political assembly, was set up after the 1905 revolution. In February 1917, after another revolution, the Romanov dynasty fell from power, leaving the Mensheviks (the orthodox Marxist faction of the Russian Social Democratic Labour Party) in control of the provisional government.

Although these post-defeat reforms were recognizably Western in character, their execution was partial and half-hearted. After the juridical abolition of serfdom, many of its features survived de facto, at least until Stolypin's later agrarian reform. The Duma provided a forum for debate and opposition speeches but the Tsar never trusted it with any executive power. The Mensheviks, once in power, continued with the policies of the former imperial government, and thereby created the opportunity for the Bolsheviks to seize power from them in the October Revolution of 1917.

Russia was too culturally divided to carry through a strategy of development by imitation. Although Russia had experienced bouts of Westernization under Peter the Great and Catherine the Great, the nineteenth century saw the rise of the Slavophile movement. This was determined to protect Russian traditions and culture, especially the powerful cultural and political role of the Russian Orthodox Church. Slavophiles rejected individualism in favour of organic unity, and rationalism in favour of Russian mysticism. Tsars Alexander III and Nicholas II adopted a version of Slavophilia as the imperial ideology. The Slavophile political thrust was grandiose, nothing less than the unification of all ethnic Slavs, whether inside Russia or outside, under Russian leadership. The Slavophile economic thrust was one of rejection of both capitalism and socialism as undesirable foreign imports and the assertion that neither system was suited to the cultural traditions of Russia.

When Vladimir Lenin arrived in Petrograd in April 1917, calling for revolutionary action modelled on the Paris Commune of 1870, at first blush he was another Westernizer in socialist revolutionary dress. However, after the October Revolution had unleashed civil war and the economic chaos of the brief period of 'war communism', Lenin, Trotsky, and Bukharin had to face up to the realities of governing Russia. They did so by abandoning the Commune model of popular administration and embracing the model of the dictatorship of the proletariat, led by the Bolshevik revolutionary vanguard. The priority now became the maximization of production, for which industry was indispensable, but democracy was not. A new, but distinctly Russian, autocracy was to be built as the political instrument to achieve central control of all production, distribution, and exchange (Harding 2003: 258–61).

Although that goal was not immediately realizable during the New Economic Policy before 1928, Joseph Stalin's two Five-Year Plans were the basis of the world's first attempt at a planned economy. The strategy was one of rapid, state-led industrialization, plus the collectivization of agriculture. In reality it was not a planned, but a hastily improvised strategy, and one carried out using maximum coercion. The collectivization of agriculture produced disastrous, immensely destructive results in the countryside, but released a flow of rural-urban migrants who could be absorbed into the tasks of building infrastructure and industrial equipment in the cities.

Stalin certainly thought that he was constructing a new and specifically Russian socialist mode of production, and the millions of workers and peasants whom the regime provided with higher education shared that conviction. A new social stratum of educated and upwardly mobile engineers, doctors, researchers, and managers supported the regime precisely because the regime had created them. Stalin cast Marx's internationalism unceremoniously aside. He argued—against Trotsky—that it was possible to build socialism in one country, despite the fact that the prospects of an international proletarian revolution had evaporated. This would enable Russia to attain its rightful, leading role in the world. In this, as in his autocratic methods, Stalin's Russian nationalist and Slavophile tendencies are reflected.

Despite the novel elements in the Stalinist strategy, it included obvious elements of borrowing from capitalist countries, particularly from the USA. In the industrial sector, the regime used foreign designs and foreign state-of-the-art equipment. Much use was made of Frederick Taylor's scientific management techniques and Henry Ford's mass production methods. In the rural sector, the drive to collectivize farming was influenced by the example of the large-scale farms of the American Midwest. Stalin once declared: 'the combination of the Russian revolutionary sweep with American efficiency is the essence of Leninism'. Later during the Cold War, however, both sides wanted to play down the importance of American influence in shaping the forms of Soviet socialism. Yet it was the product both of nationalism and of imitation.

Stalin believed that the new socialist society would demonstrate its superiority to the capitalist system from which he had borrowed much. In Stalin's Marxism–Leninism, socialism had ceased to be a successor to bourgeois society, and had turned into a parallel type of society that could outperform its competitor. Stalin's development strategy was actually a success on its chosen criteria. Economic growth in the Soviet Union from 1928 to 1937 at somewhere between 6 and 9 per cent a year was much faster than in the West, where economies were mired in the Great Depression.

Rapid growth was achieved by ruthlessly holding down consumption and raising the share of GNP devoted to investment from 12.5 per cent (1928) to 26 per cent (1937). The labour force expanded three times as fast as the population, eliminating unemployment and drawing a much greater proportion of women into education and employment. The managers of workplaces controlled access to social benefits, thereby excluding from state benefits all who were not workers. The economic structure shifted in favour of the non-agricultural sector, and within that from light to heavy industry. Illiteracy in those aged under 50 was ended, and higher and technical education was greatly expanded (Maddison 1969: 99–107).

However, these economic successes were bought at enormous human cost. Many peasants died resisting collectivization of agriculture, and animal livestock was slaughtered on an extensive scale. Large numbers of people were sent to labour camps, or compelled to migrate to areas where conditions were hostile. The peasants were turned into proletarians. They were deprived of their landed property, except for small private plots, were paid annually in kind, and were subject to heavy taxation. The Soviet state had created an enduring problem of feeding its growing urban population, and this was a problem that contributed to its ultimate demise.

Further down China's long road

Bolshevik ideas and influence spread widely in China after 1919. The newly formed Chinese Communist Party was ordered by the Comintern to ally itself with Sun Yat-sen's nationalist party, the Kuomimtang (KMT), as it engaged in military struggle. Lenin's Bolshevik government gave the KMT its support. For the duration of the alliance (1922–7), Mao Zedong formed a peasant army and organized land reform. When the KMT's Chang Kai-shek broke off the alliance, Mao formed a Communist peasant militia and with the People's Liberation Army turned on the KMT in what became a long civil war.

Under these conditions, the KMT was unable to do much for the economic development of China. Nevertheless, its vision was set out in in H. D. Fong's *The Post-War Industrialization of China* (1942). This was a manifesto for scientific planning, large development projects, heavy industries, and state ownership and operation (Easterly 2013: 72). The KMT was also much involved in researching and discussing Western social policies, such as the New Deal and the Beveridge report, as a means of gaining international legitimacy during the war (Ma 2014: 254–75).

Although conflict was suspended during the Japanese invasion of 1935–40, hostilities with the Communists were then resumed, leading to the expulsion of the KMT from mainland China in 1949. After years of guerilla warfare, and the deindustrialization of the east coast during the Japanese invasion, Mao identified the agrarian peasantry, rather than the industrial working class, as the true revolutionary force capable of replacing capitalist society with socialism. Asserting that 'political power grows out of the barrel of a gun', Mao believed that an armed peasantry engaging in guerilla warfare is capable of overthrowing existing institutions. Viewing urban and industrial capitalism as ruling and exploiting the countryside, he supported wars of national liberation as a means of ending the oppression of the countryside. At the same time, he regarded urban industrialization as a prerequisite of economic development, which was to be the prelude to the reorganization of the countryside, rural industrialization, and the ending of the division between urban and rural areas.

Chairman Mao, once in power, accelerated China's move towards socialism, initially following a technocratic and top-down strategy of development, similar to that espoused by the KMT. By late 1956, virtually all the peasants were organized into cooperatives. However, the underlying motive for this was different in the Chinese case. Mao believed that a rise in agricultural production would have to precede a rise in industrial production, not that mechanization was a necessary requirement for it.

This divergence of view led before long to Mao's distancing of China from the Soviet Union. He feared that following the Soviet model of development would have widened the gulf between the countryside and the cities, and, in

Mao's view, the peasantry could not be regarded merely as a source of surplus to be invested in industrial development. On the other hand, peasants were not natural socialists, so regular political campaigns were essential to push them further down that path. Mao led these campaigns despite the risk of the party bureaucracy losing control of the situation—hence his sponsorship of the disastrous Great Leap Forward (1958–61) and then the Great Proletarian Cultural Revolution (1966–76) in an effort to oust the moderates or 'capitalist roaders' in the party.

In all this, there are strong elements of Chinese cultural tradition. As in Confucianism, the Chinese Communists regarded the masses as inherently well intentioned, but afflicted by ignorance. They saw the masses also as essentially passive, and in need of an enlightened and ethical leadership that will take responsibility for their well-being. Mao's cult of personality drew on these Confucian cultural resources, but also on the conviction that the masses can be moved by moral appeals for self-sacrifice and the promotion of the common good. This Confucian belief seems to have influenced the extreme egalitarianism and puritanical tone of Mao's style of propaganda, even when denouncing Confucianism—as happened during the Cultural Revolution!

Despite the political divergence of Chinese communism from the Soviet Union's development model, its economic performance in the Mao period was quite similar to that of the USSR during Stalin's two pre-war plans. The growth rate of output was about as rapid at 6+ per cent a year. The most important driver of growth was the high rate of saving and investment in the physical capital stock. Next in importance was the accumulation of human capital, as illiteracy was reduced and primary school enrolment widely spread. Third, the labour force increased under the pressure of population growth. The big negative factor was the decline in total factor productivity, indicating that the entire production system was operating with increasing inefficiency as time went on (Wang and Yao 2001). This was a portent of the growing pressure for a more decisive departure from the Soviet development model.

After the death of Mao (1976) and the downfall of the Gang of Four led by Mao's wife, the capitalist roaders took their opportunity. Deng Xiaoping, who had survived two purges during the Cultural Revolution, was reinstated in leading offices in 1977. Though he never occupied the positions of President, Prime Minister, or Secretary of the Chinese Communist Party, he was able to oust from them Mao's chosen successor Hua Gufeng and install his own supporters instead. When he had secured a position of de facto paramount leader, he turned to an economic strategy of development by imitation.

In November 1978, Deng visited the capitals of Singapore, Malaysia, and Thailand and became even more convinced that China needed to adopt a new development strategy. He did not look to Western liberal capitalism, but to the authoritarian Asian variety practised successfully by the neighbouring states of Hong Kong and Taiwan. The initial emphasis was on agriculture, and involved dismantling the commune system of organization. In 1979, collectivized land was placed in the hands of farming families (Dillon 2012: 357). Peasant farmers were allowed to cultivate returned land as private plots and sell the produce for profit. The restoration of private property and private incentives accelerated the growth of agricultural output. The country was opened to foreign trade and selected forms of foreign investment. Special economic zones in coastal areas provided platforms for the development of light industries capable of exporting. Instead of imposing an overall top-down plan, Deng permitted local experiments which if successful were scaled up.

Both China and Russia were marched down the path of socialism, which was believed to be the path of the future because of its superiority to the old bourgeois civilization. Yet, since no one was very sure exactly what socialism looked like, there was scope for its creation to be shaped by the varied historic cultures of the societies within which this new social formation was to be realized. By the end of the twentieth century, the experiment with socialism in both countries was acknowledged to have failed because its initial economic dynamism had faded. Their different transitions away from socialism began, and again the contrasts were strong (Nolan 1995).

The suddenness of the collapse of the Soviet Union ushered in a furious scramble of Soviet ex-bureaucrats to buy public assets at knock-down prices. Wealthy oligarchs emerged who sought to use their wealth to build political power through the new Russia's fledgling democratic institutions. At the same time the social protection of workers in their workplaces disappeared, leading to significant reductions in life expectancy of the Russian population. Weak institutions swiftly permitted the re-emergence of political strongmen playing to Russian nationalist sentiment.

The Chinese leadership permitted a gradual and unobtrusive return to private property and individual economic incentives and welcomed the rapid higgledy-piggledy growth that they stimulated in the 1980s and 1990s. Party officials still held the ring and were able to make adjustments to the pace and direction of change, as well as benefit corruptly from it. When Japanese investment led China down the capitalist road and thereby stirred up political opposition, this was crushed by military might.

In both countries, economic activity still carries considerable political risks. In neither does one see the image of the bourgeoisie, except as in a distorting mirror.

India and imitation

India differed from Japan, China, and Russia in having been militarily conquered by Britain in the eighteenth century and in undergoing a long period of foreign rule before embarking on its path of development as an independent country. That meant that India did not have a blank sheet on which to draw its development plans, but was always reacting both to the economic scars of colonialism and to what the British had previously attempted by way of development policies. The British, despite using the policy rhetoric of laissez-faire, had at times promoted state-owned industrial enterprises. By contrast, Indian nationalist opinion favoured using state powers (such as tariffs, procurement, and banking) to support Indian private enterprise. It was the American economy driven by its dynamic capitalists that Indians were often urged to imitate.

Sir Mokshagundam Visvesvaraya, for example, was an engineer and a successful builder of modern industries when he was Dewan of Mysore during the British era. Yet his book *Planned Economy for India* (1934) does not delve at all into methods of economic planning. It is simply a plea for the industrialization of India on the grounds that 'no modern nation whose national policies are not guided by the two forces of industrialism and nationalism has gained military power or become rich and prosperous'. The way to ensure that India became a modern nation, he believed, was imitation. 'It is necessary that Indians should ... assimilate the beneficial experience of other countries in order to raise their own level of working capacity and material prosperity' (Visvesvaraya 1934: 220–2, 256–7). These are the authentic accents of mimetic nationalism.

However, when the time came, the development of independent India did not proceed by the imitation of any single country's development experience. One driver was the economic and political predispositions of Jawaharlal Nehru, who became Prime Minister after independence was granted in August 1947. Like the British Fabian socialists, he was impressed by the apparent economic success of Soviet planning in building up the country's heavy industries and educating its illiterate population. The early five-year plans that the statistician P. C. Mahalanobis devised were an adaptation of the model of the Russian economist G. Feldman. Nehru wanted key industries to be state owned, and the outbreak of war prevented Gandhi, who favoured the promotion of light industries in the private sector, from effectively challenging Nehru's Fabian strategy.

The other driver was the wartime legacy of economic controls that the British left behind. Independent India inherited an arsenal of wartime legislation on its statute book that could be used to impose detailed microeconomic controls over private sector economic activity. This opportunity suited politicians who were distrustful of private sector business and thought that national security required the economy to be substantially closed to world trade and investment.

As the post-independence economic strategy was elaborated through the 1950s and early 1960s, the principle of an industrializing course was accepted almost unanimously, with little understanding of how the neglect of the agricultural sector would slow the growth of the economy after a decade or so. The strategy of state ownership of industries was more contested. The Congress Party, with its credentials from the independence struggle, was able to dominate electorally the new political arena of universal suffrage, but it was also big enough to be the site of struggles between its left and right wings. Nehru's development strategy was held in check and at the height of enthusiasm for 'the socialist pattern' in 1956, the second Industrial Policy Resolution closed only four industries to the private sector. Nevertheless, substantial investment in state-owned industries pushed up the public sector share in the national capital stock from 15 to 35 per cent by the mid-1960s.

The results of this investment were not particularly impressive. The growth of net national product per head never exceeded 2 per cent. For the first three decades following independence, India was unable to break through this barrier, which came to be known as 'the Hindu rate of growth'. More worrying was the slow acceleration in inflation from 6 to 8.6 per cent, mainly due to rising food prices, and the gradual increase in the capital-output ratio, which indicated the diminishing return to investment skewed towards heavy industry in the public sector. By the early 1980s, the economic signs were pointing to the need to try different policies, but Congress politicians put their energies into factional infighting.

The varieties of mimetic nationalism

None of the countries whose development trajectories have been sketched in this chapter fit with the Marx and Engels prediction of how the European bourgeoisie would transform the rest of the world. The idea of development by imitation of the West certainly influenced them all, to a greater or lesser degree. The most dramatic example was Japan, which felt the most militarily threatened, but reciprocally produced the most militaristic response. Russia had no hesitation about importing Western industrial techniques, but only as a way of constructing what was a distinctively Russian type of new society— 'socialism in one country'. Its distinctness made it the most interesting example of economic development for the West, and some of their politicians and public called for the West to imitate it. China was much more hesitant about what it imported and what it proscribed, and was much more wracked by internal conflict. It eventually began to imitate the Russian example, but first adapted then abandoned it in favour of an Asian authoritarian capitalism. India tried a Fabian version of socialism for a few decades, but its democratic system eventually moved it closer towards a standard liberal capitalist economy. These varieties of mimetic nationalism bear out the important influence of national cultures on the forms of development achieved under policies of imitation of Western models, and underline again the intellectual failure of Marx in downplaying the force of nationalism in shaping both national economies and international economic relations.

References

Arndt, H. (1987). *Economic Development: The History of an Idea*. Chicago: University of Chicago Press.

Ball, T., and R. Bellamy, eds (2003). *The Cambridge History of Twentieth-Century Political Thought*. Cambridge: Cambridge University Press.

Chang, J. (2014). *Empress Dowager Cixi: The Concubine Who Launched Modern China*. London: Vintage Books.

Dillon, M. (2012). *China: A Modern History*. London: I. B. Tauris.

Easterly, W. (2013). *The Tyranny of Experts: Economists, Dictators and the Forgotten Rights of the Poor*. New York: Basic Books.

Fernbach, D., ed. (1973). *Karl Marx: Surveys from Exile*. London: Allen Lane at the Penguin Press.

Fong, H. D. (1942). *The Post-War Industrialization of China*. Washington, DC: National Planning Association.

Harding, N. (2003). The Russian Revolution: an ideology in power, in T. Ball and R. Bellamy, eds, *The Cambridge History of Twentieth-Century Political Thought*, 219–66. Cambridge: Cambridge University Press.

Ma, T. (2014). 'The common aim of the allied powers': social policy and international legitimacy in wartime China, 1940–7. *Journal of Global History* 9, 254–75.

Maddison, A. (1969). *Economic Growth in Japan and the USSR*. London: Allen and Unwin.

Morishima, M. (1982). *Why Has Japan 'Succeeded'? Western Technology and the Japanese Ethos*. Cambridge: Cambridge University Press.

Nolan, P. H. (1995). *China's Rise, Russia's Fall: Politics, Economics and Planning in the Transition from Stalinism*. Basingstoke: Macmillan.

Sun Yat-sen, (1922). *The International Development of China*. New York: Putnam.

Visvesvaraya, M. (1934). *Planned Economy for India*. Bangalore: Bangalore Press.

Wang, Y., and Yao, Y. (2001). *Sources of China's Economic Growth, 1952–99: Incorporating Human Capital Formation*. Washington, DC: World Bank.

5

Liberal development, 1925–46

When the facts change, I change my mind. What do you do?

—Saying attributed to J. M. Keynes

The Soviet economic experiment and development economics

The question of which policies are most conducive to the acceleration of economic development was a central item on the twentieth century's agenda.[*] Lenin's revolutionary attempt to create Marxist socialism in Russia posed this question with urgency and sharpness. Russia was a backward country in which capitalism had not by 1917 made much impression. Marx and Engels would have deemed the creation of socialism there wholly unfeasible, yet this experiment was being undertaken in their names, and undertaken using a combination of mercantilist policies that had never previously been put into practice. In the 1920s, before Stalin's rise to power, this Soviet economic experiment was fiercely debated within the revolutionary leadership, but the terms of debate were, as one might expect, more political than economic (Erlich 1960). Nevertheless, it was fraught with heavy consequences for economics and economists. As Alec Nove later remarked: 'Development economics could be said to have been born here' (Nove 1983). Evsey Domar thought that Soviet society provided an economic laboratory in which a (Western) social scientist could re-examine his whole intellectual apparatus in the light of a different social and economic system. Surprisingly, one social scientist who was quick to undertake such a re-examination was the economist John Maynard Keynes. The result was his reaffirmation of liberal economics as a guide to development.

[*] This chapter is based on John Toye, 'Keynes, Russia and the state in developing countries', in *Keynes and the Role of the State*, ed. Crabtree and Thirlwall (1993), St Martin's Press, reproduced with permission of Palgrave Macmillan.

Why should the link between the Soviet economic experiment, development economics, and Keynes be a surprise? Keynes's major contribution was *The General Theory of Employment, Interest and Money* (1936), which laid out the new subject of macroeconomics, the analysis of the short-term behaviour of the aggregates of a monetary production economy. Even his admirers thought that Keynes's macroeconomics has very limited relevance to the problem of economic development, while his detractors emphasized the baleful influence of his alleged 'collectivism' on the economic policies of developing countries. Talk of a Keynesian approach to economic development is commonly dismissed as far-fetched, and his essay on 'Economic Possibilities for Our Grandchildren' is regarded as the nearest he ever got to the topic of economic development.

It is also a surprise because commentators on Keynes's career seem to believe that he never visited a developing country in a professional capacity. Elizabeth Johnson, for example, refers only to his travels on Treasury business to Europe and the USA (Johnson and Johnson 1978). Anand Chandavarkar claims that 'the only developing countries that he ever visited, Tunisia and Egypt, were for a holiday' (Chandavarkar 1989). The reality is that Soviet Russia in the 1920s and 1930s was a developing country, undergoing the changes wrought by Soviet power plus electrification, and that Keynes made three visits there, in 1925, 1928, and 1936.

Harry G. Johnson thought that *Indian Currency and Finance* was Keynes's sole contribution to development economics, however inappropriate that description is of a book devoted entirely to money and finance (Johnson and Johnson 1978). Chandavarkar assumes that development economics includes only the theoretical coinage of the 1950s—the big push, balanced growth and its antithesis, unbalanced growth, and backward and forward linkages. He observes correctly that these concepts owe little to Keynes. Yet he never considers Keynes' relevance to the neo-liberal critique of them that emerged in the 1970s. Keynes in the 1920s ('the young Keynes') was a liberal economist and a supporter of the Liberal Party (Toye 2015). It does not require a great stretch of the imagination to see the connection between his liberalism and the neo-liberalism that later reshaped development policy. That there was a clear affinity, demonstrated by his writing on Soviet Russia, is the theme of this chapter.

The economics of Soviet Russia

Keynes emerged onto the world stage in 1919 as a result of his searing criticism of the Versailles peace treaty in *The Economic Consequences of the Peace*. This turned him into a prominent public intellectual, whose views were taken seriously even by those whose policies he criticized. He wrote extensively about the reconstruction of Europe and attended the Genoa Conference of April 1922, where he talked with Soviet finance officials about the working of Russia's post-revolution financial system. This involved a dual currency of 'gold roubles' for foreign transactions and 'paper roubles' for domestic transactions. Keynes noted that the fact that the internal purchasing power of the rouble was much less than its external purchasing power was 'doubtless due to the stringent prohibitions on imports combined with the excessive internal distrust of the rouble due to its catastrophic collapse in recent months'. That collapse was in turn attributed to the fact that the printing of paper money financed some 20 per cent of government expenditure. The causal link from inflationary government finance, plus strict import controls, to an overvalued foreign exchange rate was clearly postulated (CW XVII: 404–5).[1]

One of Keynes's key informants in Genoa was E. A. Preobrazhensky, who as chairman of the financial commission of the central committee oversaw the preparation of the financial aspects of the New Economic Policy (Preobrazhensky 1980). Preobrazhensky wrote a report on the Genoa Conference in November 1922 in which he stated his strong belief that 'proletarian power must not ... give up a single decisive economic position, especially not key positions such as large-scale industry, banking, foreign trade, and the wholesale trade in monopoly and foreign commodities'. In another report to the 1922 Congress he specified the Soviets' economic objectives as 'to subordinate the peasantry to large-scale production' and 'to maintain control over the country's entire trade with foreign capital in grain and agricultural raw material' (Preobrazhensky 1973/1922).

The emphasis on control of foreign trade is noteworthy. Preobrazhensky believed that access to foreign markets was absolutely essential to the success of a socialist revolution in a backward country. He fiercely opposed the strategy of 'socialism in one country' that Stalin advocated. Preobrazhensky's concern for sustaining trade with the capitalist West on advantageous terms was evidently one to which Keynes responded, with his characteristic opportunism, by writing a pamphlet advocating a large British credit to promote their agricultural production and exports. (Tsarist Russia had been a major grain exporter to the rest of Europe, but was then in the grip of famine.)

In 1922 Keynes was still optimistic that the value of the paper rouble could be stabilized, by a sufficient increase in tax effort. By 1923, however, he was not. In his *A Tract on Monetary Reform*, the concept of the inflation tax is clearly presented as 'the form of taxation which the public find hardest to evade and even the weakest government can enforce, when it can enforce nothing else' (CW IV: 37). Soviet finance officials are said to be 'more self-conscious and

---

[1] 'CW' refers to Keynes's thirty-volume *Collected Writings* (Keynes 1971–89), followed by volume and page numbers.

deliberate than others in their monetary policy'. A footnote adds that 'the Soviet Government have always regarded monetary inflation quite frankly as an instrument of taxation'. When Keynes states that 'it would be too cynical to suppose that...governments...depreciate their currencies *on purpose*', he adds 'except, possibly, the Russian government' (CW IV: 37, 49). He had by now lost his confidence of the previous year that the paper rouble would soon be stabilized.

After Keynes had married Lydia Lopokova, a Russian-born ballet dancer, they paid an official visit on behalf of Cambridge University to the Russian Academy of Sciences in 1925. On his return, he published three articles in his *A Short View of Russia*. What is most striking is the second article of the three on the economics of Soviet Russia. His general view of the Soviet economic system was that 'at a low level of efficiency [it] does function and possesses elements of permanence'. 'A certain equilibrium had been established between the urban proletariat of 20 million living at a higher standard of living than its output justifies and the 120 million strong rural peasantry which, in spite of its exploitation, desired no change in government because it had been given the land' (CW IX: 263–4).

This system of what would now be called 'urban bias' was maintained, according to Keynes, by 'the official method of exploiting the peasants'. This method he described as follows.

> [It] is not so much by taxation...as by price policy. The monopoly of import and export trade and the virtual control of industrial output enable the authorities to maintain prices at levels highly disadvantageous to the peasant. They buy his wheat from him at much below the world price, and they sell to him textile and other manufactured goods appreciably above the world price, the difference providing a fund out of which can be financed their high overhead costs and the general inefficiency of manufacture and distribution. The monopoly of import and export trade, by permitting a divorce between the internal and external price levels, can be operated in such a way as to maintain the parity of foreign exchange in spite of a depreciation in the purchasing power of [domestic] money.   (CW IX: 264)

Before his first Russian visit, Keynes had identified three linked instruments of the Soviet government's management of the economy. They were the state monopoly of the import and export trade, use of the inflation tax to part-finance government spending, and maintenance of a foreign exchange rate that was overvalued in terms of the domestic currency. In the *Short View* he explained how these policy instruments were used to exploit the peasantry by underpricing their sale of the exportable agricultural surplus and overpricing the consumer goods that they needed. Exploitation of the peasantry by means of distorted prices created the fund from which the new urban industrial enterprises were subsidized.

From liberalism to neo-liberalism

By the 1970s many newly independent countries had adopted industrialization strategies using policy instruments very similar in design and effects to
those of the Soviet strategy that Keynes had described and explained. The
results in terms of increases in welfare and decreases in poverty and inequality
were judged to be highly disappointing. Disillusion triggered a number of
studies that described and explained the reasons for the disappointing consequences. In the synthesis volume that summarized a number of the country
studies sponsored by the Organization for Economic Cooperation and Development (OECD), the authors' opening statement says:

> The main theses in this book are that industry has been over-encouraged in
> relation to agriculture and that, although there are arguments for giving special
> encouragement to industry, this encouragement could be provided in forms that
> would not, as present policies do, discourage exports, including agricultural
> exports; which would promote greater efficiency in the use of resources; and
> which would create a less unequal distribution of income and higher levels of
> employment in both industry and agriculture.   (Little et al. 1970: 1)

In this one can hear echoes of the advice of the young Keynes.
   Compare it with Keynes's diagnosis of the trouble with the Soviet economy:

> The low value of agricultural products in terms of industrial products is a serious
> deterrent to the output of the former, which is the real wealth of the country. The
> fundamental problem of the Soviet government is to get itself into a sufficiently
> strong financial position to be able to pay the peasant more nearly the real value of
> his produce—which would surely have the effect of giving him both the means
> and incentive to a far higher output.   (CW IX: 264)

The Soviet government never succeeded in resolving the agricultural problem. It
persisted throughout the Soviet era until the regime collapsed in the early 1990s.
   Preobrazhensky's strategy of squeezing the peasantry in order to subsidize
industry and the living standard of the urban proletariat was also the target of
Lipton's (1977) critique of the phenomenon of urban bias in developing
countries. This documented both the 'price twists' by means of artificially
low farm gate procurement prices not compensated by subsidies to farm
inputs, and the inefficient and inequitable allocations of public investment
between the agricultural and non-agricultural sector. However, Lipton does
not refer in his analysis to the previous analysis of the young Keynes's and his
critical account of urban bias in Soviet Russia.
   That account anticipated the Harris and Todaro analysis of the migration
consequences of urban bias. It argued that artificially boosting urban wages
would draw excessive numbers of rural-urban migrants into the towns,

because they will fail to calculate correctly their probability of finding a job there. The flow would be checked only 'after the towns have become over-crowded and unemployment reached unheard-of proportions' and a 'a vast army of unemployed is a heavy burden on the financial resources of the state establishments' (CW IX: 265).

Keynes had visited the new economic laboratory and re-examined his whole intellectual apparatus in the light of the Soviet economic system. What did he conclude from it? His verdict was:

> This state of affairs serves but to enforce a lesson of bourgeois economics as being equally applicable in a Communist [as in a liberal] state, namely that it impairs wealth to interfere with the normal levels of relative prices or with the normal levels of relative wages.   (CW IX: 265)

One hears in this pronouncement two propositions much repeated in the neo-liberal counter-revolution in development economics of the 1970s and 1980s. The first is the importance of 'getting the prices right', particularly the exchange rate, the interest rate, and factor and commodity prices. The second is the claim that there is just one type of economics that applies universally—in Bangladesh much as in Belgium, and in Ghana as much as in Greece. The idea that there is an economics of development that is separate from the economics of developed countries is one that the young Keynes did not entertain.

The element of the later neo-liberal analysis that the young Keynes failed to anticipate was its connection of rent seeking and corruption to the three policy instruments that the Soviet government used to control the economy. Some of his observations did bear on this connection, however. He noted that the new system removed any possibility of large gains except by taking the same sort of risks that attach to bribery and embezzlement elsewhere, adding that bribery and embezzlement had not disappeared in Russia or were even rare. Yet he never argued that the removal by the state of legitimate oppor-tunities for private moneymaking created extra incentives and opportunities for bribery and embezzlement or that this drove the Soviet state to take extreme countermeasures of surveillance and punishment.

When he wrote *A Short View*, the young Keynes did not believe that the Bolsheviks had made any contribution to economic problems of intellectual interest or scientific value. He was, however, as a good liberal, prepared to leave his judgment provisional until Russia had enjoyed five years of peace and fair weather. Before the five years were up he concluded after his 1928 visit that the Soviet experiment had failed.

As part of his re-examination of his intellectual principles, the young Keynes had asked himself the question 'Am I a Liberal?' In the course of answering his own question he asserted: 'I can be influenced by what seems to me to be justice and good sense; but the *class war* will find me on the side of the educated *bourgeoisie'* (CW IX: 297).

Did Keynes change his mind?

To recapitulate, the argument of this chapter so far has been that those who argue for the irrelevance of Keynes's ideas to development economics have neglected his analysis of the Soviet economy in the 1920s. Further, his analysis anticipated the main points of the neo-liberal critique of development economics and policy made in the 1970s and remains influential in the twenty-first century. Moreover, his analysis led him to make policy recommendations in favour of specialization in accordance with static comparative advantage, namely the promotion of agriculture and agricultural exports. This recommendation was highly orthodox liberal economic policy. The irony of this argument is that treating 1920s Russia as an exemplar of a developing country confounds those of Keynes's critics who accuse him of spreading collectivist beliefs and other dangerous anti-capitalist doctrines. His writings on Russia reveal him as a very intelligent, but very conventional, liberal economist.

This interpretation of Keynes's views is open to one very obvious objection. All of the evidence I have cited relates to the 1920s, which is the period (it will be said) before Keynes abandoned conventional liberal economics and developed distinctively Keynesian economic ideas. It is no surprise therefore that the young Keynes analysed the Russian economy conventionally, and gave a critical verdict on the unorthodox policies of the early Soviet regime. The mature Keynes changed his mind. He responded to the fact of the post-1929 depression by embracing both protectionism and a form of state investment planning. It is precisely whether these policies, which classical liberals reject, promote economic development that lies at the heart of the question of the relevance of Keynes to development economics. So (the objectors might conclude), it was after all right to ignore the Keynes's Soviet writings in assessing the significance of Keynes for development economics.

Was it right? The mature Keynes certainly did change his mind, but only about some things. He certainly changed his mind from being a defender of free trade to being an advocate of tariffs. He also wanted to expand the functions of the state (in addition to protection) in areas that he claimed to be legitimate and socially beneficial, such as running a budget deficit in a depression. The central issue, however, is whether his change of mind led him to backtrack in any way on his earlier criticism of the Soviet strategy of development, his prescription of the removal of price distortions, and the boosting of agricultural exports. In the remainder of this chapter, I will try to establish that only trivial alterations to his views on these points occurred during the rest of his life.

Views of the mature Keynes on the Russian economy

As evidence of his continuing disenchantment with the Soviet economic experiment, one may cite his ironical review of Kingsley Martin's impressions of the Soviet Union, which were written as the textual accompaniment to *Low's Russian Sketch Book*, published in 1932:

> [It is] a little too full, perhaps, of good will. When a doubt arises, it is swallowed down if possible. Mr Martin is ready to agree on the whole that it is a grand ideal to turn peasants into machine-minders. He reflects that 'these people at least have a fuller diet than Chinese coolies, and I doubt that they are as poor as peasants are in India'. If it is pointed out to him that that the only people who really suffer from restrictions on free speech are a few educated intellectuals, he wonders doubtfully if he will find a convincing answer in Rousseau or Bentham or John Stuart Mill. When he is told that 'as to fat, they rely on sunflower oil', he remembers that the whole civilization of Greece was built up on olive oil. That is the right spirit in which to visit Russia if one wants to enjoy oneself.

Martin manfully published Keynes's review in *The New Statesman*, although he was upset and offended by it. He complained to Keynes: '[It] reads as if you thought my stuff [were] bosh and just wanted to avoid saying so because I am editor of the paper' (Rolph 1973). We do not have Keynes's reply, but Martin was surely right in his surmise.

When Keynes made his case for trade protection in *National Self-Sufficiency* (1933), it was a very modest and qualified one. He did not deny the comparative advantage argument for free trade—the conventional justification that he had previously espoused. Instead he argued that the cost of departing from free trade would be small and might well be outweighed by the opportunity that it afforded to pursue other national goals, such as an increase in employment and output beyond what was possible under free trade. Gradualness and caution in the use of protection were recommended repeatedly.

Keynes was absolutely clear that many actions taken under the umbrella of national self-sufficiency had failed to generate net benefits. On the contrary, he candidly declared that in countries where advocates of national self-sufficiency had gained power, many foolish things were being done. Notably, Russia is singled out for special criticism in this regard (CW XXI: 243–4). Keynes was adamant that he was not giving a blanket endorsement to economic nationalism, let alone to economic autarchy. However, having dropped his absolute rejection of the principle of protection, he now had to criticize trade protection schemes on different criteria than violation of the simple lessons of bourgeois economics on which he had relied in 1925.

His new criteria concern the prudence and intelligence of schemes of protection. Russia is found wanting on two grounds. Protection had been introduced in Russia with haste that was ridiculous and unnecessary. He thought that the rapidity of the transition would ensure so great a destruction of wealth that the new state of affairs would be far worse than the old. In addition to unnecessary haste, Russia had suffered from intolerance and the stifling of sensible criticism. He was horrified that Stalin had 'eliminated every independent, critical mind, even when it is sympathetic in general outlook' (CW XXI: 246). The oppressive tactics of Stalin are contrasted with the old nineteenth-century ideals of civilized debate and Keynes leaves no doubt on which side of this contrast his own engagement lies.

Keynesian versus Soviet planning

When, in 1932, Keynes publicly advocated a form of state planning, he began that advocacy by denying that it rested on the alleged achievements of Russia's economy under planning. Instead he was ironical about the tendency to exaggerate these achievements, as a reaction to an initially excessive skepticism about whether Bolshevism could succeed economically.

> We have been taught to think of Communism as involving so complete a destruction of human organization, that when we learned that, after enormous suffering an incredible national effort of self-denial and the exercise of will, a Russian peasant can positively build a tractor of which the wheels go round and that there is a large electric power station in Leningrad, we gape with wonder and rush to the opposite conclusion that Communism is a roaring success. (CW XXI: 85)

In this quotation Keynes contrasts the huge costs and limited benefits of planning in the Russian style. This was all mere ground clearing. He wanted to make a case for planning that rested entirely on the gap between the actual and the potential achievements of the capitalist economies. As he put it, with reference to Italy and the Soviet Union:

> To establish a *prima facie* case for planning, we do not need to seek or discover success in the planned regimes to the south or to the east. It is sufficient to apprehend failure, as compared with opportunity, in the unplanned regions here at home or to the west of the ocean. (CW XXI: 86)

The type of planning that he advocated differed dramatically from the Soviet method of exploitation that he had analysed in 1925. The difference from socialism and communism was that it was not an attempt to aggrandize the state for its own sake, but to supplement the activity of private enterprise, modifying through the use of deliberate central foresight the environment in which the private economy operated. The purpose of Keynes's type of planning was not to replace private activity, but to do those things which in the nature of the case lie beyond the scope of any individual. Keynes pointed to examples of this type of planning that already existed—taxation, tariffs, exchange control, physical town planning, and the regulation of public transport.

Keynes explored problems of negative externalities to speculate on additional examples of state planning that might be needed in the future. He contemplated control over the location of industry, given the social costs of wasted infrastructure in areas that industry deserts. He also contemplated controls on immigration and emigration to regulate the size of the population. He advocated state support for the arts and a state lottery.

Most famously, Keynes advocated state action to increase employment during a depression. In 1934, he was challenged by R. H. Brand to confirm that he did not want the complete revolution that would be involved in the Soviet practice of constraining consumption and arranging production to match the planned pattern of consumption. Keynes replied:

> demand will be free in the sense that consumers will themselves decide how to spend their incomes. The sort of management I have in view would not interfere with this... or the great bulk of private enterprise. Apart from taxation it would interfere very little... except insofar as it was necessary to control the volume of investment,—subject to the reserve that the taxation or its equivalent might be deliberately aimed at discouraging saving.   (CW XXI: 342–6)

He also proposed the socialization of risk by increasing the proportion of investment undertaken by public institutions. Here we have a sketch of Keynes's new macroeconomic policy in explicit contrast with Soviet-style planning.

In the *General Theory*, he asserted that 'a somewhat comprehensive socialization of investment will prove to be the only means of securing an approximation to full employment' and that 'the central controls necessary to ensure full employment will, of course, involve a large extension of the traditional functions of government' (CW VII: 378). However, to these sweeping and imprecise assertions, two important riders were added. First, that all manner of compromises and devices could be used by the public sector to cooperate with the private to achieve the required levels and directions of investment. Second, that the reasoning behind the proposal for the socialization gave no warrant for a system of state socialism that would embrace most of the economic life of the community.

In his advocacy of both protection and planning, Keynes very emphatically separated his proposals for selective protection and moderate planning of the framework for private enterprise from communism, state socialism, and the actual management of the Soviet economy. In his writings this separation could hardly be clearer and in his correspondence it is equally clear. The editor of *Soviet Heavy Industry* wrote to Keynes in 1934, asking him to explain why industrial production in the USSR was growing while capitalist economies remained severely depressed. Keynes immediately cabled this reply:

> It is, however, certainly true that the growth of industrial production is much facilitated in a state which starts at a very low level and is prepared to make great sacrifices to increase industrial production without making a close calculation as to whether it is strictly speaking profitable and advantageous for the existing generation of workers.   (King's College Library, Keynes Archive, folio L.34)

Keynes changed his mind about whether capitalism could survive without more state planning, but he did not change his mind about the Soviet strategy of economic development.

Did Keynes remain a liberal?

It is common to attribute to Keynes a Platonist view of the state, that is, that benevolent and intelligent guardians, such as he was, should guide its policies. This is the opinion of Maurice Cranston, for example (Thirlwall 1978). Such a view labels Keynes as an elitist and a technocrat, rather than a political liberal. There is a grain of truth in this image, but it is misguided in that it ignores much weightier liberal leanings in Keynes's political stance.

His true position is perfectly clear and he stated it succinctly in the early 1930s. 'My own aim', he declared, 'is economic reform by the methods of political liberalism' (CW XVIII: 29). The methods of political liberalism in a democracy are manifold and Keynes made use of most of them, although he declined to stand for elective office. In order to influence and persuade, he wrote books and articles, wrote journalism for newspapers, gave radio talks, gave evidence to committees of enquiry, and held positions of high responsibility in the civil service, private firms, national boards, and the House of Lords. The ideal state in his view was one that kept open all these channels of influence on a government that was itself democratically elected. Keynes had plenty of criticisms of individual politicians and of the cumbrous working of the liberal democratic political process. Yet he never tried to subvert it.

The grain of truth in the accusation of Platonic sympathies is that he greatly valued the injection of intelligence into government. He was not simply on the side of the bourgeoisie, but of the *educated* bourgeoisie. He praised political parties whose leadership was able to control the details of its election manifesto and the techniques by which its principles were to be put into practice. This was because he believed that the right solution to problems of the underlying economic framework would involve intellectual and scientific reasoning that would be above the heads of the vast mass of more or less illiterate voters.

A Platonic state is not necessarily committed to the maintenance of liberal institutions. An elite determines the laws, according to its concept of the public good. Indeed, the Soviet state in the 1920s could correctly be dubbed a Platonic state. Keynes thought Leninism was a missionary religion, and that the Bolsheviks had swapped a new form of tyranny for the old one. Karl Popper (1945) thought Plato, Marx, and Lenin were all enemies of an open society.

When Keynes changed his mind to favour an enlarged role for the state in shaping the economic framework of society, critics accused him of betraying liberalism. He replied that his proposals would lead neither to Bolshevism nor to Fascism. Although state planning was obviously easier in an autocracy, Keynes thought that autocratic planning had two fatal flaws. Its lack of legitimacy leads to popular apathy and an inability to recruit the best talent into the planning administration. Nonetheless, his critics attacked him on the ground that he was constructing a slippery slope that would frustrate the separation between liberalism and autocracy that he wanted to preserve. They argued that to try to advance beyond the existing framework of capitalism would jeopardize what Keynes evidently cherished—the old nineteenth-century ideals of liberty. Their contention was that the next step forward (reformed capitalism) would be at the expense of losing a previous valued reform (liberal institutions). Further, it would happen irrespective of the intentions of the reformers. This is the jeopardy thesis, one of the three classic argument used to shoot down proposals for social progress (Hirschman 1991).

Late in his life Keynes debated this point with Friedrich Hayek. In 1944, he wrote to Hayek about his diatribe against planning, *The Road to Serfdom* (Hayek 1962/1944). He reiterated his view that, in evaluating the practice of planning, the moral and political climate in which planning is done is all-important in determining its social consequences. He believed that his type of modest planning, where the state supplements but does not substitute for private enterprise, would be much less of a threat to liberal values than Hayek had prophesied, provided that a liberal moral and political culture could be preserved and strengthened (CW XXVII: 385–8).

Even closer to his premature death, Keynes fired a parting shot, in which he repudiated a key instrument of Soviet economic management. In April 1945 he considered the international settlement for which Britain should aim after victory. He rejected any turning away from a return to multilateral trading, after discussing extensively the pros and cons of Britain opting for Russian-style controls over foreign trade. He called it a 'frantic and suicidal' alternative to multilateralism; he was certain that it would be a disaster

(CW XXIV: 256–7). He simply brushes aside Joan Robinson's enthusiasm for trade controls.

Revolution and counter-revolution

Keynes's modest planning turned out to be a great success. In the field of economic theory, his invention of macroeconomics was received as a veritable intellectual revolution, though from the start it never went uncontested (Backhouse 1999). In terms of practical economic policies, when coupled with the tools of national accounting, it worked the miracle for two decades of maintaining full employment, and in some countries over-full employment, along with low inflation rates.

The success of the Keynesian revolution had unintended consequences for the economics of development emerging in the 1940s and 1950s. Keynes had distinguished two systems of economics—the Classical, which applied only to the special case of full employment, and the Keynesian, which applied when there was unemployment because of deficiency of demand. This step from one to two systems of economics gave the idea that there might be yet another system of economics, instant credibility, especially among keen young converts to Keynesian economics who wanted to create another revolution in economics. Dudley Seers was one such would-be revolutionary. Whereas Keynes took the full employment economy to be a special case, Seers dubbed the economics of advanced economies to be the special case and the economics of development to be the general case (Seers 1963; Hirschman 1981: 6 and n.3). Unfortunately, this extension of the special/general distinction to capitalist and developing countries has no foundation in Keynes's writings about developing countries, which reflect a robust 'monoeconomics' approach.

Keynes's mission was to save capitalism from its self-destructive tendencies. Once he began to work out the logic of the fiscal and monetary policies to that end, his criticisms of Soviet economic management became ever sharper. The enormity of the mistakes that planning regimes can make if they are hugely ambitious, too weak in administration, and too unfettered by liberal and democratic institutions impressed him ever more strongly as the era of Stalin unfolded its horrors. Joan Robinson must be given the last word. She had it exactly right when she wrote of Keynes: 'Capitalism was in some ways repugnant to him, but Stalinism was much worse' (Robinson 1975).

The sixty years from 1925 to 1985 was the heyday of economic narratives of development, stretching from the liberalism of Keynes through heterodoxy and orthodox responses and back to neo-liberalism. In Chapters 6 to 8 we will look at the highlights of these economic narratives of the acceleration of economic development, before coming to the debates in which disenchantment with them found its expression.

References

Backhouse, R. E., ed. (1999). *Keynes: Contemporary Responses to the General Theory*. South Bend, IN: St Augustine's Press.

Chandavarkar, A. (1989). *Keynes and India: A Study in Economics and Biography*. Basingstoke: Macmillan.

Erlich, A. (1960). *The Soviet Industrialization Debate, 1924–1928*. Cambridge, MA: Harvard University Press.

Hayek, F. A. (1962/1944). *The Road to Serfdom*. London: Routledge and Kegan Paul.

Hirschman, A. O. (1981). *Essays in Trespassing: From Economics to Politics and Beyond*. Cambridge: Cambridge University Press.

Hirschman, A. O. (1991). *The Rhetoric of Reaction: Perversity, Futility, Jeopardy*. Cambridge, MA: Belknap Press of the Harvard University Press.

Johnson, E. S., and Johnson, H. G. (1978). *The Shadow of Keynes: Understanding Keynes, Cambridge and Keynesian Economics*. Oxford: Blackwell.

Keynes, J. M. (1971–89). *The Collected Writings of John Maynard Keynes*, 30 volumes. Basingstoke: Macmillan. Cited as 'CW'.

Keynes, M., ed. (1975). *Essays on John Maynard Keynes*. Cambridge: Cambridge University Press.

Lipton, M. (1977). *Why Poor People Stay Poor: A Study of Urban Bias in World Development*. London: Temple Smith.

Little, I. M. D., Scitovsky, T., and Scott, M. F. (1970). *Industry and Trade in Some Developing Countries*. Oxford: Oxford University Press for the OECD.

Nove, A. (1983). *The Economics of Feasible Socialism*. London: Allen and Unwin.

Popper, K. R. (1945). *The Open Society and its Enemies*. London: Routledge.

Preobrazhensky, E. A. (1973/1922). *From NEP to Socialism: A Glance into the Future of Russia and Europe*. London: New York Publications.

Preobrazhensky, E. A. (1980). *The Crisis of Soviet Industrialization: Selected Essays*. New York: M. E. Sharpe.

Robinson, J. (1975). What has become of the Keynesian revolution?, in M. Keynes, ed., *Essays on John Maynard Keynes*. Cambridge: Cambridge University Press.

Rolph, C. H. (1973). *Kingsley: The Life, Letters and Diaries of Kingsley Martin*. London: Victor Gollancz.

Seers, D. (1963). The limitations of the special case. *Bulletin of the Oxford University Institute of Economics and Statistics* 25(1), 77–88.

Thirlwall, A. P. (1978). *Keynes and Laissez-Faire*. Basingstoke: Macmillan.

Toye, R. (2015). Keynes, liberalism, and 'The Emancipation of the Mind'. *English Historical Review* 130(546), 1162–91.

6

Colonial development by intersector labour transfer, 1950–69

> *The conquest of the earth, which mostly means the taking it away from those who have a different complexion or slightly flatter noses than ourselves, is not a pretty thing when you look at it too much. What redeems it is the idea only. An idea at the back of it; not a sentimental pretence but an idea; and an unselfish belief in the idea.*
>
> —Charlie Marlow in *The Heart of Darkness*

From nationalism to imperialism and colonialism

The last quarter of the nineteenth century witnessed a transition from the nationalism that had unified Italy and Germany to a new phase of European territorial conquest—imperialism and colonialism. This transition, well illustrated in the political career of Benjamin Disraeli, was later spelt out in J. A. Hobson's *Imperialism: A Study* (1902). Hobson presented the change as a corruption of genuine nationalism. Imperialism, in his view, was 'a debasement of this genuine nationalism, by attempts to overflow its natural banks and absorb the near or distant territory of reluctant or unassimilable peoples' (Hobson 1902: para.9 Introduction).

Hobson documented the huge extent of European imperial and colonial expansion, not least the persistent extension of British India into Burma and Afghanistan, but including the colonial acquisitions of France, Germany, Italy, Belgium, Portugal, and the United States. He pointed out that nowhere had the new imperialism and colonialism extended the political and civil liberties of the metropolitan country to any of the newly acquired territories. They involved the extension of autocracy to mainly tropical lands where European people would not be able to settle and undertake genuine colonization.

The popular justification for imperialism was a form of Social Darwinism. The argument was that human progress depended on continuing military competition. Competition was allegedly beneficial both between the 'socially efficient' European nations and inferior weak races, and between the European nations themselves in their attempts to subjugate the weak races. This justification rested on dubious assumptions about European social efficiency and non-European racial weakness that derived from eugenics. It may come as a surprise that the young Keynes was among the many adherents of the doctrines of both imperialism and its justification by eugenics (Toye 2000).

By the 1930s, as Keynes was embarking on his famous change of mind about the functions of the capitalist state, official and public attitudes to Western colonialism and imperialism were beginning to change. Eugenics was being revealed as a spurious science, and the natives were getting restless. At the end of the decade labour disturbances broke out in the British West Indies, and a royal commission was set up to investigate. The possession of colonies began to seem problematic. The official response was to consider offering constitutional advances to colonial governments, but the state of development and welfare was regarded as inadequate to provide firm foundations for the delegation of power to local assemblies. The Second World War brought with it the imperative of maintaining 'a contented Empire' and a reliable source of food and raw materials. These pressures were the occasion for the launch of long-term policies of colonial development and welfare (Morgan 1980: I xvii, 72–5).

The war accelerated advances in science, technology, and production engineering. Science and technology became more integrated into the operations of businesses and government. As a result, the prestige of the natural sciences reached new heights, and so did the ambitions of natural scientists. For example, the British Association for the Advancement of Science organized an international conference in September 1941 on 'science and world order'. The scientists claimed to be able to effect a rational reconstruction of the world once the war was won. The scope of the action envisaged was very broad, including the application of medical, nutritional, and agricultural science, the management of global natural resources, and the economics and anthropology of colonized peoples. The ageing H. G. Wells in his plenary address expressed the grand Enlightenment ambition that he still harboured:

> We are the small beginning that may start an avalanche which will cleanse the world. Men of science have the alternative of being like Greek slaves and doing what they are told by their masters, the gangsters and profiteers, or taking their rightful place as the servant-masters of the world.   (Crowther et al. 1942: 11)

Not all the conference participants shared the messianic vision of Wells. Lord Hailey's paper on science and colonial responsibilities struck a much more sober note. He noted the growing gap between the material conditions of the colonizers and the colonized. 'From our anthropological study' (presumably his *African Survey* (1938)), he concluded that the cultural gulf between colonial and European populations was so great that it could not be closed 'by a hasty substitution of our own social conceptions and practices'. What was needed was 'a studied adaptation of custom to modern uses' (Crowther et al. 1942: 124–6). The outcome of the adaptation process could not be specified in advance and would probably be decided in due course by the dependent people themselves, but in the meantime Hailey accepted that the colonial administration, acting as trustees for their future, should provide adequate welfare, in the three dimensions of nutrition, health, and education.

Hailey's caution on the prospects for modernization in the colonies contrasted with the vaulting ambition of the natural scientists on the prospects for post-war world agriculture, food, health, and nutrition.

All the same, his vision of development was a technocratic one, in which colonial administrators delivered material welfare so that the autocratic political basis for colonial rule could be gradually eroded (Easterly 2013: 86–9, 339).

Arthur Lewis and colonial economic development

One of the well-established traditions of British colonial administration at that time was that non-whites were barred from becoming colonial administrators. That applied in St Lucia, a small island in the Eastern Caribbean where Arthur Lewis was born and brought up. Lewis won a scholarship for undergraduate study in the UK; he wanted to be an engineer, but knew the colour bar in the West Indies would keep him out of that profession. Instead he chose to study for the Bachelor of Commerce Degree at the London School of Economics (LSE). It contained some economics, but at the time Lewis did not know what economics was (Breit and Hirsch 2005: 1). Yet by 1937 he had his degree with first class honours and by 1940, after his doctorate, he was appointed as a junior lecturer at the LSE.

In August 1941, Lord Hailey (then at the Colonial Office) invited the LSE to prepare a memorandum on the financing of mining and industrial development in the Caribbean and African colonies. The task fell to Lewis. The young lecturer showed extraordinary self-confidence and ambition in expanding the scope of the requested research to include plantations, and in making a series of policy recommendations, contrary to Hailey's cautious preference for limiting the memorandum to purely objective factual statements (Ingham and Mosley 2013: 27–31).

By this time, Lewis had joined the Fabian Society, for whom he had written a pamphlet on *Labour in the West Indies* (1939), which reported on the labour unrest in St Kitts, Trinidad, and Jamaica. He had also become a member of the

Fabian Colonial Bureau, set up in 1940 as a separate organization from the society. Both institutions gave him moral and practical support. He formed a firm friendship with Evan Durbin, a fellow economist at LSE and Fabian. When in 1943, Lewis was appointed as Secretary to a new Colonial Economic Advisory Council (CEAC) within the Colonial Office, he co-authored with Evan Durbin a twelve-page paper on 'Colonial Economic Development'.

It emphasized four key messages. The first was that laissez-faire was not a suitable policy for colonial development, because of extensive market failures in the colonies. Lewis and Durbin appealed for the use of List's instruments of government intervention and protection, even in tropical colonial countries. The second message was that investment in secondary industries should be selective, rather than the across the board 'big push' industrialization that Paul Rosenstein-Rodan had advocated in his seminal article on development in south-eastern Europe (Rosenstein-Rodan 1963/1943). The third was the need to raise agricultural productivity by consolidating land holdings up to an economic size. Finally, they advocated mass education in the rural sector through agricultural extension work.

The significance of this paper was that, along with Rosenstein-Rodan's article, it marked a shift from descriptive analysis of colonial economies to analysis that was strongly prescriptive and tackled the question 'What should be done?' However, before the Secretary of State had considered the paper's policy advice, Lewis had resigned from the CEAC in bitterness and frustration (Ingham and Mosley 2013: 53–66). It was the first of a number of impetuous resignations that would mark his career.

In 1948, the Fabian Society commissioned Lewis to write a pamphlet that grew eventually into his book *The Principles of Economic Planning* (1949). He did not favour what he called 'planning by direction', but advocated forms of government intervention that were less coercive and less inefficient. Like many Fabians, he believed in economic science as a guide to the rational administration of the economy. Like many Fabians, he supported colonial reform. He declared himself an 'anti-imperialist' and associated with the mixed bag of anti-imperialists living in London in the 1940s, but the main targets of his wrath were the institutionalized racism of the colonial system and the neglect of the social and economic needs of the local populations. Like Lord Hailey, he saw these as the primary objectives of colonial reform, rather than political decolonization.

Given the activist recommendations of his joint CEAC paper with Durbin, he was surprisingly tentative in *The Principles of Economic Planning* about the use of economic planning in tropical colonial countries. In an appendix, Lewis acknowledged that planning in backward countries faced a whole raft of inter-linked problems. Planning by corrupt administrations would provoke violent revolutions; but building greater administrative capacity was impossible because of the prevailing poverty. Backward agriculture was the cause of the poverty problem, but popular revolutions would only worsen matters if they resulted in splitting up large estates. Large-scale agriculture would need to be complemented by new employment opportunities outside agriculture, but in order to industrialize the government must first invest in infrastructure. Industrialization therefore implied strict exchange control and borrowing capital from abroad. Yet backward countries did not have the strong, competent, and noncorrupt administrations required to carry out these tasks.

The thrust of the argument was that the problems of backward countries are cumulative and self-reinforcing. So what to do? Lewis's first thought was that 'it is often better that such governments should be *laisser-faire* than that they should pretend to plan' (Lewis 1949: 121). However, he could not leave the matter there. He had already written defiantly in his pamphlet on *Labour in the West Indies* 'there is no vicious circle for men of determination'. In a sudden leap, he concluded on a more optimistic note. 'Popular enthusiasm is both the lubricating oil of planning and the petrol of economic development—a dynamic force that almost makes all things possible' (Lewis 1949: 128).

The theory of intersector labour transfer

The idea that manufacturing industry has distinctive features that made it a superior form of economic activity to agriculture has a very long pedigree. In 1691, for example, Sir William Petty wrote: 'There is much more to be gained by Manufacture than Husbandry; and by Merchandise than Manufacture'. He was reflecting on the fact that throughout the seventeenth century in England, the structure of male employment had already been shifting away from agriculture and in favour of manufacturing and services. 'Petty's Law' captures the idea that differences in labour productivity in the different occupational sectors of an economy can become the dynamic for its development (Clark 1940: 176–7, 181). In his book *The Conditions of Economic Progress* (1940), Colin Clark provided statistical evidence for an association of intersector labour transfer with rising average real income per head. His main correlation was on a cross-section basis, but he also showed that the process had occurred in developed countries over time. His data are largely restricted to developed countries, because it was only for them that this indefatigable data hunter could find the numbers that he needed. Nevertheless, his correlations raised the question whether Petty's Law was a universal process that would also characterize the development of poor colonies in the tropics. What was not clear was whether changes in the sector composition of output and employment were the causes or consequences of economic development.

It was a question that Clark himself was unable to give a definitive answer, as his preferred method of working was wholly inductive and empirical.

Arthur Lewis believed in the idea of development by means of intersector labour transfer. He believed that it had characterized the Industrial Revolution in Britain, citing the work of the Fabian economic historians J. L. and Barbara Hammond. Lewis did not doubt the relevance of British economic history to the problems of colonial societies, and held that the absorption of surplus rural labour into manufacturing could also be the dynamic of economic development in colonial countries. The neoclassical economics of wages determined by marginal productivity in which he had been trained had no relevance there, he thought. Accordingly, he looked to the works of the English classical economists to inform a long period theory that would better suit the colonial case. He was impatient with those who, like List, thought that in tropical countries people held attitudes and values inconsistent with economic development (Tignor 2006: 88–93).

Curiously, he made no reference to the work of Ida Greaves. A Barbadian, she was that rare thing, a female economist, who had written a brilliant doctoral thesis at the LSE about development. She succeeded Lewis there as a lecturer in colonial economics after he moved to a chair at Manchester University. Her thesis, *Modern Production among Backward Peoples*, had been published in 1935. She argued that relegating people in tropical countries to some pre-economic state of society was an invalid and unnecessary assumption. However, at the same time she provided a detailed analysis of the conditions of labour supply in the public and private sectors of colonial economies. Her challenging message was: 'The means by which a satisfactory supply of workers for all these classes of demand can be obtained has been one of the leading problems of the administration in every tropical territory' (Greaves 1968/1935: 112).

A major reason for this difficulty, she suggested, was that most indigenous people still had the option of working on their own land and did not constitute a genuine proletariat reliant solely on wage labour to survive. Colonial administrations therefore resorted to undermining the independence of indigenous people through land confiscation or the imposition of new obligations that could be satisfied only through earning money by labour. In addition, they encouraged the large-scale immigration of Indian and Chinese indentured labour to augment the labour supply, often creating fresh disincentives for indigenous labour in the process. Lewis did not engage at all with these realities of colonial economic history, but focused instead on the history of the Industrial Revolution in Britain. This ignored Greaves' prescient warning: 'the problem of establishing a capitalistic system in backward territories is that of grafting a structure which arose in one place in consequence of a certain set of conditions on to a completely different set of conditions in another place' (Greaves 1968/1935: 153).

The UN Report 1951: from full employment to development

Arthur Lewis was the principal author of a major United Nations report in 1951 on economic development, a report that shaped the UN's approach to the subject for a decade. In mid-1950 the UN Economic and Social Council (ECOSOC) was interested hardly at all in the problems of economic development. Instead it was wrestling with the problem of how to deal with the expected return of recession that a sudden downturn in the US economy in late 1949 seemed to pre-figure. Meanwhile, Brazil, Chile, India, Pakistan, and Peru complained that, although the General Assembly had pressed for action to overcome unemployment and underemployment in underdeveloped countries, none had followed. In July 1950 a new expert group was appointed 'to prepare, in the light of the current world situation and of the requirements of economic development, a report on unemployment and under-employment in under-developed countries, and the national and international measures required to reduce' them. The UN Secretary General, Trygve Lie, invited Arthur Lewis to join the expert group, consisting of George Hakim (Lebanon), Alberto Baltra Cortez (Chile), D. R. Gadgil (India), and Theodore W. Schultz (USA).

Lewis was mainly responsible for drafting the group's report, which was agreed unanimously and published in May 1951. The report had remarkably little to say specifically about its ostensible topics, unemployment and under-employment. It boldly finessed the whole debate on these issues. The tactic adopted by the group was to put its emphasis on specifying 'the requirements of economic development', and then argue that employment problems would be resolved once rapid economic development had got going (Dadzie 1988: 140). Hence, they entitled their report *Measures for the Economic Development of Under-developed Countries*. According to the Introduction:

> It will be seen that we are led by the analysis of technological unemployment and of under-employment to the same point, namely, that new employment must be created rapidly. This is the task of economic development. And this is the reason why the emphasis of our report is upon economic development rather than upon employment.

Yet the report never spelled out what it meant by either 'economic progress' or 'economic development'. These terms were used interchangeably, and the report simply assumed their meanings to be self-evident. Nevertheless, the report established a powerful paradigm of the process of economic development, while at the same time establishing this as a central mission for the UN.

The report made three optimistic economic assumptions. The first was that underdeveloped countries could draw on an ever-increasing stock of technologies, which had made each latecomer country's period of catching-up shorter than its predecessor's (Arndt 1987: 62–3). The second was that the marginal productivity of capital must be higher in underdeveloped countries, because of its scarcity there relative to labour. The third was that, because of gross underemployment of labour in the agricultural sector, labour was available at very low real cost, and that this could be put to work with additional capital to produce labour-intensive manufactures for export.

> The disguised unemployed are those persons who work on their own account and who are so numerous, relatively to the resources with which they work, that if a number of them were withdrawn for work in other sectors of the economy, the total output of the sector from which they were withdrawn would not be diminished even though no significant reorganization occurred in this sector, and no significant substitution of capital.   (UN 1951: 7)

The report affirmed the quantitative significance of agricultural surplus labour, at least in 'overpopulated' countries. In Egypt, India, Pakistan, and parts of the Philippines and Indonesia, the surplus population was estimated as not being less than 25 per cent of the total.

The doctrine that 'effort has to be concentrated upon creating new industries off the land, of which manufacturing industries comprise the largest and usually the most promising category' was also clearly stated. The justification for this proposal was that, where underemployment was the most acute, nearly all land that could be cultivated was already being cultivated. The report assumes that the raising of agricultural yields, which it also encouraged, would be achieved by adopting a better agrarian technology, but that this process would not be enough to absorb additional productive labour in agriculture, nor would it require any additional capital.

The report emphasized the need for the rate of investment to increase as a share of GDP from 5 to 10 per cent. The share of savings would also have to rise similarly, and while foreigners could supply some of the increase, some would have to come from domestic sources. The report goes on to consider how the state could be enabled to take on a larger role as an agent of capital formation. Issues of taxation, inflation, and financial intermediation are all reviewed in that context.

The main empirical contribution of the report was to make estimates of the external capital that would be required to achieve a 2 per cent annual increase in income per head in developing countries. It was assumed that this increase would be brought about in two ways—first, by transferring population out of agriculture into nonfarm occupations with a fixed endowment of capital per person, and, second, by spending 4 per cent of national income on agricultural extension and research and new agricultural capital. The expert group, while acknowledging a skill shortage in underdeveloped countries, thought that the remedy was large-scale technical assistance. These estimates of required rates of capital accumulation for industrial and agricultural growth (para.239–41) then led naturally to further calculations of the savings gap (para.246–8 and Table 2) and to targets of capital exports from developed countries (para.268).

The popularity of both planning and foreign aid was much influenced by the UN Report on Economic Development (Dadzie 1988: 141). It advised developing country governments to establish a central economic unit to carry out national economic surveys, make development programmes, recommend policy measures for implementing them, and report on the outcomes. The report called for the drawing up of a national capital budget, showing how much new investment could be financed from domestic and how much from foreign sources (Meier 1984: 18).

On politics, the UN report was something of a counsel of perfection. It stressed that a country's institutions must be conducive to development, not only its economic institutions, but also its social, legal, and political institutions (para.23). It stressed that the political leadership of a country must be committed to a strategy for development, rather than the entrenchment of its own privileges (para.37–8). It stressed that governments must do more than provide basic services, and that they must be able to regulate economic activity, whether in the public or the private sector (para.39). This has all been rediscovered and forms the basis of the 'governance' initiatives of today's development cooperation agencies.

However, having laid out these fundamental political and social preconditions for successful economic development, the report did allow the reader to assume that they were, or easily could be, fulfilled in the underdeveloped countries. It then proceeded to elaborate a much more narrowly economic design of development. Between the sociopolitical preconditions and the working through of the economic design, there was an enormous—and often unobserved—leap of faith. This was a leap that was hardly avoidable given the unwritten diplomatic conventions of the Cold War era, and Lewis made it.

Lewis's 1954 article

Lewis published his famous article on 'Economic Development with Unlimited Supplies of Labour' in 1954, for which (jointly with Theodore Schultz) he was awarded a Nobel Prize in Economics. Paul Krugman described it as 'probably the most famous paper in the literature of development economics', but added a twist in the tail, 'in retrospect, it is hard to see exactly why' (quoted by Tignor 2006: 82, note 5). The reason was not its discovery of rural surplus labour, which had already surfaced in the work of Joan Robinson and Paul Rosenstein-Rodan. The theme of agriculture to industry transfer of labour as an engine of economic development was also already familiar from the writings of Friedrich List and Colin Clark. What Lewis's article did was to spell out the assumptions on which economic dualism, intersector labour transfer, capital accumulation, and factorial income distribution could be packaged together in a simple model depicting the transition to a fully capitalist economy. His model was, above all else, in an era of increased technical sophistication in economics, *readily accessible*.

The fame of the 1954 article may also have rested on Lewis's claim that he had created a new branch of economics. While at the LSE, Lewis had never joined other colleagues like Nicholas Kaldor in converting from the classical liberalism of Lionel Robbins to the new economics of Keynes's *General Theory*. He believed that the *General Theory* had nothing to offer developing countries, despite assuming an unlimited supply of labour at the current price. That was because it also assumed that land and capital were also unlimited in supply. Once the monetary tap is turned on, bringing capital and labour together, it is the absence of more labour at the point of full employment that limits growth. So, once Keynes's remedies have been applied, neo-classical economics comes into its own again. Hence, says Lewis, 'from the point of view of countries with surplus labour, Keynesianism is only a footnote to neo-classicism'—adding magnanimously 'albeit a long, important and fascinating footnote' (Lewis 1963/1954: 401). Hence, he saw the need to work right back to the classical political economists on whom Robbins had lectured so learnedly. In this way Lewis drew a line in the sand marking off development economics as a new and separate subdiscipline of economics (Hirschman 1981: 8).

Critics of the model lighted on its assumption that the marginal productivity of labour in the subsistence sector was zero and strained to demonstrate that this was both theoretically and empirically incorrect. This objection was, however, something of a red herring. Lewis later argued that his conclusions would follow provided only that the supply of labour at the given wage in industry exceeds the demand for it—i.e. the model relied only on a much weaker condition. The real problem with the model was that it depended on capitalists continually reinvesting a rising share of their surplus in their own sector, irrespective of the state of demand, including consumption demand. Lewis assumed that only the capitalist sector could use capital productively, that it could do so without limit, and that the investment of capital was the driver of economic growth.

As Lewis soon realized during his subsequent short period as economic adviser to Kwame Nkrumah in Ghana, capitalist profits in developing countries were not automatically reinvested, because investment was not savings-constrained. So even though his use of the classical assumption of a constant real wage rate in the capitalist sector often proved to be empirically correct, economic growth was less rapid than he had expected. In the high expectations sparked by independence, rural people did migrate to the towns, but their migration was excessive because, as he noted in Ghana, rural migrants remained jobless urban slum-dwellers unable to transfer their labour into capitalistic employment.

If the practical consequences of this famous model were disappointing, what of the intellectual consequences? Ingham and Mosley (2013: 110) write:

> Before Lewis wrote this text, the economics of growth was based on single-sector, closed-economy models in which all markets cleared and the role of government was not specified. After the publication of 'Unlimited Supplies of Labour', all that had to change.

This conclusion needs to be modified. In fact, 'all that' did not change, but was reinforced very soon afterwards. Doubt about Lewis's claim that raising the saving rate could raise the growth rate prompted Robert Solow to design his neoclassical model of economic growth in 1956. It put 'all that' together again with a high degree of mathematical elegance. The Solow model, its variants, and its analytical tools (e.g. development accounting) have since, for better or worse, come to dominate the macroeconomics of economic development.

Although short-lived in relation to macroeconomics, the Lewis model did have particular relevance to the microeconomics of development, specifically in the field of investment appraisal. Lewis believed that in developing countries, wages bore no relation to marginal productivity and therefore policy must be in defiance of prices if the true situation were to be met. Social cost–benefit analysis (SCBA) was later developed as a method of investment appraisal that uses 'shadow prices' in substitution for actual prices. The Lewis model is the foundation of the calculation of the shadow wage rate and the device of income weighting. That is Lewis's true theoretical legacy to development economics.

The popularity of SCBA has ebbed over the past thirty years, as neo-liberalism reached its high tide. The debt crisis of developing countries in the 1980s opened an opportunity for developed countries to leverage policies of economic liberalization in countries applying for structural adjustment loans. SCBA was declared redundant when people asked this question: 'Why bother with shadow pricing, a second-best policy, when economic liberalisation could succeed in getting the actual prices right?' When this neo-liberal ambition was embraced politically, the idea of determining investment in the light of *social* prices—by which, for example, the income of the poor was valued more than the income of the rich—was rejected as an unacceptable form of social engineering.

After sixty years, the Lewis model poses a number of neglected questions that remain important for researchers to investigate. Lewis simply takes the differences in productivity between the sectors as given. What is it that causes them in the first place? More significantly, why are they still so large in the twenty-first century when rural-urban migration is not restricted, and indeed in many countries has been excessive? What are the underlying constraints inhibiting the equalization of sector labour productivity? Some are hopeful that these questions can be answered. '[With] new data sources and more ability than ever before to collect and analyze data, it seems reasonable to aim for an updated and improved understanding of dualism—one that is consistent with the data and can guide policy choices in the years ahead' (Gollin 2014: 86). A renewed and deeper curiosity about the axioms of his model may also be a part of Lewis's theoretical legacy.

The Theory of Economic Growth

Arthur Lewis always regarded *The Theory of Economic Growth* (1955) as his magnum opus. It was very wide in its scope, and comprehensive in the spirit of John Stuart Mill. When Peter Bauer reviewed it in the prestigious US economics journal *The American Economic Review*, he was critical: 'The book fails in its principal purpose, especially its aim to serve as a basis of policy. The broad-brush technique neglects distinctions without which it is not possible to frame or assess meaningfully particular measures of policy.' He added, perhaps to soften the blow: 'A book can be very important and valuable in spite of its shortcomings' (Bauer 1956: 641). Lewis was angered by the review and complained to the editor of the *AER*, though without securing any redress.

The queries raised in the review were not unreasonable—whether subsistence agriculture was indeed stagnant; whether increased output was necessarily welfare improving; and whether the rise in the saving ratio was a cause or consequence of development. However, the reviewer's critical slant indicated that he was out of sympathy with the Fabian policies of government intervention that Lewis advocated (Durbin 1984).

Lewis made it perfectly clear that while he advocated forms of government intervention to speed up development, he held no brief for planning by direction and did not approve of coercive economic controls.

His 1966 book *Development Planning: The Essentials of Economic Policy* makes a clear distinction between a controlling plan, which authorizes investment and production and an indicative development plan that 'authorizes nothing' but sets out 'expectations, aspirations and intentions' (Lewis 1966: 19–20). The planning method that he expounds is concerned with ensuring the consistency of inter-related targets and testing their realism in the light of available resources. His emphasis is as much on the soundness of the underlying economic strategy and policy as it is on the techniques of ensuring the internal consistency of the plan.

Lewis initially took a rosy view of planning as the instrument for mitigating the harsh excesses of early industrialization. By the 1960s he had become rueful about how many bad plans he had seen during his work as an economic consultant in developing countries. His early leap of faith that planning would drive development in developing countries when popular enthusiasm was mobilized rarely came to pass. He attributed his disappointment to the poor quality of political leadership. His critique of the first generation of post-independence African leaders in *Politics in West Africa* (1965) was robust. Their espousal of the one-party state, their promotion of the cult of the leader, and their relish for the perquisites of office undermined both nation building and economic development. One-party rule stoked ethnic tensions and acted as a licence to suppress voices of opposition and dissent. Regional favouritism in the allocation of investment was divisive, promoting rivalry and resentment. Lewis's disillusion with the real-life politics of planning, based on his difficult personal experience with Nkrumah in Ghana, was sharp enough.

Two decades after the publication of his *Principles of Economic Planning*, he remarked wryly: 'making Development Plans is the most popular activity of the governments of underdeveloped countries since the war, and is also nearly their biggest failure' (Lewis 1969: 37). Despite this and other disappointments, Lewis never stepped back from his fundamental Enlightenment outlook. In 1977, he wrote to Carlos Diaz Alejandro:

> As a child of the French Enlightenment, I think that all mankind will gain from, and come to be steeped in, the scientific outlook, egalitarian vision, the civil freedom of the common man, and the restricted pluralist state. The things that separate mankind—cultural patterns, religion, language, racial and regional affiliations—to the extent that they survive in the future, they will be of small importance. (Tignor 2006: 253)

References

Agarwala, A. N., and Singh, S. P., eds (1963). *The Economics of Underdevelopment*. New York: Oxford University Press, Galaxy Books.

Arndt, H. W. (1987). *Economic Development: The History of an Idea*. Chicago: University of Chicago Press.

Bauer, P. T. (1956). Lewis on economic growth. *American Economic Review* 46(4), 632–41.

Breit, W., and Hirsch, B. T., eds (2005). *Lives of the Laureates*. Cambridge, MA: MIT Press.

Clark, C. (1940). *The Conditions of Economic Progress*. London: Macmillan.

Crowther, J. G., Howarth, O. J. R., and Riley, D. P. (1942). *Science and World Order*. Harmondsworth: Penguin Books.

Dadzie, K. (1988). The United Nations and the problem of economic development, in A. Roberts and B. Kingsbury, eds, *United Nations, Divided World: The UN's Roles in International Relations*. Oxford: Clarendon Press.

Durbin, E. (1984). Fabian socialism and economic science, in B. Pimlott, ed., *Fabian Essays in Socialist Thought*. London: Heinemann for Fairleigh Dickinson University Press.

Easterly, W. (2013). *The Tyranny of Experts: Economists, Dictators and the Forgotten Rights of the Poor*. New York: Basic Books.

Gollin, D. (2014). The Lewis model: a 60-year retrospective. *Journal of Economic Perspectives* 28(3), 71–88.

Greaves, I. C. (1968/1935). *Modern Production Among Backward Peoples*. New York: Augustus M. Kelley.

Hirschman, A. O. (1981). *Essays in Trespassing. Economics to Politics and Beyond*. Cambridge: Cambridge University Press.

Hobson, J. A. (1902). *Imperialism: A Study*. New York: James Pott & Company.

Ingham, B., and Mosley, P. (2013). *Sir Arthur Lewis: A Biography*. Basingstoke: Palgrave Macmillan.

Lewis, W. A. (1949). *The Principles of Economic Planning*. London: George Allen and Unwin.

Lewis, W. A. (1955). *The Theory of Economic Growth*. London: George Allen and Unwin.

Lewis, W. A. (1963/1954). Economic development with unlimited supplies of labour, in A. N. Agarwala and S. P. Singh, eds, *The Economics of Underdevelopment*, 400–49. New York: Oxford University Press, Galaxy Books.

Lewis, W. A. (1965). *Politics in West Africa*. Oxford: Oxford University Press.

Lewis, W. A. (1966). *The Essentials of Development Planning*. London: George Allen and Unwin.

Lewis, W. A. (1969). *Some Aspects of Economic Development*. Accra: Ghana Publishing Corporation.

Meier, G. M. (1984). The formative period, in G. M. Meier and D. Seers, *Pioneers in Development*. New York: Oxford University Press for the World Bank.

Morgan, D. J. (1980). *The Official History of Colonial Development*, Vol. 1: *The Origins of British Aid Policy 1924–1945*. London: Macmillan Press.

Pimlott, B., ed. (1984). *Fabian Essays in Socialist Thought*. London: Heinemann for Fairleigh Dickinson University Press.

Roberts, A., and Kingsbury, B., eds (1988). *United Nations, Divided World: The UN's Roles in International Relations*. Oxford: Clarendon Press.

Rosenstein-Rodan, P. N. (1963/1943). Problems of industrialization of eastern and south eastern Europe, in A. N. Agarwala and S. P. Singh, eds, *The Economics of Underdevelopment*, 245–55. New York: Oxford University Press, Galaxy Books.

Tignor, R. L. (2006). *W. Arthur Lewis and the Birth of Development Economics*. Princeton, NJ: Princeton University Press.

Toye, J. (2000). *Keynes on Population*. Oxford: Oxford University Press.

United Nations (1951). *Measures for the Economic Development of Under-developed Countries*. New York: UN Department for Economic Affairs.

7

Development as take-off, 1950–75

How often misleading words generate misleading thoughts
—Herbert Spencer, *Principles of Ethics*, book I

The USA and the end of empire

From its birth the United States of America should have had a staunchly anti-colonial political disposition, having fought a successful war of independence to throw off British colonial rule.[*] However, by the end of the nineteenth century, in line with its increasing economic and military strength, the USA was securing its share in the spoils of China, and in the Spanish-American war of 1898, acquiring the remnants of the Spanish empire—Cuba, Puerto Rico, and the Philippines—much as Friedrich List had expected, and indeed recommended. Cuba gained formal independence in 1902, but its government remained under US control. The Philippines proved hard to defend, even after cutting a canal through Panama, and the USA granted the country full independence in 1946. Puerto Rico remains a commonwealth controlled by the USA.

Presidents Wilson and Roosevelt were both opposed to European countries retaining their empires. That resolve to strip the Europeans of their empires became entangled in the late 1940s with the outbreak of the Cold War with the Soviet Union and America's so-called 'loss of China' to the Communists in 1949. When France, the relevant European colonial power, resolved to fight to retain its hold on Indo-China, the USA was willing to provide the French with supplies and finance. Notwithstanding American aid, the Viet Minh under General Giap defeated French forces at the battle of Dien Bien

[*] This chapter is based on John Toye and Richard Toye, 'Competitive coexistence and the politics of modernization', in *The UN and Global Political Economy: Trade, Finance, and Development*, Indiana University Press (2004), reproduced with permission of Indiana University Press.

Phu (1954)—the first time that any colonial independence movement had defeated an occupying power in pitched battle.

At the ensuing negotiations in Geneva, Vietnam was divided into North and South, pending elections in which, at American instigation, the South refused to participate. The Eisenhower administration was now deeply committed to the prevention of a Northern takeover of South Vietnam, even to the extent of being ready to commit US forces to the area (Brogan 1999: 648–9). The incoming Kennedy administration was left to balance a robust anti-communist stance against its desire to improve relations with developing countries who were its potential allies in the Cold War.

The theory of the economic take-off

At this time, American economists were analysing the prospects for accelerating growth in the (what were then described as) underdeveloped countries. A key figure in this endeavour was W. W. Rostow, an economic historian, a US diplomat and the inventor of a novel theory of economic development. Rostow was the son of Jewish parents who had emigrated from Russia to the USA. They were socialists, but he took a very different intellectual and political tack. Having studied the British Industrial Revolution at Yale, he expressed much optimism that the underdeveloped countries could readily follow Britain's and other industrial countries' successful growth experience, given the free flow of technical knowledge and increased international flows of capital.

If the anti-communism of the Eisenhower years in the United States had a prophet, it was Walt Whitman Rostow. After the Second World War, he entered the State Department, and advocated the unification of Europe as the primary goal of US foreign policy. Seconded to the UN Economic Commission for Europe, he was ambitious to make that goal a reality. Gunnar Myrdal noted Rostow's ambition: 'he thinks we [in UN ECE] have a chance to make history (or at least to be involved in it) and, as a historian, he wants to be on the spot'. As the Soviet-backed takeover of Czechoslovakia and other parts of Eastern Europe unfolded, his dream of a united Europe faded away and he returned to Boston in 1950.

There he joined the Center for International Studies (CENIS) at the Massachusetts Institute of Technology. This was essentially a government-controlled Cold War operation, funded by the Ford and Rockefeller Foundations with money from the CIA. With Max Millikan, Rostow produced *A Proposal: Key to an Effective Foreign Policy* (1957). The authors criticized the fact that US foreign aid was directed mainly to political allies for military purposes, as to France in Indo-China, and was essentially reactive and short term in nature. *A Proposal* argued that a successful US foreign policy required that aid also be given for longer-term purposes of economic development to uncommitted nations who were unwilling to enter into formal anti-communist military pacts with the USA. It aroused much interest among State Department officials, but Eisenhower could not override his fear of the budgetary consequences of this new type of aid and did not approve it.

Together with the Social Sciences Research Council's Committee on Comparative Politics, CENIS was the main force behind the production of a new body of theory on the politics of underdeveloped countries—modernization theory. Rostow made his chief intellectual contribution at MIT as an economic historian with a penchant for schematic thinking. He approached the development problem from a starting point very similar to that of Arthur Lewis, aiming to understand the role of capital accumulation in the process of economic growth. Like Lewis, he took the British industrial revolution as his paradigm of economic development. However, modernization theory went beyond economic history. It was a cross-discipline effort that integrated social psychology and political and social change into the economic account of the factors promoting modern economic growth and development. Rostow collaborated with Harold Lasswell, Lucian Pye, and Daniel Lerner on the project. Unlike Lewis, however, they had little first-hand knowledge of the underdeveloped countries to which modernization theory was to be applied in the attempt to contain the spread of communism.

In the course of formulating his ideas, Rostow developed a taxonomic scheme of the so-called stages of economic growth. He turned this taxonomy into a history of capitalism that was the polar opposite of the self-destructive version in Marxism–Leninism—now the official ideology of the USSR. Marx's stage theory tended inevitably towards the overthrow of capitalism in its economic, social, and political manifestations. While still a Yale undergraduate, Rostow had decided to 'do an answer one day to Marx's theory of history'. His answer was modernization theory—the stages by which economies were able to surmount the problems of poverty, alienation, and plutocracy that capitalist development generated in its early phases. It would present an entirely different and optimistic vision of the future viability of capitalist society. It had obvious, powerful attractions for American politicians of the Eisenhower, Kennedy, and Johnson era and exponents of the American Dream.

Analytically, Rostow wanted to go behind the Keynesian economic aggregates of savings, consumption, and investment that were the key ingredients of the mature Keynes's macroeconomics. He wanted to examine the role of individual sectors during the growth process, and particularly the role of the different industrial sectors. He also wanted to introduce more flexible and realistic psychological assumptions about economic motivation, recognizing that people differ in their propensities to create and accept innovations, to take risks, to value large families, and so on. Modernization theory was intended to provide a multidiscipline framework according to which the variety of growth experiences could be systematically classified. In *The Process of Economic Growth*, Rostow posed the problem of formulating an answer to Marxism, the harshness and simplicity of which he criticized, but he did not disclose his alternative at this point.

In a classic article in 1956, he took a crucial next step. He argued that it was useful to think of the process of economic growth as centring on 'a relatively brief time interval of two or three decades' during which the rapid transformations that occur make economic growth thereafter more or less automatic (Rostow 1956). During these decades, the initial impulses of developmental change, whatever they may be, are transcended. If they are water-based energy and water-borne transport, they can be replaced by coal and steam power; if iron, it can be replaced by steel; if gas, by electricity. During this short period, innovation becomes routinized and so economic growth becomes the norm, not the exception. For Rostow, learning how to transcend the exhaustion of the initial impulses for change was what constituted an industrial revolution.

His signature metaphor was 'the takeoff into self-sustaining growth'. The traditional economy was visualized as like an aircraft that, once it was moving sufficiently fast, could get off the ground and stay in the air without further support. Rostow stressed that 'in the end takeoff requires that society find a way ... to apply the tricks of manufacture ... Only thus, as we have all been correctly taught, can that old demon, diminishing returns, be held at bay'. Like Arthur Lewis, Rostow thought that a large upward shift in the investment share of net national product was essential for economies to be able to take off (Toye and Toye 2004: 169–70).

Rostow's other distinctive contribution was an empirical one. He claimed to have identified and dated nine completed episodes of economic take-off. These were Great Britain, France, Belgium, the USA, Germany, Sweden, Japan, Russia, and Canada. He also asserted that four underdeveloped countries had begun, but not completed the take-off. These were Argentina, Turkey, India, and China. This led him to suggest dropping the dichotomy of developed and underdeveloped areas and replacing it with a sequence of stages of growth.

Finally, in *The Stages of Economic Growth: A Non-Communist Manifesto* (1960) he offered a set of five stages of growth as a way of generalizing the sweep of modern economic history. The stages were the following: the traditional society, the pre-conditions for take-off, the take-off, the drive to maturity, and the age of high mass consumption. Ironically, in thus setting out his stages of growth, Rostow reverted to an earlier, nineteenth-century way of thinking about development. 'Doing an answer to Marx's theory of history' involved him in imitating the evolutionary approach to development that Marx had refined. To change the trajectory of his evolutionary scheme, however, he had to install a different dynamic from Marx's; the entrepreneurial application of technology was his new motor of socioeconomic development. Casting aside Marx's dynamic of the conflict of classes over modes of labour exploitation, Rostow delineated the social and political driver of economic progress as the triumphant emergence of a new elite entrepreneurial class. For him, the connotations of the rise of this entrepreneurial elite were wholly positive because it was the embodiment of all the desirable modern attitudes and values.

From the development decade to the Vietnam War

Rostow was already attracting attention in high US political circles at the end of the Eisenhower era. While in Washington, he was contacted by the then Senator John Kennedy, who disclosed that he would be running for the presidency. Rostow wrote campaign speeches for him on the economic gap between rich and poor countries, and the danger that this posed for America. When Kennedy became president in 1961, he appointed Rostow as deputy to his national security adviser, McGeorge Bundy. His new colleagues saw him in the same light as Gunnar Myrdal had previously. He was described as a leading member of the 'Charles River School of action Intellectuals' (Schlesinger 1965: 588–9). Robert McNamara, Kennedy's Secretary of Defense, later described Rostow as 'an extraordinarily bright man with a warm personality and an open approach to his colleagues'. Others saw him as 'this verbose, theoretical man, who intended to make all of his theories work' (Halberstam 1972: 43).

Rostow made the initial report to Kennedy recommending a substantially increased support to South Vietnam, including more advisers, equipment, and even small numbers of combat troops. McNamara recalled: 'Optimistic by nature, he tended to be skeptical of any report that failed to indicate that we were making progress' in Vietnam (McNamara and Van de Mark 1995: 235). Is discounting all reports contrary to a prior belief in victory not the defining characteristic of an extraordinarily bright man, one wonders?

Aside from Vietnam, Rostow encouraged Kennedy to make the 1960s the 'economic development decade'. Remarkably, he predicted that, with US foreign assistance, Argentina, Brazil, Colombia, Venezuela, India, the Philippines, Taiwan, Turkey, Greece—and possibly Egypt, Pakistan, Iran, and Iraq—could all attain self-sustaining growth by 1970. Within a decade, he forecast, 80 per cent of Latin America's population and half the population of the developing areas would be 'off the international dole'. Citing 'my ideas as an economist', Rostow assured Kennedy and Congress that the 1960s would see the requirement for foreign aid peak and then decline. Kennedy went ahead and declared the 1960s the 'decade of development'.

Rostow irritated some powerful figures, including Dean Rusk, Kennedy's Secretary of State. In December 1961, Rostow was moved to become chairman of the State Department's policy planning council. After Kennedy's assassination, Rostow stayed loyal to President Johnson. As the situation in Vietnam became more confrontational, the message of development was blended more strongly with anti-communism. As he put it in 1964: 'The process of modernization involves radical change not merely in the economy of underdeveloped nations but in their social structure and political life. We live, quite literally, in a revolutionary time. We must expect over the next decade recurrent turbulence in these areas; we must expect systematic efforts by the Communists to exploit this turbulence.'

In May 1964, Johnson's staff asked Rostow to set out his policy for dealing with Vietnam. He produced a long report, complete with a draft speech for the president. His draft was the one that Johnson used after the alleged North Vietnamese naval attacks in the Gulf of Tonkin, to announce the escalation of American involvement and the US bombing of the North. When in 1966 he became Johnson's special assistant for national security affairs, he remained fiercely loyal to the belief that the war in Vietnam must be won and would be won. He regarded negotiations with Hanoi as a waste of time and recommended a continuing military build-up. In 1968 Johnson decided to withdraw from the forthcoming presidential race and Rostow's political career came to a sudden end.

It took seven more years for the USA to extract itself from the morass in Vietnam, and for the North and South of the country to be reunited. After Richard Nixon's presidential victory in 1968, Rostow's attitude to Vietnam was adopted by the new administration. In 1969 Nixon pronounced that North Vietnam could not defeat or humiliate the United States, adding (perhaps more truly than he knew) that 'only Americans can do that'. Henry Kissinger saw more realistically that a conventional army, such as the Americans', loses if it does not win, while guerilla forces win if they do not lose—and negotiated a ceasefire in 1973, which the North Vietnamese ignored in their victorious spring offensive in 1975.

Back to the academic debate

Walt Rostow returned to academic life, but not to the Ivy League institutions that he had once inhabited. Neither Yale, where he did his undergraduate and doctoral studies, nor MIT, where he had taught economic history and international affairs for eleven years, found a post for him. Instead, he went into a kind of academic exile at the University of Texas at Austin, which at that time had a distinctly provincial air. He remained there as part of LBJ's circle until his death in 2003. His exile from the East Coast universities has been attributed to their revulsion from his policies in Vietnam (which he continued to justify for the rest of his life), or at least their wariness about the revulsion that others might feel. No doubt such considerations played their part, but the other side of this coin was that his theory of economic take-off was regarded as academically suspect.

Rostow and his fellow modernization theorists claimed that an ideal of modern society based closely on the actual United States could be realized if the societies of underdeveloped areas would only give sufficient authority to the representatives of their entrepreneurs and innovators. In any underdeveloped country, once power begins to gravitate into the hands of a modernizing elite, they implied, a self-sustaining economic take-off can be expected. Like Lewis, Rostow asserted that the elite need not be a private sector elite, but could also be operating through its control of public sector institutions. This assertion in itself placed him at variance with right wing, conservative US academics; Milton Friedman and Peter Bauer said they suspected him of socialist sympathies!

Other colleagues were not convinced, though they were not convinced on different grounds. Albert Fishlow of Berkeley pointed out that Rostow had never really explained how changes in the national income aggregates were integrated with developments in the leading sectors of the economy in the period of most rapid growth, or with technical changes in the leading industries. The ambition to get beyond the Keynesian aggregates had not been fulfilled because these different levels of analysis had never been tied together. The result of this failure, Fishlow argued, was to divert attention from those interesting cases where economies had entered well into the transition to modern economic growth, but eventually failed to take off. He noted: 'some of the nations of Latin America seem to be so beset'.

Hollis Chenery, who was a Harvard professor and Vice-President for Development Policy at the World Bank, objected to the linear view of development that all stage theories, including Rostow's, implied. He did not agree that all countries that developed had to pass through the same succession of stages. Although from his empirical studies he could see that there were different patterns of development, those patterns implied that different developing countries might have different experiences of development and could find ways of short-circuiting some of the stages of any linear scheme.

An even weightier critic was Professor Simon Kuznets of Harvard University. Like Rostow, Kuznets was the son of Russian parents. He emigrated from the Ukraine to the USA for his education—not at Yale but at Columbia University. He joined the US National Bureau of Economic Research in 1927. His research was on the comparative study of the economic growth of nations. He undertook very careful analysis of national income and its components, in whose conceptualization and measurement he was a leading pioneer. His research showed that for modern economic growth the rate of increase of real per capita income typically averaged about 15 per cent or more per decade over periods of a century or more. Significantly, although he found evidence of fluctuations in growth, such as business cycles, he did not find evidence of systematic long-term retardation or acceleration of growth.

Accordingly, he rejected Rostow's notion of a distinct and commonly found take-off stage when the growth rate accelerated. He wrote: 'the doubling of capital investment proportions and the implicit sharp acceleration in the rate of growth of national product, claimed by Professor Rostow as characterizing his "takeoff" periods, are not confirmed by the statistical evidence for those countries on the list for which we have data' (Kuznets 1963: 40). He found Rostow's definition of this and the other stages so analytically fuzzy that 'there is no solid ground on which to discuss Professor Rostow's view of the analytical relation between the take-off stage and the preceding and succeeding stages'.

All in all, Kuznets's review constituted crushing criticism of the theory of economic take-off, although Rostow long afterwards continued to maintain that the differences between his and Kuznets's empirical estimates were trivial or nonexistent.

Kuznets's alternative view of economic development

Despite his rejection of a stage theory centred on a take-off, Kuznets did accept that the reality of the idea of 'modern economic growth', a phenomenon of a new era of economic history. For him, three features marked out this phenomenon from all previous forms of economic organization—a higher growth rate of per capita income, changes in the sector and occupational distribution of the labour force, and new forms of population settlement. The foundation of these three features of the new era was the technological changes stemming from the scientific revolution of the seventeenth century—the shift from animate to inanimate sources of power, to minerals rather than fibres as raw materials, and the consequent spread of mechanization and large-scale operation in industry, agriculture, mining, and services.

However, Kuznets did not identify modern economic growth with any particular institutional system, such as capitalism. He saw it as compatible with different institutional frameworks, those of the USA and the Soviet Union, of Western and Eastern Europe, and with those as contrasting as China's, India's, and Brazil's. In that sense, while distancing himself from Marx, he also distanced himself from Rostow. Moreover, he was far more sensitive than Rostow to the powerful impact that faster growth and its accompanying transitions would have on the labour force. They induced internal migration, movements out of occupations in one economic sector and into new ones in different sectors. Change on this scale caused social and political conflict, as established groups, experiencing or foreseeing the contraction of their economic base, struggled to resist or slow down the process. For Kuznets, the important point was 'the inevitable presence, in a society within which social groups [rapidly] shift from one set of conditions of work and life to another, of a mixture of gains and losses for which the market does not provide an agreed-on social valuation' (Kuznets 1980: 420). Consequently, the cost (or benefit) of rapid transitions within the economy cannot be found by inspecting changes in the national accounts totals.

Social conflicts induced by structural changes must be resolved so as to preserve a sufficient consensus for growth and change—and yet not at a cost that would retard it unduly. The state must be so constituted that it can act as an authoritative referee, able to facilitate consensus decision-making to mitigate the negative effects of economic change, in order to reduce social resistance to the continuation of growth. Kuznets thus was a pioneer in pointing towards a better understanding of the critical role institutions play in facilitating or retarding modern economic growth.

Kuznets envisaged the spread of modern economic growth as a unified and unique historical phenomenon. That implied that the Industrial Revolution in Britain was not just one case among many similar experiences. He argued that the Industrial Revolution had been preceded by a period of sustained preparation that lasted for several centuries, but, once modern economic growth had taken hold in Britain, it gradually diffused to other parts of the world. This implied that other countries had to develop within an environment in which Britain's economic ascendancy was already established—the key point that for List justified economic nationalism.

John Hicks endorsed this view, and stressed its importance for the methodology of analysing economic development:

> [T]he long run growth of the economy is not a thing that repeats itself; it does not repeat itself in different nations; their growth is all part of a single world story. One cannot argue from what did happen in the United States in a certain period so as to establish laws of economic development. (Hicks 1960: 132)

Kuznets protested against the assumption of uniformity of national experiences implicit in the stages of growth theory. He noted that Rostow 'assumes that the characteristics of the take-off are broadly the same for all countries undergoing modern economic growth, regardless of whether the countries were recently settled by European emigrants (USA, Canada, Australia, New Zealand) or were traditional societies attempting to transform themselves' (Kuznets 1963: 28).

Modernization theory tended to be blind to the differences between the initial conditions of countries pursuing the aim of modern economic growth, lumping them all together under the heading 'traditional society'. This lumping approach provoked two very different sorts of reactions, one emphasizing the advantages of being a late-starting economy and the other emphasizing its disadvantages.

The advantages of backwardness

Like Rostow and Kuznets, Alexander Gerschenkron was Russian born, but left with his family for Vienna after the revolution. After the Anschluss, he went to England and then to a position at the University of California, Berkeley. He pursued a career there as an economic historian, writing on the Prussian estate owners as an obstacle to modernization in *Bread and Democracy in Germany* (1943) (Adelman 2013: 205). Like many US economists, he went on to do Cold War-related research, estimating the economic strength of the Soviet Union. Working for the Rand Corporation, he produced articles on the Soviet production of machinery, petroleum, iron and steel, and electric power—the sinews of military power. This was difficult work, because it required a form of statistical translation from the conventions of the Soviet statisticians into a form that could be compared accurately with equivalent US production estimates valued in dollars.

Later, as a professor at Harvard, Gerschonkron published *Economic Backwardness in Historical Perspective* (1962), which surveyed the cases of Russia and of other late starters on the path of economic development. Although his conclusions have often been contrasted with those of Rostow, they share an underlying similarity, in that both held a linear stages theory of economic development. Where they differed was that Gerschenkron added an important qualification, arguing that there were positive advantages to being a late starter, because late starters could shorten the length of the sequence of stages.

He also observed a number of differences in the development paths of late starters like Germany, Japan, and Russia, compared with early starters like Britain and France. The former relied less on indigenous technologies, and more on borrowed ones. Their production methods were on a larger scale and were more capital-intensive. Special institutions, such as banks and the state, were more in evidence as channels that directed capital investment. Producer goods took priority, while consumption was kept in check. These differences, he argued, generated a faster rate of economic growth for those countries still at an early stage in the process of growth. They were 'the advantages of backwardness', and they caused the period of time during which backward countries caught up with advanced ones to be reduced.

Gerschenkron did not give a precise definition of backwardness, but his thinking was largely centred on Europe, and the contrast between the least backward at the start of their economic development, like Britain and France, and the most backward, like Russia and the Balkan countries, with Germany somewhere in between. How the advantages of backwardness applied to the backwardness of colonial and ex-colonial countries was far from clear.

The Great Divide

The opposite reaction to the stages of growth theory was to argue that the coexistence of more with less advanced countries could impact negatively on the development prospects of the less advanced. Rostow brushed aside this criticism, claiming that any disadvantage arising was surmountable. In doing so, he could find some support in Gerschenkron's observations. Nevertheless, the notion had long been spreading that the conditions under which countries entered on the quest for modern economic growth were not only different, but also unequal. Not only that, but that the existence of countries that had already become developed acted as a barrier to those that had not.

This proposition could be made more concrete in a number of ways. One was to argue that colonial rule in a previous era had long-lasting negative effects on the prospects for development, such as the monopoly of political power by minority settler elites. Another was to argue that the institution of slavery and the slave trade before their abolition created high levels of distrust among the affected populations, which persisted into the present, inhibiting the investments needed for economic development. Both were assertions that a history of colonialism was a very powerful shaping force, rendering countries less able to meet the current challenges of modernization. However, these assertions had not been rigorously tested, so it was easy to dismiss them as a form of special pleading.

It was precisely this notion of a geographical cleavage hampering the development of latecomers that produced the greatest challenge to the modernization approach, both in theory and in practice. This cleavage was given a variety of names. While in terms of geopolitics, the West was accurately described as in opposition to the East, for the purposes of development discourse, 'the West' became 'the North', juxtaposed with the developing countries in 'the South'. Other labels identified the West as 'the Centre' and the remainder as 'the Periphery'. Although countries are spread out along a spectrum of levels of development, the search was on to find a geography-bending vocabulary to express the idea of a Great Divide. Yet important questions remained to be answered. If colonial history was to be dismissed as special pleading, what exactly was it that marked off one side of the Great

Divide from the other? And how exactly did being on the wrong side of the divide create disadvantages for future development? How could the nature of the malign interaction be specified in terms of current circumstances?

Ever since the Great Depression, many in Latin America maintained that the crucial distinction was between those countries that exported agricultural products and those that exported industrial products. As Sanford A. Mosk noted in 1944, when reviewing trends in the continent's economic thought: 'The relatively unfavorable price position for raw materials and foodstuffs that prevailed in the interwar period and especially during the depression of the 1930s, profoundly affected the outlook of Latin Americans' (Whitaker 1944). Primary commodity exporting countries like Argentina and Brazil were starting to see their future economic security in terms of promoting industrialization. Even the US economist Charles Kindleberger suggested that industrialization was the path of the future, invoking Engel's Law as his justification. He wrote in 1943: 'inexorably . . . the terms of trade move against agricultural and raw material countries as the world's standard of living increases (except in time of war) and as Engel's law of consumption operates' (Kindleberger 1943). Although he later referred to this view in his memoirs as a 'youthful indiscretion', it had influence at the time with Latin American economists.

One of those who read his 'indiscretion' was Raul Prebisch. An Argentinian economist who had become a successful central banker, he had struggled with effects of the precipitous export price declines of the 1930s. When Juan Peron ousted him from his post in the central bank, he moved to the University of Buenos Aires. When Peron ousted him again, this time from the university, he moved to Santiago de Chile where the UN Economic Commission for Latin America (ECLA) had just been set up. There he was tasked to write an overview of economic conditions in the entire Latin American region, which was subsequently published under the title *The Economic Development of Latin America and its Principal Problems* (1950).

He was asked to incorporate the results of a statistical study that Hans Singer, then employed at UN headquarters in New York, had recently completed, showing Latin America's long-term decline in its terms of trade. Singer's report carried a clear implication of injustice in the trade relations of industrialized and underdeveloped countries. It dovetailed neatly with the categories of Centre and Periphery that Prebisch had begun to use in the late 1940s and with Kindleberger's deduction from Engel's Law. The declining terms of trade for primary producers was now included in Prebisch's overview along with other material on balance of payment disequilibria and low saving rates, culminating in the rallying cry that 'industrialization is the only means by which the Latin American countries may fully obtain the advantages of technical progress'. When his overview was presented at ECLA's Havana conference in May 1949, it received great acclaim from the Latin American delegates. Singer's thesis had become the Prebisch–Singer thesis and declining terms of trade of primary commodity producers became the accepted explanation of the Great Divide between the Centre and the Periphery in the achievement of modern economic growth.

The dependency approach

Another variation on the theme of the disadvantages of a large agricultural sector was the work of those, like Paul Baran and Andre Gunder Frank, who sought a less economistic and a more class-based rebuttal of modernization theory. According to it, in the Periphery foreign merchants had formed an alliance with domestic elites (the class of *compradors*) and thereby gained control of the agricultural export trade and the associated shipping, insurance, and banking businesses. The profits made from them were either exported or used for conspicuous consumption with a high import content. The surplus that should have been used for investment was thereby drained abroad and could not be used for development in the country of origin. Instead it was used in the Centre to strengthen its economic and technological superiority, the preservation of which became an incentive for frustrating the beginnings of industrial development in the Periphery. They argued that only a Cuban-style political revolution could demolish these structures of dependency.

It was the theory of a zero-sum game, where the development of the Centre produced 'the development of underdevelopment' in the Periphery—the phrase was the title of an influential book by Walter Rodney about the failure of development in Africa, *How Europe Under-developed Africa* (1972). Popular as this narrative was both with nationalists on the Periphery and with radicals at the Centre, this crude and mechanical version of the Great Divide fairly quickly lost credibility to a much more nuanced version, with reformist rather than revolutionary implications.

The reformist strand of dependency theory, represented by Fernando Henrique Cardoso and Enzo Faletto (1979), was a much more fruitful, if not entirely successful enterprise. They never lost sight of the conflict-ridden nature of development, arising from the fact that late developers must develop within a pre-existing global nexus of economic and political power over which they have little control. Yet they never claimed that all the possibilities for national development are determined by these external factors. They acknowledged that the development experiences of peripheral countries could vary, depending on the balance between domestic and foreign capital in the structure of production and the vibrancy of their civil society and politics.

Cardoso and Faletto viewed authoritarian rule, such as had been adopted by Fidel Castro in Cuba and by military dictators in Latin America, as problematic. In this they differed from economists who thought that the political regime had neutral effects and those who positively pleaded for authoritarian regimes as a means to accelerate development. They analysed the costs of authoritarianism in terms of the increasing marginalization of vulnerable social groups, both economically and ethnically. Economic policy issues had to be analysed in their social and political context, and not as simple technical issues with standard solutions. They were genuinely committed to poverty alleviation and a more democratic polity. All of these features made their conception of the Great Divide both subtler and more realistic than the earlier deterministic and pessimistic version.

Prebisch, structuralism, and trade policies

Although Prebisch had absorbed Singer's findings on the declining terms of trade, he continued to wrestle with other aspects of the problem of balance of payments disequilibria that he regarded as particularly widespread in the Periphery. He was dissatisfied with the classical theory of the balance of payments. He believed that it focused excessively on the equilibrating effects of the price changes that alteration in the foreign exchange rate induces. This narrow focus ignored two important factors that produced disequilibrium. The first was the difference between the Centre and the Periphery in the income elasticity of demand for each other's exports. The second was the time lags involved in the Periphery's sucking in of additional imports and the boost that this provided to the Periphery's exports.

Because the Centre's demand for peripheral exports was weaker than the Periphery's for central exports, any expansion of the Periphery's exports quickly led, Prebisch argued, to a current account deficit as imports were sucked in. Although in time the Centre, too, would begin to draw in more peripheral exports, there was a long transitional period, during which the Periphery would lose foreign exchange reserves. This drain of foreign exchange would bring its economic growth to a halt.

Prebisch's account of the Periphery's growth as constrained by balance of payments disequilibria assumes that the rate of growth of its primary commodity exports is restricted by the state of external effective demand. However, external demand was never the whole story. Primary exports are especially vulnerable to failures of supply and to the growth of domestic consumption demand. His account also was inconsistent with the finding of declining terms of trade for the Periphery's exports, which might have been expected to stimulate the Centre's demand for them. Prebisch played this down, arguing that such relative price changes were not an effective adjustment mechanism. This contention was in line with the view of his colleagues in ECLA, Celso Furtado and Juan Noyola. All shared the perspective that a balance of payments constraint cannot be corrected by relative price changes. This was the essence of the ECLA doctrines of 'structuralism' in relation to the balance of payments (Boianovsky and Solis 2014: 23–59).

In the 1950s, developing countries agitated for a new international body to regulate trade, in the hope that it would assist their aspirations for economic development. Prebisch agreed to be the Secretary-General of a UN conference on trade and development in 1964. He undertook an extensive round of diplomatic consultations in key capitals on his proposals, later published as *Towards a New Trade Policy for Development*. They made the fundamental point that developing countries should be compensated for past and future losses through deteriorating terms of trade, either by means of international commodity agreements or by mechanisms of compensatory financing. He also wanted a new system of trade preferences for all manufactures exported by developing countries to developed countries.

The final stop on Prebisch's diplomatic itinerary was Washington, DC. There he met Walt Rostow, the chair of the State Department's Policy Planning Council and later President Johnson's key adviser on Vietnam, nation building, and North–South relations in general. He had set up a 'Modernization Institute' inside the Special Group on Counter-Insurgency. Rostow told Prebisch that his proposals for the international trade conference were on entirely the wrong track. His advice for developing countries was that they should remedy their own internal deficiencies and assist the United States in developing new technologies as the route to faster economic growth. In any case, the US Administration was unable to support Prebisch's proposals, since 'protectionist lobbies are protected by Congress and fiats established in the State Department can do little about it' (Dosman 2008: 396–7). It was an uncomfortable interview that dramatized the Great Divide in both intellectual and political terms.

Eventually in 1967, in a moment of political weakness, the USA conceded the principle of establishing a General System of Preferences (GSP) for manufactured exports from all developing countries. In the case of the USA, it was not until 1976 that Congress passed a Trade Act incorporating industrial trade preferences. Even then, as Rostow had warned Prebisch, Congress loaded the legislation with protectionist-inspired limitations.

The preferences granted, by both the USA and the European Economic Community, were in reality neither 'general' nor a 'system', but a ragbag of nationally determined trade concessions. The GSP, which had seemed to be Prebisch's greatest achievement, turned out to be a great disappointment.

In his confrontation with Prebisch on trade policy, Rostow showed that he understood very well the politics of the Great Divide. As for his modernization theory, it has been rightly characterized as 'the initial social scientific rationalization of the post World War II American drive to achieve global free trade and American geopolitical hegemony' (Gilman 2003: 191).

References

Adelman, J. (2013). *Worldly Philosopher: The Odyssey of Albert O. Hirschman*. Princeton, NJ: Princeton University Press.

Boianovsky, M., and Solis, R. (2014). The origins and development of the Latin American structuralist approach to the balance of payments, 1944-1964. *Review of Political Economy* 26(1), 23–59.

Brogan, H. (1999). *The Penguin History of the USA*. London: Penguin Books.

Cardoso, F. H., and Faletto, E. (1979). *Dependency and Development in Latin America*. Berkeley and Los Angeles: University of California Press.

Dosman, E. J. (2008). *The Life and Times of Raul Prebisch, 1901–1986*. Montreal: McGill Queens University Press.

Gerschenkron, A. (1962). *Economic Backwardness in Historical Perspective*. Cambridge, MA: Harvard University Press.

Gilman, N. (2003). *Mandarins of the Future: Modernization Theory in Cold War America*. Baltimore, MD: Johns Hopkins University Press.

Halberstam, D. (1972). *The Brightest and the Best*. New York: Random House.

Hicks, J. (1960). Thoughts on the theory of capital—the Corfu Conference. *Oxford Economic Papers (N. S.)* 12(2), 123–32.

Kindleberger, C. P. (1943). Planning for foreign investment. *American Economic Review: Papers and Proceedings* 33(1) Supplement.

Kuznets, S. (1963). Notes on the take-off, in W. W. Rostow, ed., *The Economics of Take-Off into Sustained Growth*, 22–43. London: Macmillan.

Kuznets, S. (1980). Driving forces of economic growth: what Can we learn from history. *Weltwirtliches Archiv* 116, 409–31.

McNamara, R. S., with Van de Mark, B. (1995). *In Retrospect: The Tragedy and Lessons of Vietnam*. New York, Random House: Times Books.

Millikan, M. F., and Rostow, W. W. (1957). *A Proposal: Key to an Effective Foreign Policy*. New York: Harper and Brothers.

Prebisch, R. (1950). *Economic Development of Latin America and its Principal Problems*. Lake Success: United Nations.

Rodney, W. (1972). *How Europe Under-developed Africa*. London: Bogle-L'Ouverture Publications.

Rostow, W. W. (1952). *The Process of Economic Growth*. Oxford: Clarendon Press.

Rostow, W. W. (1956). The take-off into self-sustained growth. *Economic Journal* 66(261).

Rostow, W. W. (1960). *The Stages of Economic Growth: A Non-Communist Manifesto.* Cambridge: Cambridge University Press.

Schlesinger, A. M. (1965). *A Thousand Days: John F. Kennedy in the White House.* Boston: Houghton Mifflin.

Toye, J., and Toye, R. (2004). *The UN and Global Political Economy: Trade, Finance and Development.* Bloomington, IN: Indiana University Press.

United Nations (1964). *Towards a New Trade Policy for Development.* New York: United Nations.

Whitaker, A. P., ed. (1944). *Inter-American Affairs 1944,* 143. New York: Columbia University Press.

8

Development as economic growth, 1956–

Growth is the only evidence of life.
—Cardinal Newman

The transformation of American economics

The Second World War transformed the prospects of the economics profession in the United States, although the number of US economists had multiplied rapidly in the previous four decades, European economists had remained intellectually dominant, their different schools operating at national level—Cambridge and the LSE in the UK, the Vienna school in Austria, the Stockholm school in Sweden, the Swiss school in Lausanne, and so on.* Political turmoil in Europe drove many hundreds of economists to migrate to the USA, those from Germany and Austria joining others who had fled from the Russian revolution. A statistic reflecting the extent of economists' immigration is that by 1945, half of the articles published in the *American Economic Review* were written by economists who were born outside the USA but who held positions in US universities. Earlier in the century, the equivalent figure was five per cent (Backhouse 2010: 38).

American economists had a 'good war', in the sense that in their wartime employments they had shown themselves able to work alongside engineers and others in successfully solving urgent practical problems. Walt Rostow, for example, worked in the Office of Strategic Services planning the most efficient distribution of bombing raids on Nazi Germany. US economists' record in wartime raised their profile and prestige, so that the subsequent onset of the Cold War produced generous government funding for the continuation of

* This chapter is based on the article 'Solow in the Tropics', John Toye, *History of Political Economy* annual supplement to Vol.41, eds Mauro Boianovsky and Kevin. D. Hoover, copyright 2009 Duke University Press, with permission of Duke University Press.

economic work relevant to the Cold War context, e.g. in the Rand Corporation or at the Massachusetts Institute of Technology.

Economists' wartime experience also had a powerful effect in turning economics into a more technical discipline. The wartime construction of the national income accounts provided a powerful statistical tool for macroeconomic planning and management. Linear programming in engineering provided a mathematical technique that could also be used to solve more general resource allocation problems. Game theory was developed for strategic planning but could be applied to economic problems that involved strategic interaction. The more extensive use of quantitative methods such as mathematics and mathematical statistics in economics became an attractive route for new recruits to the profession to explore.

A crucial use of mathematics in economics was to make formal links between economic theory and empirical economic data. The US National Bureau of Economic Research (NBER) had been set up in 1927 and had pursued very detailed statistical investigations of the US economy and accumulated extensive stores of empirical data. Yet the world of the empirical researcher remained disconnected from that of the economic theorist. Many of those collecting data were skeptical of the neoclassical doctrines that theorists like John Bates Clark were expounding. What was missing was a way of linking theoretical work with data that had been gathered to describe the real world economy.

Increasingly, theories tended to be formulated as mathematical models, usually in algebraic form, so that their implications could be derived with logical rigour. The derived propositions could then be treated as hypotheses to be tested. Data gathering became oriented less to providing fuller descriptions of the economic world, and more towards the testing of theoretical hypotheses using methods based on probability theory. The mathematical 'model' was a term hardly used before 1945, but since then has become almost universal, connecting theory and empirical research in a formal and rigorous procedure (Backhouse 2010: 41).

Full employment models of economic growth

Mathematical modelling provided a new and very different way of thinking about economic development. Its effect was to put the focus on the process of economic growth, and not on economic development conceived more broadly. Neoclassical growth theory, as formulated in a model, makes a grand initial simplification: that the economy produces only one commodity and that this single commodity can be used either for consumption or for investment. The theory of economic growth is therefore quite unlike the theory of economic dualism, which depends on the transfer of labour between at least two economic sectors. There is no possibility in a one-commodity model of intersector factor transfer; this is excluded by assumption. It is also quite unlike modernization theory, the economic element in which focuses on a series of leading industrial sectors as drivers of aggregate growth. Technologically advanced (or backward) industrial sectors are also excluded by assumption. Economic growth in a model of an economy with one commodity can only be a process of undifferentiated expansion. Indeed, neoclassical growth of an economy is often described by analogy as a balloon expanding as it is inflated with air.

After war service, Robert Solow taught at Harvard and Columbia and then joined the economics staff of MIT. Simultaneously with Trevor Swan of Australia, he produced a neoclassical model of economic growth (1956) as a modification of the Harrod–Domar model of economic growth. Harrod and Domar had formulated the dynamic aspect of Keynes's thinking on employment, based on the idea that if the capital/output ratio is fixed, the savings rate and the population growth rate would have to stay aligned with each other to ensure the steady growth of per capita income at full employment. However, their model was unstable in the sense that if these two variables did not remain aligned with each other, the economy could suddenly veer off a steady growth path.

The Solow model solved this instability problem by introducing the feature of diminishing returns to capital per head. Making the capital/output ratio variable instead of fixed would ensure that any deviation from the alignment of the two variables would be counteracted and that the economy would be returned to a path of steady-state growth at full employment. This modelling device had a beautiful simplicity, and was quickly recognized as 'a major step in the history of growth theory' (Sen 1970: 21).

Harrod's model was a theory of the requirements of steady-state growth at full employment. When Sen asked whether Solow's model should be read as a description of how capitalist economies actually work, or of the consequences of maintaining full employment, Solow's clarification was: 'The idea is to trace full employment paths, no more' (Sen 1970: 23–4, n.15). Yet within what was still a requirements theory, Solow presumably would have held—as had Harrod (1951: 272, n.1)—that his account of the forces that lead to and maintain equilibrium growth was intended to be an account of causes.

Solow has subsequently sounded slightly rueful that his model concentrated on the price and interest rate dynamics that would support an equilibrium path of growth. He regretted unleashing 'a standing temptation to sound like Dr Pangloss' (Solow 1988: 309). Dr Pangloss held that *this is the best of all possible worlds*. By contrast, if its price and interest rate dynamics were indeed an account of causes, the Solow growth model tells us that, in the long term, there is another, better world—a world of full employment growth, and that it is possible to reach it. Far from imitating the complacent conservatism of Dr Pangloss, the vital characteristic of the initial Solow growth model was that it had a visionary quality. It was a theory in both senses: a programmatic idea of how things should be, and a scheme of explanation of how that programme would come to be realized.

Development economics derived from a different part of Keynes's legacy, the one that focused on identifying practical policy problems, on public advocacy, and on persuading policy makers to adopt intelligent solutions. The key problem of development economics had emerged during the Second World War in the less developed regions of Europe, where disguised unemployment was believed to prevail. The problem was how to raise incomes in these regions, *under specific constraining conditions*: namely, without waiting on further technical progress; without making any impact on existing international trade flows, and in the absence of much local entrepreneurship. The recommended policy was for the government to undertake large-scale capital investment in a range of complementary light industries, drawing labour out of disguised unemployment and into productive employment (Rosenstein-Rodan 1943). Development economics and policy began as an exercise in thinking *inside* the box—evaluating what to do for the best in a specific constrained situation.

Walt Rostow promoted his stages of growth theory on the grounds that its features related to the realities of the developing world. 'Its structure can be recognizably linked', he asserted, 'to the phenomena [economists there] see about them and the problems they must try and solve from day to day.' Rostow thought that the failure to make this link was the flaw in Solow's model. 'The neoclassical growth models that absorbed so much theoretical talent in the 1960s ran into the sand precisely because their method ruled out changes in most of the variables relevant to the process of economic growth' (Rostow 1984: 237).

Does the Solow model apply to the tropics?

Yet one may ask: was the austerely beautiful Solow model ever intended to apply to economic growth in developing countries? Bill Easterly says that Solow 'never mentioned tropical countries in any of his writings; in fact, he never applied his model to any other country besides the United States [so] Solow is not to blame for how his model was applied to the tropical countries' (2002: 55–6). This is not quite correct. Justifying the omission of land from the aggregate production function, Solow stated that 'one can imagine the theory applying as long as arable land can be hacked out of the wilderness at essentially constant cost' and then cited Ethiopia as an underdeveloped country that had no shortage of land (Solow 1956: n.2).[1] Moreover, the fact that he applied his model only to the USA does not entail that he believed that it did not apply elsewhere.

On the contrary, he explains the motivation for his model in terms of intellectual discomfort not simply with the Harrod and Domar models, but 'also [with the model] by Arthur Lewis in a slightly different context'.

> I believe I remember that writings on economic development often asserted that the key to a transition from slow growth to fast growth was a sustained rise in the savings rate. The recipe sounded implausible to me.   (Solow 1988: 307–8)

His intellectual discomfort with the Lewis model was misplaced, however, because that model does not address the issue of steady-state growth in a capitalist economy; rather, it asks how a transition occurs from an economy that is subsistence based to an economy that is fully capitalist (Lewis 1954: 155). Lewis's proposed answer was: by means of a capitalist sector that continually reinvests its profits, while drawing surplus labour from the subsistence sector at a constant real wage rate. Whatever the defects of this answer, the important point is that it addressed a different issue from the one that Solow was tackling. The crossing of purposes is explained thus.

> This process [of economic development] could be seen as inherently a transition, from one form of economy to something very different [and] the stylized apparatus of balanced growth paths might have little to say about many events that are central to this transition.   (Temple 2005: 436)

The Lewis model gave this transition a formal shape in his model of economic dualism (1954), although he always referred back to its links to the socio-political complex set out in his subsequent *Theory of Economic Growth* (1955). Perhaps inevitably it was his formal model that was more attractive to many economists of development. In this he placed underemployment was a key stylized fact about underdeveloped countries, so that his model was not a full employment model. Moreover, until surplus labour in the economy is exhausted, the accumulation of capital does not run into diminishing returns. The neoclassical and the economic dualism models simply used different assumptions to portray different processes of growth.

---

[1] Solow assumed unlimited supplies of land, rather than (with Lewis) unlimited supplies of labour.

Solow's remark about Ethiopia, however, implies that the geographical scope of his model was intended to include underdeveloped countries, at least those with unlimited supplies of cultivable land. Solow gave his own understanding of the limits of the application of his model in 2001:

> In my view growth theory was conceived as a model of the growth of an industrial economy... I have never applied such a model to a developing economy, because I thought the underlying machinery would apply mainly to a planned economy or a well developed market economy. *This is not a matter of principle, just wariness.*
>
> (Solow 2001: 283, with emphasis added)

The convergence debate

The Solow–Swan model opened up a debate on a topic of global importance. Its assumptions of a single universally available technology, diminishing returns to capital per head, and constant returns to scale provided the basis of a hypothesis that poor countries will grow faster than rich ones, and thus that levels of per capita income will converge across the world.

In response to different initial stocks of capital, and thus different rates of return to investment, domestic savings should temporarily increase (in poorer countries) or decrease (in richer countries). This implies that, before reaching their steady-state growth path, poor countries will grow faster than rich countries. However, since the steady-state growth rate is determined only by the rate of technical progress, and since technical progress is assumed to be available to all countries as a free good, ultimately all countries, whatever their initial incomes per head, will converge on the same steady-state rate of growth (Ray 1998: 74–82).

A naive rejection of the prediction of the unconditional convergence hypothesis does less than justice to the Solow model. It was argued that the convergence prediction should be conditional on intercountry differences in savings and population growth rates, implying different steady-state growth paths and the absence of an inverse relation between initial income level and the rate of income growth. When capital accumulation is augmented to include both physical and human varieties, about eighty per cent of the observed differences in per capita incomes were estimated to be attributable to differences in these two variables (Mankiw et al. 1992). Yet this rehabilitation of the Solow model in an augmented version runs into the difficulty mentioned earlier, and has not proved wholly convincing either. Theoretically, conditional convergence might be the result of the transfer of resources from a low productivity sector (agriculture) to a high productivity sector (industry), i.e. the process that Lewis modelled, rather than a decline in the marginal product of capital (Thirlwall 2002: 33–4).[2] Moreover, estimates of the pace of conditional convergence suggest that it is very slow.

Growing doubts about conditional convergence by the mid-1980s[3] prompted Paul Romer and Robert Lucas to devise growth models in which technical progress is endogenous, essentially as a result of the externalities of knowledge production or education.[4] While retaining the framework of competition and diminishing returns to capital, these models exhibit increasing returns in the aggregate. They explain why capital does not necessarily accumulate faster in poor countries or, when capital is mobile, flow from high to low per capita income countries. Thus, they neither imply even conditional convergence nor rule out any catching up. Endogenous growth models added some limited degrees of realism to the Solow model, and in not making any definite prediction about convergence are compatible with key facts many development economists were beginning to observe—examples of failure to converge (in sub-Saharan Africa) coexisting with a few remarkable examples of rapid catching up (in East Asia).

Growth models, trade models, and trade policy

The original Solow model was a closed economy model. Thus, the context of the convergence debate was a set of isolated Solow-type economies, each of which was responding to its initial position relative to its own steady-state growth path. This setup contrasted with the concerns of the pioneer development economists, like Raùl Prebisch and Hans Singer, who focused on the consequences for growth and global inequality of the actual linkages through investment and trade of developed and undeveloped economies (Toye and Toye 2004: 110–36). The spirit of Prebisch and Singer could be captured in global North–South models of dependent development. Ronald Findlay (1979, 1980) did so by yoking a Solow model (representing the North) to a Lewis model (representing the South) via deteriorating Southern terms of trade.

However, in a world where Solow-type economies are linked up by perfectly integrated capital markets, a uniform rate of profit will be established, and

---

[2] Once structural change is added to the augmented Solow model, it can do a better job of mimicking the actual growth rates of developing countries, even China's. In the doubly augmented model, the assumption that technical progress is exogenous, and is the same for all countries, is retained, however.

[3] Econometrically, the Mankiw, Romer, and Weil result has attracted a volley of objections, along the lines that the estimates are systematically biased (see, for example, Temple 1999: 134–5; Bosworth and Collins 2003: 124–5; Helpman 2004: 27–8; McCombie 2006: 151–6; Bliss 2007: 73–85).

[4] The basic idea for neoclassical endogenous models comes from Arrow's classic paper on the economic implications of learning by doing (Arrow 1962).

with access to identical technology, will move capital per worker to a common level. Despite differences in population growth and savings, economies will converge in terms of output per worker. Even without capital mobility, Solow-type economies that engage in trade will, using the standard assumptions of trade theory, tend to equalize factor prices, which implies a considerable move towards income equalization, though factor quantities in each economy would still differ (Ros 2000: 184–7). However, 'there is a makeshift feel to these [trade and growth] models, [which] is unsurprising if one considers that both growth, and trade, have been modeled independently, according to their particular requirements' (Bliss 2007: 238).

Development accounting and the complex sociological tangle

Apart from the arcane issues of convergence, the neoclassical model can be used as a theoretical framework to estimate the empirical contribution of increases of the factors of production (capital and labour) to the growth of total output. Solow wrote a paper on growth accounting (1957) of which the main conclusion was that US output growth resulted from capital accumulation hardly at all, and (approximately seven-tenths of it) was the result of the famous 'residual', i.e. other variables not specifically included in the model.

Development accounting (the cross-country analogue of growth accounting) has been used to derive conclusions about economic performance in developed and developing countries. Solow's wariness about this enterprise has not dampened the enthusiasm of newcomers to this field. Hall and Jones (1999), for example, have produced output-to-input decompositions that show that the differences in output levels between rich and poor countries result less from differences in capital inputs (of both physical and human kinds) than from differences in total factor productivity (TFP). Is this a useful exercise? There are well-known measurement problems involved in making estimates of TFP levels. These include the crudeness of the underlying data on inputs and the fact that the method assumes that the share of the inputs in income is the same in all countries. This creates a major problem for interpreting the TFP estimate because, as a residual, it includes both specification error and measurement error. It includes all unmeasured differences in the quality of inputs—technological differences; differences in organizational efficiency in the use of inputs; differences in government regulations and policies. It has been noted that more refined methods of measuring inputs normally lead to reductions in the TFP estimate.

One might be inclined to attribute the large estimated differences in productivity levels between developing and developed countries to (a) the concentration of most of the world's research and development (R&D) expenditure in the latter countries and (b) the existence of a threshold level of income or skill that must be passed before technology transfer to developing countries can take place (Baumol et al. 1994). Differences in TFP levels between countries indicate that some countries (the now industrialized countries) started accumulating capital earlier than others, and have continued longer and more persistently than others.

When one turns to decompositions of output growth rates, it becomes clear that there are major contrasts between groups of countries in different parts of the developing world. Where, over the past fifty years, the growth of capital inputs per worker has been low (say, less than two per cent a year), i.e. in sub-Saharan Africa, Latin America, and the Middle East, the rate of growth of measured TFP has been slight or even negative. Where the growth of capital inputs per worker has been high, i.e. in East and South Asia, the growth of TFP has also been high (Bosworth and Collins 2003: 122–3). In this connection it is interesting that Hicks, for example, suggested the very small share of output growth explained by capital accumulation in Solow (1957) might be 'an illusion which has only arisen because the particular production function chosen does not allow sufficient scope for the effect of capital accumulation on productivity' (Hicks 1960: 129).

This suggests that the policy advice to developing countries often derived from levels accounting results; namely, to de-emphasize savings and investment, and emphasize technical change and technology adoption, does not make a great deal of sense. As Solow (1959) suggested with his vintages model, improvements in technology and upgraded labour skills are embodied in each new vintage of physical and human capital. Policies that emphasize technology at the expense of capital formation, or vice versa, ignore their close interdependence and are therefore incoherent.

Perhaps for that reason, these development and growth accounting exercises often provoke a desire to push one stage further back. Accounting for the proximate causes of growth (capital inputs, productivity) provokes the researcher to go further back into the complex sociological tangle to find more fundamental causes of productivity disparities than induced technical change and technology adoption. Hall and Jones (1999), for example, hypothesized that the fundamental determinant of a country's economic performance was its social infrastructure (a combination of institutions and policies). This conjecture was tested by growth regressions employing various proxy indices for social infrastructure. While their hypothesis is plausible, their tests of it—using an ad hoc methodology and employing less than convincing institutional proxies—were not sufficiently challenging. Other so-called fundamental variables have been proposed, such as geography, entrepreneurship, financial deepening, religion, ethnic fractionalization, and natural resources, but none have been found to be robust determinants of growth.

International trade, the World Bank, and neo-liberalism

Hicks wrote over fifty years ago:

> 'Growth Economics' is often taken to be particularly associated with the problem of 'developing the underdeveloped'. The appearance of a branch of theory called Growth Theory, at a time when the economics of underdevelopment has been a major preoccupation of economists, has made it look as if there must be a real connexion. I much doubt if there is.

He distinguished the two subjects as follows. Growth theory treats economic growth in general, while development economics is a practical subject that draws on any theory relevant to it (including sociological theory). He made a significant additional point: 'if there is any branch of economic theory which is especially relevant to [development economics], it is the Theory of International Trade' (Hicks 1965: 3–4).

A key tool for estimating the impact of obstacles to trade was Max Corden's measure of the effective rate of protection, which calculated the degree of protection not in relation to the price of the final good, but to the domestic value added of the good (Corden 1966; 1971). This measure was employed in a number of multicountry studies of developing countries' trade regimes in the 1970s. The Organization for Economic Cooperation and Development's (OECD) studies are summarized in Little et al. (1970). Balassa (1971) presented the results of World Bank sponsored research. The US NBER series on foreign trade regimes and economic development (1974–8) concluded with summary volumes by Jagdish Bhagwati (1978) and Anne Krueger (1978).[5] All of these series of studies revealed very high levels of effective protection in many developing countries.

The substantial intellectual effort sunk into these studies had important and varied consequences for development economics and policy. It showed what could be done by the sustained application of formal economic analysis, and encouraged the appearance of new academic journals that featured formal analysis of trade and payments problems, such as the *Journal of International Economics*. It also opened up important political economy questions about why trade was distorted by government policies, in the process undermining the naive idea of governments being motivated solely by the public interest. Finally, it could be cited in support of trade liberalization as a growth-promoting reform in developing countries, despite Solow's assertion that 'sheer efficiency gains from trade cannot [raise the steady-state growth rate] except temporarily' (Snowdon and Vane 1999: 280).

---

[5] Other economists who were closely involved in this group of studies and who later became influential in the World Bank were Michael Michaely and Michael Bruno.

When the World Bank expanded its lending to developing countries in the 1960s, it turned hardly at all to growth models for guidance. In 1973, its first historians could declare: 'one will look in vain in the Bank files, both current and old, for any evidence of accepted theories of development or models of the development process' (Mason and Asher 1973: 458). The World Bank was (and indeed remains) an organization that takes a pragmatic view of economic doctrines. Its activities revolve around the central functions of borrowing and lending, and its views of the development process have been closely related to achieving success in its operational activities.

The arrival as President of the Bank of Robert McNamara (1970–81) and Hollis Chenery (as his Economic Adviser) initiated big changes at the bank—both a rapid expansion of lending and zeal for managing lending by quantitative methods. Countries' capital needs were now estimated from Chenery and Strout's (1966) two-gap model, which became embodied in the bank's minimum standard model—and subsequently its revised standard minimum model (RMSM). Although the two-gap model soon fell from academic favour, it lived on in the bank's operational practice, and the RMSM's investment–growth relation is derived from the original Harrod–Domar model that Solow had refined (Easterly 2002: 34–5). Like the even longer-lived Polak model at the International Monetary Fund (IMF), RMSM survived because it is serviceable. It facilitates, standardizes, and makes routine the tasks of the agency, whatever it may lack in intellectual sophistication (Chenery 1983).

Solow's conception of technology as a universal library of blueprints freely available ruled out the existence of a technology gap that required countries to import technology from others endowed with different factor proportions, because they had no alternative source. In the Solow model, the problem of inappropriate technology simply could not arise: there was no technology gap for trade to close. The bank, however, sought to stimulate a new intermediate technology, i.e. one that was neither the capital-intensive technology imported from the West nor the traditional labour-intensive but low-productivity technology. In an effort to change project design choices to make them more pro-poor, the bank's project evaluation criteria were modified to give greater weight to the incomes of the poor. There were, however, many influential people in whose eyes this modification was too radical, indicating excessive government intervention in the marketplace.

When McNamara retired before appointing Chenery's successor, the new President, Tom Clausen, a former commercial banker, selected Anne Krueger. Krueger had built her reputation in the 1970s, while at the University of Minnesota, by her contributions to the NBER foreign trade regimes studies already mentioned (Krueger 1974a, 1978). She also showed how controls on foreign trade could produce corruption and unproductive activities (Krueger 1974b).

Coining the term 'rent seeking' to describe them was perhaps her most original intellectual contribution. Krueger was something of an outsider to Washington circles, but as a tough-minded economic liberalizer she soon made her mark. Once installed as the Research Director of the Bank, she purged the Chenery regime, which she regarded as both too relaxed about government intervention in the economy and insufficiently technically competent. She made it her mission to be the main conduit by which neoclassical economics permeated the bank. The new policy message was to be the pro-market one that price signals work, that the effects of market liberalization favour the poor, and thus that special anti-poverty strategies are redundant. Research that threw doubt on these messages was actively discouraged (Kapur et al. 1997: 1193–5, ns. 47 and 48).

Part of her agenda was to pour cold water on the claim that developing countries faced a technological gap. Ian Little, who was closely associated with the bank's research department during her tenure, argued that empirically there was a wide range of capital/labour ratios for the production of the great majority of products. Even when equipment was imported, there were different ways to use it that could make its operation more labour-intensive (Little 1984: 176–81). Little also rejected the idea that the proprietary knowledge of multinational corporations contributed to the technological dependency of developing countries. In his view, since there are always ways to get around such problems, excessive capital intensity in production in developing countries must be attributed to ignorance, plus the prejudices of local politicians, engineers, and managers in its favour (1984: 249).

It was Anne Krueger's relatively short tenure at the bank (1982–6) that established the dominance of neo-liberal policy agenda. This provided the basis of 'the Washington Consensus' on desirable economic reform in developing countries. She had the full political backing of the Reagan administration, but even so it was an impressive personal achievement. Sheer energy and determination made her perhaps the most influential development economist of her generation in policy circles.

Growth theory and development theory

Was there a real connection between growth theory and the economics of development? The answer is 'yes and no'. Yes, in that, as Solow tells us, his desire to work on growth theory was stimulated by the fact that he, like everyone in the 1950s, was interested in economic development.

> I was passively interested in economic development, but I have never been actively interested—in a research way—in what happens in underdeveloped

countries... I knew I was not going to work on development issues, but it did get me interested in the area of economic growth. (Snowdon and Vane 1999: 273)

No, in that, as Solow also tells us, 'growth theory, *par excellence*, yielded to model building' while 'on the whole the personality types in the profession who became interested in economic development were not model builders... So even Arthur Lewis thought of his 1954 paper as a minor sideline to his book *The Theory of Economic Growth*' (Snowdon and Vane 1999: 275).

Thus, for a generation after the original Solow model, growth theory and development economics remained at cross purposes, since the latter was occupied principally with the question of transition between different types of economy, while the former was not. The prediction extracted from the original Solow model of convergence in per capita income levels in the long run provided the main link between growth and development economics. Although the claim that an augmented Solow model performs well in respect of this prediction has been disputed, it has stimulated new types of growth model, using a double augmentation, i.e. incorporating both human capital and intersector labour transfer as a source of average productivity increase (Temple and Woessmann 2006). Thus, today the original Lewis theme has been absorbed into neoclassical macroeconomic theory, and nested inside the augmented Solow framework, as part of a more comprehensive approach to formal growth modelling.

The endogenous growth models of the 1980s introduced into formal growth models some features that development economists had previously identified as significant for development, but which the original Solow model did not accommodate. These include induced innovation, investments with aggregate increasing returns, and the transfer of technology from developed to developing countries. Their incorporation into endogenous growth models has re-awakened research interest in institutions—the security of property rights, patent and intellectual property laws, competition policy, and international business regulation.

Growth (and development) accounting, which the original Solow model rationalized and enabled, has since the 1980s been applied to developing countries and estimates of differences in TFP levels and growth rates have been interrogated for their meaning and their contribution to policy formulation. They have provided a springboard for a revival of interest in the fundamental causes of growth, including historical differences in institutional trajectories. Other than that, their findings have been used to castigate development economists at large as 'capital fundamentalists' (i.e. believers that capital accumulation, but not technical progress, drives growth).[6] Yet as

---

[6] Easterly presents capital fundamentalism as the first of a series of failed panaceas advocated by development economists, others being education, population restraint, and debt relief.

Kenneth Arrow said: 'no economist would have denied the role of techno-logical change in economic growth' (1962: 155).

What remains at issue is the true size of the residual. Unfortunately, this empirical question is still hard to settle decisively and is, in any case, moot in its policy implications. 'The question that refuses to go away is this: whether all the fuss over TFP is increasing the stock of effective policy instruments and institutions, and helping us to understand why growth is so persistently uneven' (Yusuf 2014: 56).

I have suggested that the increasing formalization of analysis within devel-opment economics during the past fifty years derives less from various growth theories, or—as in Easterly's view—from what growth accounting tells us about the components of growth, than from advances made in trade theory, which (as Hicks so acutely noted) is especially relevant to development economics. Further, within trade theory, the conduit of change was not so much the pure theory of international trade as the close analysis of particular trade policies and their undesirable consequences. In this subject area, the combination of formal treatment, standard assumptions, and, above all, the ability to speak directly to policy issues has proved to be persuasive. By that I do not mean that more formal analysis inevitably produces a superior understanding of the dilemmas of economic development—only that, since the 1980s, under the decisive influence of Anne Krueger, it succeeded in changing the whole tenor of the economic development debate.

As with all innovations, Solow's growth model brought both benefits and costs. The benefits were obvious: the extension of the scope of formal analysis and a new model that was fully articulated, amenable to clear demonstration, and therefore also an excellent research tool. Today, the original and aug-mented Solow models, along with several varieties of endogenous growth model, have become obligatory components in the development economics curriculum, and indeed hold the pride of place in many development economics textbooks, e.g. Ray (1998).

However, the cost of the dominance of growth models have also been noted. Douglas Gollin (2014: 86) has expressed reservations in the following terms. 'Both academic economics and the world of development policy were arguably hurt by the relative neglect of dual economy models for several decades, beginning in the mid-1960s. The long dominance of one-sector models in the growth literature meant that questions of importance to devel-oping countries were not really addressed.'

Shahid Yusuf has an even more critical view, emphasizing how the debate on economic growth still remains pretty much the province of economists trained at a few North American and European universities. Western fashions in research methodology still dominate the research that is done, and despite its great volume, it follows established lines of thinking, though with innumerable minor variations. He laments how unproductive recent research has been in terms of contributing to convincing analysis and policies to accelerate growth. He sees economists' obsession with mathematical modelling and hypothesis testing as a sure route to their professional marginalization and impotence in the face of the need for practical proposals for policy action (Yusuf 2014: 60).

The well-chosen simplification that a good model requires can often eclipse ideas that contribute to the better understanding of development, but cannot be rendered in formal mathematical terms. These ideas, however important, remain exiled in the catch-all category of 'the complex sociological tangle'.

References

Arestis, P., McCombie, J., and Vickerman, R., eds (2006). *Growth and Economic Development: Essays in Honour of A. P. Thirlwall*. Cheltenham: Edward Elgar.

Arrow, K. J. (1962). The economic implications of learning by doing. *Review of Economic Studies* 29(3), 155–73.

Arrow, K. J., Karlin, S., and Suppes, P., eds (1959). *Mathematical Models in the Social Sciences*. Stanford, CA: Stanford University Press.

Backhouse, R. E. (2010). Economics, in R. E. Backhouse, and P. Fontaine, eds, *The History of the Social Sciences since 1945*, 38–70. Cambridge: Cambridge University Press.

Backhouse, R. E., and Fontaine, P., eds (2010). *The History of the Social Sciences since 1945*. Cambridge: Cambridge University Press.

Balassa, B. (1971). *The Structure of Protection in Developing Countries*. Baltimore, MD: Johns Hopkins Press.

Baumol, W., Nelson, R. R., and Wolff, E. N. (1994). *Convergence of Productivity*. New York: Oxford University Press.

Bhagwati, J. N. (1978). *Anatomy and Consequences of Exchange Control Regimes*. Cambridge, MA: Ballinger.

Bliss, C. (2007). *Trade, Growth, and Inequality*. Oxford: Oxford University Press.

Bosworth, B. P., and Collins, S. M. (2003). The empirics of growth: an update. *Brookings Papers on Economic Activity* 2, 113–206.

Chenery, H. B. (1983). *Oral History Interview*. Washington, DC: World Bank.

Chenery, H. B., and Strout, A. M. (1966). Foreign assistance and economic development. *American Economic Review* 56(4, part 1), 679–733.

Corden, W. M. (1966). The structure of a tariff system and the effective protective rate. *Journal of Political Economy* 74, 221–37.

Corden, W. M. (1971). *The Theory of Protection*. Oxford: Oxford University Press.

Easterly, W. (2002). *The Elusive Quest for Economic Growth: Economists' Adventures and Misadventures in the Tropics*. Cambridge, MA: MIT Press.

Findlay, R. (1979). Economic development and the theory of international trade. *American Economic Review* 69(2), 186–90.

Findlay, R. (1980). The terms of trade and equilibrium growth in the world economy. *American Economic Review* 70(3), 291–9.

Gollin, D. (2014). The Lewis model: a 60-year retrospective. *Journal of Economic Perspectives* 28(3), 71–88.

Hall, R. E., and Jones, C. I. (1999). Why do some countries produce so much more output per worker than others? *Quarterly Journal of Economics* 114(1), 83–116.

Harrod, R. F. (1951). Notes on trade cycle theory. *Economic Journal* 61(242), 261–75.

Helpman, E. (2004). *The Mystery of Economic Growth*. Cambridge, MA: Belknap Press.

Hicks, J. (1960). Thoughts on the theory of capital—the Corfu Conference. *Oxford Economic Papers (N. S.)* 12(2), 123–32.

Hicks, J. (1965). *Capital and Growth*. Oxford: Clarendon Press.

Kapur, D., Lewis, J. P., and Webb, R. (1997). *The World Bank: Its First Half Century*, vol. 1. Washington, DC: Brookings Institution Press.

Krueger, A. O. (1974a). *Foreign Trade Regimes and Economic Development: Turkey*. Cambridge, MA: Ballinger for the National Bureau of Economic Research.

Krueger, A. O. (1974b). The political economy of rent-seeking. *American Economic Review* 64(3), 291–303.

Krueger, A. O. (1978). *Foreign Trade Regimes and Economic Development: Liberalization Attempts and Consequences*. Cambridge, MA: Ballinger for the National Bureau of Economic Research.

Lewis, W. A. (1954). Economic development with unlimited supplies of labour. *Manchester School* 22(2), 139–91.

Lewis, W. A. (1955). *The Theory of Economic Growth*. London: George Allen and Unwin.

Little, I. M. D. (1984). *Economic Development: Theory, Policy, and International Relations*. New York: Basic Books.

Little, I. M. D., Scitovsky, T., and Scott, M. F. (1970). *Industry and Trade in Some Developing Countries*. Oxford: Oxford University Press.

McCombie, J. (2006). The nature of economic growth and the neoclassical approach: more questions than answers?, in P. Arestis, J. McCombie, and R. Vickerman, eds, *Growth and Economic Development: Essays in Honour of A. P. Thirlwall*, 135–61. Cheltenham: Edward Elgar.

Mankiw, N. G., Romer, D., and Weil, D. N. (1992). A contribution to the empirics of economic growth. *Quarterly Journal of Economics* 107, 407–38.

Mason, E. S., and Asher, R. E. (1973). *The World Bank since Bretton Woods*. Washington, DC: Brookings Institution.

Meier, G. M., and Seers, D., eds (1984). *Pioneers in Development*. New York: Oxford University Press for The World Bank.

Ray, D. (1998). *Development Economics*. Princeton, NJ: Princeton University Press.

Ros, J. (2000). *Development Theory and the Economics of Growth*. Ann Arbor: University of Michigan Press.

Rosenstein-Rodan, P. (1943). Problems of industrialization in eastern and south-eastern Europe. *Economic Journal* 53(210–11), 202–11.

Rostow, W. W. (1984). Development: the political economy of the Marshallian long period, in G. M. Meier and D. Seers, eds, *Pioneers in Development*, 229–61. New York: Oxford University Press for The World Bank.

Sen, A., ed. (1970). *Growth Economics*. Harmondsworth: Penguin Books.

Snowdon, B., and Vane, H. R. (1999). *Conversations with Leading Economists. Interpreting Modern Macroeconomics.* Cheltenham: Edward Elgar.

Solow, R. M. (1956). A contribution to the theory of economic growth. *Quarterly Journal of Economics* 70, 65–94.

Solow, R. M. (1957). Technical change and the aggregate production function. *Review of Economics and Statistics* 39, 312–20.

Solow, R. M. (1959). Investment and technical progress, in K. J. Arrow, S. Karlin, and P. Suppes, eds, *Mathematical Models in the Social Sciences.* Stanford, CA: Stanford University Press.

Solow, R. M. (1988). Growth theory and after. *American Economic Review* 78(March–June), 307–17.

Solow, R. M. (2001). Applying growth theory across countries. *World Bank Economic Review* 15(2), 283–8.

Temple, J. (1999). The new growth evidence. *Journal of Economic Literature* 37(March), 112–56.

Temple, J. (2005). Dual economy models: a primer for growth economists. *The Manchester School* 73(4), 435–78.

Temple, J., and Woessmann, L. (2006). Dualism and cross-country growth regressions. *Journal of Economic Growth* 11, 187–228.

Thirlwall, A. P. (2002). *The Nature of Economic Growth.* Cheltenham: Edward Elgar.

Toye, J., and Toye, R. (2004). *The UN and Global Political Economy: Trade, Finance, and Development,* Bloomington: Indiana University Press.

Yusuf, S. (2014). Fifty years of growth economics, in B. Currie-Alder, S. M. R. Kanbur, D. Malone, and R. Medhora, eds, *International Development: Ideas, Experience and Prospects.* Oxford: Oxford University Press.

9

Development doctrines doubted, 1951–77

Progress has its drawbacks and they are great and serious.

—Sir James Fitzjames Stephen

Measures for the Economic Development of Under-developed Countries (1951) soon acquired a special status in the embryonic literature on economic development. It was comprehensive in its coverage of national strategies and international financing, and it was the first pronouncement of the United Nations on these issues of global concern. The report was generally regarded as a repository of conventional wisdom on economic development. However, the report was a product of one style of working, the expert group, that lacked the heavyweight economic research that the League of Nations had commissioned from Gottfried Haberler, Jan Tinbergen, and others. The report of an expert group tended to reflect the views of the person who drafted it, which in this instance was the youthful Arthur Lewis (Ingham and Mosley 2013: 100–1).

Lewis was an outspoken and headstrong figure. In the circumstances, it is not surprising that, though written to create a consensus, the report attracted a series of sceptical challenges. The earliest challenge came from S. Herbert Frankel, a South African economist, whose family had emigrated from Germany to South Africa. In 1945 he became Oxford University's first Professor of Colonial Economic Affairs. Like Arthur Lewis, Herbert Frankel had been born and brought up in an underdeveloped country and had come to Britain to study economics at the London School of Economics (LSE). Unlike Lewis, who was there in the 1930s, Frankel's period of study was in the 1920s, before the subject of economic planning had become fashionable. His LSE mentors were Edwin Canaan, Theodore Gregory, Hugh Dalton, and Lilian Knowles.

Herbert Frankel on the official concept of progress

More than by any of these LSE figures, however, Frankel was influenced by the work of W. M. Macmillan, which he had absorbed as an undergraduate.

Macmillan's most important book was *The South African Agrarian Problem and its Historical Development* (1919). In this work, Macmillan sought explanations for South Africa's political and economic backwardness. He found it in the sudden imposition, in the 1870s and 1880s, of modern forms of economy and society on a country previously characterized by a backward agriculture. In the earlier period, farms and farmers had been very isolated, as a result of a primitive transport network, the physical insecurity resulting from sporadic wars, and poorly integrated agricultural markets. The discovery of gold and the wave of immigration that followed it changed everything. They suddenly brought a new, modern economic psychology into a country with a structurally backward agriculture.

In terms of economic motivation and behaviour, Macmillan painted South Africa as a deeply divided society struggling with the consequences of the sudden onrush of modernization. It was this account of the pathological development of his homeland that Herbert Frankel absorbed as an undergraduate student. It seemed to him increasingly relevant as the political position of English-speaking liberals in South Africa was eroded and Afrikaner nationalists began pushing the country steadily towards an *apartheid* regime.

Also unlike Lewis, Frankel's family environment was one of business—the grain marketing business about which he wrote his MA thesis at the University College of Johannesburg (soon to become the University of Witwatersrand). Frankel was conscious that South Africa's economic development was bound up with wide political and social issues and did not proceed simply by the investment of capital under normal competitive conditions. His doctoral study of South African railways indicated that the country's development relied on discriminatory and coercive policies. The railways' employment policy followed the government's 'whites only' directives, while the development of the mining industry was possible only by using coercive methods to regiment the black labour force. In 1945, as public opinion drifted in favour of Afrikaner nationalism, Frankel left his homeland for the chair of Colonial Economic Affairs that Lord Hailey had proposed and that Oxford University had established.

Frankel attacked the UN report (1951) root and branch as a representation of conventional mid-twentieth-century thinking about development, which he derided as 'something like an Official Concept of Progress' (Frankel 1953a). He disputed the fundamental assumptions on which it rested. Given Macmillan's interpretation of South Africa's experience, he denied that rapid economic change was a desirable policy goal. He further denied that progress could be measured in terms of increases in national income. This was pretty surprising, coming from the man who had pioneered the task of estimating South Africa's national income (Frankel 1941, 1943, 1945) It derived from two different critical viewpoints. One was that the incomes of a country's residents do not reflect just their own efforts or national policies, but 'the income-creating activities of individuals all over the world' (Frankel 1942: 182–3). The other objection was to the excessive individualism of the view that income is a measure of utility, something alien to societies where satisfaction is derived from communal activities and shared purposes (Frankel 1953a). The use of national income estimates for comparisons of welfare over space or time was therefore, in his view, without any substance or meaning.

He denied that beneficial change in underdeveloped countries was dependent on government action. His experience of the family grain dealing business made him a long-standing critic of South African government economic policies. His MA research had been on the government's introduction of a cooperative system for grain farmers, which, he found, failed to raise farm gate prices or provide sustainable agricultural credit. The farm cooperatives did, however, become an active lobby for extra privileges not available to commercial grain traders—an early example of regulatory capture. His doctoral research on the South African railways found evidence of government manipulation of the railways' accounts to provide additional government revenue at the expense of the rail user, and of railway investment being allocated on political criteria, rather than according to expected rates of return on capital. He thus doubted governments' ability to act in the public interest, rather than to pursue its own hidden agendas that distorted economic activity.

He was therefore an opponent of government economic planning. This was partly because he rejected the positivist notion of representing the working of the economy by a set of equations, which planners could then manipulate to reveal future problems or indicate appropriate remedies. For him, this mechanical analogy was a fundamental error, an illegitimate abstraction of the economy from the society in which economic activity was embedded. Although he was an economic liberal, he did not agree with Margaret Thatcher that 'there is no such thing as society'. He did regard planning as an authoritarian practice, by which governments used their power to determine the distribution of future incomes amongst different sections of the community—something that he thought was wrong in principle.

The need for the large-scale international transfers of public capital recommended by the UN report was something that Frankel regarded as doubtful. In his book *Capital Investment in Africa* (1938), written as an input to Lord Hailey's *African Survey* (1938), he had shown how inward investment was closely linked to the mining industry and, following Macmillan, increased social division. Moreover, additional public capital transfers might actually damage the prospects of underdeveloped countries in two ways. They might be invested in relatively less productive projects. They might also reinforce governments' persistence with harmful discriminatory or autarchic trade regimes.

Frankel launched his full-frontal onslaught on the presuppositions of modernizing development in the Harvard-based *Quarterly Journal of Economics* in an article reprinted in a subsequent book (Frankel 1953a). Arthur Lewis took it upon himself to respond to this grand remonstrance, and it is very instructive to see how he did it. In essence, his reply plays on the ambiguity inherent in H. G. Wells's description of scientists as 'servant-masters of the world'. Lewis switched into servant mode. He defended only two substantive criticisms that Frankel advanced—one relating to the need for agricultural exports and the other relating to mass education as a method of raising agricultural yields. Apart from that, Lewis argued that the presuppositions that Frankel rejected were not his own, but the presuppositions of the UN member governments who sought his advice as a technical expert. What the UN report does is to answer the question that the UN asked him to answer, Lewis argued; namely, what governments of developing countries and the international community should do if they want to stop the income gap between industrial and developing countries from widening further (Lewis 1953: 267–75).

Frankel's rejoinder did not really penetrate this defence (Frankel 1953b: 280–5). Lewis effectively won the immediate debate, yet his reply, though deft and superficially plausible, was also extremely disingenuous. While still a junior lecturer at the LSE, Lewis had served on the Colonial Economic Advisory Committee of the British Colonial Office in 1943–4. The evidence shows that he used his position to promote what was then a radical development agenda. It included the idea that economic development should proceed 'as rapidly as possible', that it should be assisted by government planning, that it required a 'sudden jump into industrialisation', and that it needed an increased flow of capital into the colonies (Ingham and Mosley 2013). Although the Colonial Office had succeeded in blocking his development agenda, for Lewis to give the impression that the presuppositions of the 1951 UN report were not his own was to be grossly misleading.[1]

The result of sidestepping Frankel's critique, rather than engaging with it head on, was to leave the fundamentals of the modernizing development agenda without any substantial defence. In a curious way, Lewis had managed to give the impression that there really was an official concept of progress—a set of presuppositions owned by the United Nations, but not by himself personally. These presuppositions continued to occupy much of the intellectual space of

---

[1] In a letter to the journalist Honor Croome dated 17 November 1953, Lewis wrote: 'Here we part company with poor old Frankel who is horrified by the notion of trying to speed up development in these fragile societies. I have much sympathy with him, as with all ostriches.' The mention of 'fragile societies' and 'sympathy' with Frankel shows a certain ambiguity in Lewis's own position, one could argue. I am grateful to Barbara Ingham for drawing my attention to this letter, which is in the Princeton University archives.

development economics in the 1950s and their critics remained isolated. Yet the Official Concept of Progress was left vulnerable to renewed assaults.

C. P. Snow on rich and poor and Leavis's counterblast

The novelist C. P. Snow was an influential bearer of the presuppositions of the 1950s modernization agenda. If it seems odd that a literary man should play that role, one should note that Snow had been a scientist. Trained in chemistry, he worked at Cambridge University as a research scientist in the 1930s. During and after the war, he was a British civil servant, responsible for the recruitment of government scientists. Snow's personal hero was H. G. Wells, who had similarly trained as a scientist with T. H. Huxley before turning to literature later in life. Wells, in his book *The Open Conspiracy* (1928), had called for the betterment of the world's backward races through the planning and development of science, technology, and industry (Ortolano 2009: 207–8). Snow saw himself as something of a latter-day H. G. Wells, a person who genuinely spanned the two cultures of science and literature and had the interests of developing countries at heart.

When Snow agreed to give the 1959 Rede Lecture in Cambridge, he originally intended its title to be 'The Rich and the Poor', and its theme global inequality. Its concluding section was written in order 'to sharpen the concern of rich and privileged societies for those less lucky' (Snow 1998/1959: 79, 53). In the event he decided to call his lecture 'The Two Cultures'. He thereby placed in the foreground of his lecture another concern of his, the cultural gap between scientists and literary intellectuals. Despite the title, the lecture gave full expression to those strong beliefs about applied science, industrialization, and poverty reduction, both in Britain and in the wider world, that the UN report had popularized, and which Frankel had already dubbed 'something like an official concept of progress'.

The question of whether the Industrial Revolution had raised or lowered the British standard of living had been brought into focus by a debate in the 1950s between economic historians in the journal *Past & Present*. Neo-Marxist historians, such as Eric Hobsbawn and E. P. Thompson, claimed that living standards fell during the Industrial Revolution, while non-Marxists, such as T. S. Ashton and Max Hartwell, claimed the opposite. Snow had no doubt that the neo-Marxists were wrong. In his lecture, he held that 'one truth is straightforward [that] industrialisation is the only hope of the poor'. This was demonstrated, he said, by the response of the poor whenever they had the option of industrial employment. 'For, with singular unanimity, in any country where they have had the chance, the poor have walked off the land into the factories as fast as the factories could take them'. Better medical care, better food, better education—these gains for the poor were, for Snow, the basis of social hope (Snow 1998/1959: 25–7).

In global terms, he said, 'the main issue is that the people in the industrialised countries are getting richer, and those in the non-industrialised countries are standing still: so that the gap between the industrialised countries and the rest is widening every day'. Nevertheless, he thought that the existing disparity between rich and poor countries could not long endure. He argued that a second industrial revolution had started in 1920 or 1930 and had created the potential for countries to catch up ever more easily and quickly. He singled out China, though he later admitted that this prediction had been somewhat premature.

'For the task of totally industrialising a major country, as in China today, it only takes will to train enough scientists, engineers and technicians', according to Snow. Thus, he concluded that 'it is technically possible to carry out the scientific revolution in India, Africa, South-East Asia, Latin America, the Middle East, within fifty years' (Snow 1998/1959: 41–6). However, the transformation would need capital—and this capital must come from outside because there was no alternative—plus armies of trained scientists and engineers, who did not yet exist in the numbers required in either developing or developed countries.

Such transformations as had already occurred had involved much effort, mistakes, and suffering, yet they succeeded because they could draw on popular enthusiasm. 'They've proved that common men can show astonishing fortitude in chasing jam tomorrow. Jam today and men aren't at their most exciting: jam tomorrow and one often sees them at their noblest' (Snow 1998/1959: 44).

These confident, optimistic, and inflated claims moved the literary critic F. R. Leavis, in his Richmond Lecture in February 1962, to try to demolish Snow's reputation as a public sage. He mercilessly ridiculed Snow's tendencies to talk in clichés, and selected two of Snow's phrases for particular attack. One was 'social hope', while the other was 'jam tomorrow', which was Snow's shorthand expression for the benefits of future consumption and greater leisure. Snow had said that scientists saw no reason why 'just because the individual condition is tragic, so must the social condition be', adding 'there is social hope'. Leavis could not see how the tragic condition of the individual could be reconciled with social hope. He further asserted: 'individual lives cannot be aggregated or equated or dealt with quantitatively in any way' (Leavis 1972: 53–4). In contrast to Frankel, who emphasized the value of community activity and shared purposes, Leavis offered radical individualism as the platform on which to counter what he saw as the superficial illusion of 'social hope'.

Leavis believed that the organic culture that had existed in the time of Shakespeare no longer existed. In the twentieth century, the growth of

125

journalism, films, and broadcasting had produced cultural deterioration, what today would be called 'dumbing down'. The authentic literary voices that remained were few, Eliot, Conrad, and, above all, D. H. Lawrence. They certainly did not include the literary works of H. G. Wells or C. P. Snow, 'who is the spiritual son of H.G. Wells' (Leavis 1972: 54, 57, 61).[2] Although he did not advocate trying to reverse the advance of technology (an impossible project in any case), he certainly hated and feared its accumulating cultural consequences. 'The advance of science and technology means a human future of change so rapid and of such kinds, of tests and challenges so unprecedented, of decisions and possible non-decisions so momentous and insidious in their consequences, that mankind . . . will need to be in full intelligent possession of its full humanity' (Leavis 1972: 60).

Leavis regarded Snow as a portent of the contemporary journalistic culture, according to which the standard of living is the ultimate criterion and raising it is the ultimate social priority. This priority neglected Ruskin's celebrated distinction between material wealth and well-being.

> What I am saying is that such a concern [for material wealth] is not enough—disastrously not enough. Snow himself is proof of that, product as he is of the initial cultural consequences of the kind of rapid change he wants to see accelerated to the utmost and assimilating all the world, bringing (he is convinced) . . . salvation and lasting felicity to mankind. (Leavis 1972: 59)

Since, Leavis argued, the type of felicity that a high standard of living procures is disastrously inadequate in human terms, it cannot be the ultimate human goal. Science is, he believed, only a means to an end. The end itself must be determined in the light of what it is to be fully human. This was the central element of his critique. It struck at the heart of gross domestic product (GDP) divided by population as the criterion of a society's success, although Leavis was unable to specify a different criterion that could represent quality of life in a measure of well-being. All he could do was to gesture towards the existence of some alternative.

He dismissed with contempt Snow's concern to provide the people of poor countries with 'jam tomorrow'. 'If you are enlightened,' Leavis declared sarcastically, 'you will see that the sum of wisdom lies in expediting the processes which will ensure the Congolese, the Indonesians, the Bushmen (no, not the Bushmen, there are not enough of them), the Chinese, the Indians, *their* increasing supplies of jam' (Leavis 1972: 58). This was the pinnacle, he jeered, of Snow's superficial and shallow kind of enlightenment.

---

[2] Leavis shared this opinion with the Cambridge historian Herbert Butterfield, who in 1935 had described the young Snow as 'an up-dated version of H. G. Wells' (Bentley 2011: 196).

As a fierce critic of contemporary Western culture and society, Leavis had no sympathy with its export to Asia and Africa, which he believed would impose a destructive civilization on those areas. Surviving primitive people, who still retained an organic culture, were to be found living there. 'Who will assert', he asked rhetorically, 'that the average member of a modern society is more fully human, or more alive, than a Bushman, an Indian peasant or a member of one of those poignantly surviving primitive peoples, with their marvellous art and skills and vital intelligence?' (Leavis 1972: 60).[3] This rhetorical question about the average member of modern society sat rather oddly with his prior claim that individual lives cannot be dealt with quantitatively in any way.

Snow gave a measured reply in *The Two Cultures—A Second Look* (1963). He made three important clarifications to his argument about the rich and the poor. Morally, it was based on an appeal to human solidarity in relation to meeting the elemental needs of those worse off than one was oneself. To refuse this basic solidarity was to be 'anti-human'. Politically, industrialization was not a matter of the authoritarian imposition of an alien culture. Rather, rural–urban migration was a means of social liberation and political empower-ment. It was an opportunity in a hierarchical face-to-face society to escape from the oppressions of power, and the peasantry had gratefully seized it the world over.

Educationally, the effort to understand the scientific transformation of the world, past, present, and future, was producing a third culture, bridging the gap between scientists and literary intellectuals.

> This body of opinion seems to come from intellectual persons in a variety of fields—social history, sociology, demography, political science, economics, government (in the American sense), psychology, medicine and social arts such as architecture. It seems a mixed bag, but there is an inner consistency. All of them are concerned with how human beings are living, or have lived. (Snow 1998/1963: 70)

This was the birth of cross-disciplinary development studies.

Snow's personal reputation went into eclipse in the wake of the two cultures controversy and his brief stint as a minister in the Labour government's Ministry of Technology. The public mood was changing, as faith in the white heat of technology cooled (Sandbrook 2006: 744–9). Encouraged by the response to his Richmond lecture, Leavis began a long campaign against what he called the 'orthodoxy of enlightenment'.

At the end of his career, this brought him to praise the dissenting opinions on development questions expressed in the 1970s by Peter Bauer. He deemed

---

[3] Shades here of Colin Turnbull's *The Forest People* (1962), an ethnographic study of the Mbuti pygmies in the present-day Democratic Republic of Congo, which presented them as an idyllic community of hunters and gatherers.

Bauer a worthy partner in scourging the conventional wisdom of modernity. However, he could never grant Bauer his undiluted admiration, because, as he put it, 'Bauer is, of course, an economist, but he is an intelligent one' (quoted in Ortolano 2009: 215–16). Indeed, it was an odd choice of an ally, and Bauer did not reciprocate it. Bauer was opposed to state-sponsored development planning and to large-scale foreign aid (Bauer 1959), but he strongly supported the goals of economic advance and economic achievement in poor countries. He also believed that social attitudes and institutions in those countries needed to change—to more Western and liberal forms—before such material goals could be reached. For him, economic development was a desirable objective and 'economic development requires a modernisation of the mind' (Bauer 1969: 82).

Bauer was thus no defender of traditional values and attitudes. Following his liberalizing policy advice would have closed the option for societies to conserve their traditional culture. In any case, this option was no longer available to the remaining hunter-gatherer societies, including Leavis's beloved Bushmen. The Kalahari Bushmen had already lived in intimate contact with pastoral groups for perhaps a thousand years. Moreover, for the two previous centuries they had formed part of a complex Southern African society that included Europeans and Bantu-speaking farmers. Already at the point when Leavis celebrated them, they had long ago become an underclass in a modern state (Kuper 2005/1998: 8; 211–16).

Fritz Schumacher, renegade economist

In 1973 a slim volume appeared. The author was Ernst Friedrich ('Fritz') Schumacher, a German refugee turned British national. The book was a compilation of his old lectures and articles, loosely pulled together. Its title was *Small is Beautiful*, which, though arresting, partly clouded Schumacher's real message. In fact, he did not advocate smallness of scale for its own sake (Schumacher 1973: 166). His concern was that the units of organization for economic activity should be on a scale suitable for the human beings that worked in them, and that the technology in use should be affordable by individual workers. His central message was the need for widespread access to economic opportunity in a human-friendly form.

Schumacher's career presents a curious paradox. It was a game of two halves. During the first half, despite a good intuitive grasp of economics and good professional connections with Maynard Keynes and William Beveridge, he made very little impact on policy or public opinion. In the second half, when he turned to religion (or, more precisely, to religions) and became a fierce critic of mainstream economics, his ideas were given an enthusiastic welcome, starting in the United States but spreading virtually all over the globe. His dramatic disavowal of his role as an economist, scientist, and expert magnified his little book's popular appeal.

After the war, once settled as the Economic Adviser to the National Coal Board, he slowly transformed himself from an applied economist into a prophet of development, a path that involved him first of all in the exploration of religious ideas. During the first forty years of his life Schumacher had been utterly intolerant of religion, but once the war was over, his personal quest for truth led him into religion, mysticism, astrology, and parapsychology. He would discover whole new areas of thought, become convinced of new truths, enthusiastically propagate them, and be frustrated when others were not convinced in turn. Over one weekend that he spent with Nicholas Kaldor, he enthused so intensely about flying saucers that Kaldor believed that he had been the victim of an elaborate practical joke (Wood 1984: 230–1).

Schumacher's views evolved further when he focused his interest on Buddhism. He began to practise yoga and meditation as a personal discipline. When the government of Burma invited him as a visiting adviser on economic development, he was keen to accept and went there on the mission in 1955. His advice to the Burmese government was that economic development should take place within the cultural context of the country, Buddhism. Therefore, rather than pressing ahead with Western-inspired schemes, he thought that Burma would do better following the Gandhian route of being satisfied with simple consumption goods and local, village-based production.

In 1971, he converted to Roman Catholicism, the culmination of a long period of interest in Catholic theology and philosophy. Thus, although *Small is Beautiful* has a chapter on Buddhist economics, he now declared that the choice of Buddhism had no special significance. 'The teachings of Christianity, Islam, or Judaism could have been used just as those of any other of the great Eastern traditions' (Schumacher 1973: 47). His Christian roots were Thomist, that is Christianity modified by the absorption of classical Greek philosophy (Schumacher 1973: 32, 99–100). Schumacher believed that 'the classical-Christian culture...supplied man with a very complete and astonishingly coherent interpretation...of man, the universe and man's place in the universe' (Schumacher 1973: 76). Its coherence, however, had been shattered and fragmented, and neither modern science nor the modern humanities would be able to provide a substitute.

He appealed not for a return to the metaphysics and ethics of the past, but to a metaphysics and ethics that was appropriate to the problems of the day. He finally expounded the metaphysics, epistemology, and moral philosophy that are the foundation of his post-1950 thinking in *A Guide for the Perplexed* (1977). That book is a concise statement of refurbished Thomist ideas of the Great Chain of Being and the methods of cognition appropriate to each level

129

of being, but it is not Christian in any exclusive sense. It is presented as the traditional wisdom of many religions or even of all religion, drawing on Buddhism, Taoism, and reformed Hinduism and others for corroboration. It could be another religion of humanity or a version of Christian Unitarianism.

The attack on science and experts once again

Schumacher joined the chorus of criticism of C. P. Snow's ideas (Schumacher 1973: 71–8). His basic objection to Snow's veneration of science was that, although scientific knowledge was useful in practical ways, it could not produce the moral values needed to control its own activities, so it must be made subordinate in any educational curriculum to philosophy and literature. The main implication of this objection was epistemological—that there are clear limits to what can be understood about economics, including the economics of development, by using only quantitative methods modelled on the natural sciences. The idea of using mathematics as a guide to public policy was anathema to him, and he blamed Vilfredo Pareto for pressing all sciences (including economics) into the mould of physics.

He was willing to concede that from the manipulation of scientific models 'a certain kind of "progress" is obtained; a kind of knowledge is accumulated'. Yet there was a sting in the tail, because such knowledge 'more likely than not becomes a barrier to understanding and even a curse from which it is hard to escape' (Schumacher 1977: 117). How does the curse of quantitative economic thinking operate? His answer was: 'If economic thinking pervades the whole of society, even simple non-economic values like beauty, health or cleanliness can survive only if they prove to be "economic" ' (Schumacher 1973: 41). He denied that social cost/benefit analysis, which utilitarian economists use to balance quantifiable and non-quantifiable costs and benefits alike, could produce meaningful results. He argued:

> All it can do is lead to self-deception or the deception of others; for to undertake to measure the immeasurable is absurd and constitutes but an elaborate method of moving from pre-conceived notions to foregone conclusions; all one has to do to obtain the desired result is to impute suitable values to the immeasurable costs and benefits. (Schumacher 1973: 41–2)

Schumacher's later vision was thus of an economics absolutely subordinated to meta-economic values. He believed that what he called 'science for understanding' had been supplanted in the West by what he called 'science for manipulation', a science restricting itself to visible and external low-level phenomena in the name of objectivity but for the purpose of exercising power (Schumacher 1977: 64–7). While he conceded that there was nothing wrong with manipulation per se, without a science for understanding to which it was subordinated, science for manipulation would inevitably produce inhuman consequences.

He found examples of these inhuman consequences in many areas of economic life. The use of the money metric to reduce all types of economic activity to components of an aggregate GDP, the growth of which had to be maximized, obliterates what to him were fundamental distinctions of kind between and within economic sectors. The primary sector contains both renewable and nonrenewable resources, but failure to recognize this distinction led to unsustainable growth plans. The consumption of nonrenewable natural capital, while accounting for it as if it were production that generates income, was a fundamental error. What appears in the national accounts as income growth may be no more than the depletion of the planet's original wealth. This is illusory growth, conjured up from particular definitions of what constitutes GDP. 'There can be "growth" towards a limited objective, but there cannot be unlimited, generalised growth' (Schumacher 1973: 29).

The gospel of sustainability

Sustainable development is thus a key element in Schumacher's vision. Schumacher preached that an acceptance of the right meta-economic values would give the primary renewable sector, i.e. agriculture and forestry, a new priority and reverse the economic trends of previous decades. Instead of more urbanization, investment in rural culture would draw people back to the land. Instead of greater mechanization, rural employment in worthwhile occupations would be created. Instead of chemical cultivation, there would be a reversion to organic methods. Instead of the gross exploitation of animals, their treatment would become more humane.

In the manufacturing sector, Schumacher felt that it was necessary to throw his weight against what he called industrial 'giantism'. He was, in fact, not in favour of smallness per se, despite the title of his most famous book. He saw that a balance had to be struck between the advantages of large- and small-sized organizations and judged that the contemporary need was a tilt in favour of shrinkage.

> [I]t is a matter of people. But people can be themselves only in small comprehensible groups. Therefore we must learn to think in terms of an articulated structure that can cope with a multiplicity of small-scale units. (Schumacher 1973: 68)

The goal of sustainable development, he concluded, required a profound reorientation not just of conventional economics, but also of science and technology. The forces of production themselves had to be tamed. Their trajectories must be switched away from the drive to invent machines and projects on an ever larger and ever more polluting scale towards generating methods of production that are small scale, accessible to all, and supportive of the creativity of labour. A major motive for scaling down production equipment was the promotion of full employment. This was desirable not in order to maximize production but because work could be a good activity in its own right (as the economists of happiness claim) rather than, as mainstream economists thought, a source of disutility; and, if it were a good activity, it should be widely shared. Given the way that industrialism had developed, much work had become mechanical, monotonous, meaningless, and soul-destroying. The vision of work as bringing out the creative impulses of the worker would require much more effort to be invested in the humanization of work.

In developing countries, the inhuman consequence of the then current strategy of economic development was a 'mutual poisoning' of the rural and urban sectors, according to Schumacher. The introduction of modern technology in the urban sector caused unemployment in the traditional industries in the rural sector, leading rural people without work to migrate to huge slums in the urban areas, making urban living costly and unmanageable (Schumacher 1965a: 91–2). The dual economy was intensified as a result of rural–urban migration, rather than being eroded, as Arthur Lewis had anticipated in his model of economic dualism. The answer to this lay in developing a technology intermediate between the modern and the traditional, a technology the use of which was attainable from within the boundaries of poverty and with which novel elements could be integrated into an evolutionary process of improvement.

His grand plan for the governments of developing countries and for aid donors was the adoption of an 'intermediate technology'. It was launched at the Cambridge Conference on Development (1964). It involved the creation of a large number of new workplaces whose equipment should cost on average not more than £70–100 per head in the money of the day, implying relatively simple methods of production and the use of locally available materials. The outputs should be buildings, building material, agricultural implements, and processed food and raw materials. In agriculture, the emphasis should be on the application of green manure and tree planting. Such a strategy would need to be implemented on a regional, rather than a centralized basis (Schumacher 1965a: 93–8). Schumacher recognized that a small portion of the industrial sector would continue to use modern technology, but advocated that future industrial investment should be much more broadly distributed.

At the 1964 Cambridge Conference on Development, Nicholas Kaldor, to whom he had enthused about flying saucers, dramatically attacked his proposal of intermediate technology as 'nonsense'. Where capital is scarce, Kaldor argued, it must be invested in projects with the lowest possible capital/output ratio and 'research has shown that the most modern machinery produces much more output per unit of capital invested than less sophisticated machinery that employs more people'. Despite this onslaught, the conference organizer reported: 'The consensus was that intermediate technology has big possibilities and advantages. It is emphatically not the case that intermediate techniques of manufacturing are necessarily less efficient than advanced methods... In technical jargon, the simplified production may be the optimum technique, given the characteristics of the market, the factor availability and the state of skills' (Robinson 1965: 27). The feasibility of intermediate technology was, after all, an empirical question, and knowledgeable people were willing to give it the benefit of the doubt (Robinson 1964: 440–2).

Then *The Observer* published in August 1965 a crucial article by Schumacher (headlined as 'How to Help Them Help themselves') that touched off strong public support of the idea of intermediate technology (Schumacher 1965b). George McRobie called a meeting at the Overseas Development Institute of those who had responded favourably to the *Observer* article, a meeting that agreed to set up the Intermediate Technology Development Group (ITDG). The ITDG reflected Schumacher's practical philosophy of finding out what people are doing and helping them to improve it. ITDG initially saw its role as assembling information about efficient labour-intensive technologies, publishing directories of intermediate technology for different industries, and advising people on its use.

The *Observer* article and the creation of ITDG showed that the idea of intermediate technology had gained a wide public acceptance. Even so, nobody—apart from Schumacher himself—expected *Small is Beautiful* to be the runaway, roaring success that it proved to be. *Small is Beautiful* sold over 700,000 copies world-wide, in at least fifteen different languages (Binns 2006: 218). What was the nature of its impact? First of all, it did have a considerable impact on professional and public opinion about development. At the ideological level it reinforced the retreat from 'modernism' that was already in train in the 1960s, and especially the retreat from the technocratic conception of how economic development should be promoted. It was another step towards the dethroning of the expert, whether he were a scientist or an economist (for it usually was a 'he'). The reception of the book revealed that many people were no longer willing to leave the task of development in the hands of economists claiming to be scientists and acting as servant-masters of the world.

There was something much more constructive in Schumacher's critique than in Herbert Frankel's protests about the official doctrine of progress or in Leavis's vituperation against the superficiality of the scientist/novelist Snow. *Small is Beautiful* could not have gained traction with the public unless it contained something more than the conservative laments that had played counterpoint to the Industrial Revolution for more than a century.[4]

Kaldor dubbed Schumacher's vision 'romanticism', a view that other critics also shared (King 2009: 117). Indeed, parallels with the romantic reaction to nineteenth-century industrialization were not hard to discern. However, his vision, while conservative at base, is not simply one of nostalgic melancholy. On the contrary, Schumacher turned it into an optimistic kind of romanticism, full of hope and inspiration for the future. He called for a movement away from certain 'poisonous errors' of the past and towards the development of a 'healthy' economy and society. With this medical metaphor, Schumacher looked forward cheerfully to society's recovery.

Schumacher made his positive contribution by organizing the provision of additional resources for governments and NGOs. It was not the case, as Kaldor for example believed, that the intermediate technology that he was calling for did not exist in any shape or form. Some elements of it had been invented and propagated by colonial officials who wrote many ingenious booklets on improved latrines, improved grain storage vessels, and improved stoves. Other elements would need to be invented by competent engineers. Much practical good was achieved through ITDG's efforts at documentation, distribution, and development of the scattered blueprints of intermediate technology. The ITDG survives today, now renamed Practical Action, one living memorial to Schumacher's contribution to the debates on development of the years 1950–80.

Stefan Collini points out that the cultural critic often occupies 'the discursively awkward position of appearing to speak on behalf of the ineffable' (Collini 2013: 48). This was fair comment on Frankel's idea of community and Leavis's defence of authentic culture. It was also true of Schumacher's concept of sustainability.

Sustainability in the sense of maintaining a pattern of development continuously is a concept that cannot be made concrete without definite knowledge of the future—future demands, future technologies, future institutions and policies. This is knowledge that in principle is not attainable.

Policies to ensure that vague notion of sustainability are inevitably arbitrary. Schumacher held, for instance, that nuclear energy was not sustainable and recommended instead coal-fired generation. Climate scientists now regard the burning of fossil fuels as unsustainable and tend to favour nuclear energy instead. (Schumacher was after all the economic adviser to the National Coal Board!) There is no measure of sustainability in general that will guide us in

---

[4] For example: 'The statistician will register a growing progress and the novelist a gradual decline...The useful will take the place of the beautiful, industry of art, political economy of religion, and arithmetic of poetry' (Henri Frederic Amiel in 1851, quoted by Briggs (1965/1963): 22).

making a decision, but there are indicators of past damage relevant to particular aspects of ecology (Stiglitz et al. 2010: 98). *Ex post* many types of development have been found to be unsustainable. That does not imply that *ex ante* one can know what will be sustainable. Schumacher popularized the new meta-value of sustainability but did not investigate its philosophical and practical complications.

What has changed in the sixty-five years since the publication of *Measures for Economic Development*? The UN is still in charge of the Official Concept of Progress; witness the seventeen Sustainable Development Goals adopted in 2015. Economists have lost some of their credibility as experts, but climate scientists have joined them as purveyors of specialist knowledge and advice. The cult of the expert per se is still alive and well. There is a new emphasis on a broader notion of development driven by those who criticized GDP as a measure of welfare; a better appreciation of the importance of the use of renewable resources rather than ecologically damaging ones; and a greater sense of urgency about organizing collective action. The critics did not win all of their battles, but they did make these important gains.

References

Bauer, P. T. (1969). Dissent on development. *Scottish Journal of Political Economy* 16, 75–94.

Bauer, P. (1959). *United States Aid and Indian Economic Development*. American Enterprise Association.

Bentley, M. (2011). *The Life and Thought of Herbert Butterfield: History, Science and God*. Cambridge: Cambridge University Press.

Binns, T. (2006). E. F. (Fritz) Schumacher (1911–77), in D. Simon, ed., *Fifty Key Thinkers on Development*, 218–23. London: Routledge.

Briggs, A. (1965/1963). Technology and economic development, in *Technology and Economic Development: A 'Scientific American' Book*. London: Penguin Books.

Collini, S. (2013). Introduction, in F. R. Leavis, *The Two Cultures? The Significance of C. P. Snow*. Cambridge: Cambridge University Press.

Frankel, S. H. (1938). *Capital Investment in Africa: Its Course and Effects*. London: Oxford University Press.

Frankel, S. H. (1941). Consumption, investment and war expenditure in relation to the South African national income. *South African Journal of Economics* 9, 445–8.

Frankel, S. H. (1942). World economic solidarity. *South African Journal of Economics* 10, 169–92.

Frankel, S. H. (1943). Consumption, investment and war expenditure in relation to the South African national income. *South African Journal of Economics* 11, 75–7.

Frankel, S. H. (1945). Consumption, investment and war expenditure in relation to the South African national income. *South African Journal of Economics* 13, 132–5.

Frankel, S. H. (1953a). *The Economic Impact on Under-developed Societies: Essays on International Investment and Social Change*. Oxford: Basil Blackwell.

Frankel, S. H. (1953b). United Nations primer for development: reply. *Quarterly Journal of Economics* 67(2), 280–5.

Hailey, Lord (Ormsby-Gore, W. G. A.) (1938). *African Survey*. London: Macmillan.

Ingham, B., and Mosley, P. (2013). *Sir Arthur Lewis: A Biography*. Basingstoke: Palgrave Macmillan.

King, J. E. (2009). *Nicholas Kaldor*. Basingstoke: Palgrave Macmillan.

Kuper, A. (2005/1998). *The Reinvention of Primitive Society: Transformations of a Myth*. London: Routledge.

Leavis, F. R. (1972). *Nor Shall My Sword: Discourses on Pluralism, Compassion and Social Hope*. New York: Barnes and Noble Books.

Lewis, W. A. (1953). United Nations primer for development: comment. *Quarterly Journal of Economics* 67(2), 267–75.

Macmillan, W. M. (1919). *The South African Agrarian Problem and its Historical Development*. Witwatersrand: Central News Agency Ltd.

Ortolano, G. (2009). *The Two Cultures Controversy: Science, Literature and Cultural Politics in Post-war Britain*. Cambridge: Cambridge University Press.

Robinson, R. E. (1964). Conference on the role of industrialisation in developing economies. *Journal of Modern African Studies* 2, 440–2.

Robinson, R. E. (1965). *Industrialisation in Developing Countries*. Cambridge: Cambridge University Overseas Studies Committee.

Sandbrook, D. (2006). *White Heat: A History of Britain in the Swinging Sixties*. London: Little, Brown.

Schumacher, E. F. (1965a). Industrialisation through 'intermediate technology', in R. E. Robison, ed., *Industrialisation in Developing Countries*, 91–9. Cambridge: Cambridge University Overseas Studies Committee.

Schumacher, E. F. (1965b). How to help them to help themselves. *The Observer*, August 25th.

Schumacher, E. F. (1973). *Small is Beautiful: A Study of Economics as if People Mattered*. London: Blond and Briggs.

Schumacher, E. F. (1977). *A Guide for the Perplexed*. London: Jonathan Cape.

Simon, D., ed. (2006). *Fifty Key Thinkers on Development*. London: Routledge.

Snow, C. P. (1998/1959). *The Two Cultures*. Cambridge: Cambridge University Press.

Stiglitz, J. E., Sen, A., and Fitoussi, J.-P. (2010). *Mismeasuring Our Lives: Why GDP Doesn't Add Up: The Report*. New York: New Press.

Turnbull, C. M. (1962). *The Forest People*. New York: Simon and Schuster.

United Nations (1951). *Measures for the Economic Development of Under-developed Countries*. New York: UN Department of Economic Affairs.

Wells, H. G. (1928). *The Open Conspiracy: Blueprints for a World Revolution*. London: Victor Gollancz.

Wood, B. (1984). *Alias Papa: A Life of Fritz Schumacher*. London: Jonathan Cape.

10

Development with a human face, 1980–

Lord, we know what we are, but know not what we may be.
—William Shakespeare, *Hamlet*, Act 4, Scene 5

Humanizing political economy

Long before anyone saw the need to give economic development a human face, there was a movement to humanize nineteenth-century political economy. Its protagonist was the artist and art critic John Ruskin, whose four essays on the subject were published as *Unto This Last* (1862/1906). He was a follower of Thomas Carlyle and described himself as 'a violent Tory of the old school'. Nevertheless, his opinions deeply influenced those of very different political persuasions, Liberals such as William Beveridge and socialists such as Keir Hardie and Clement Attlee.

Unto This Last has three elements—a critique of political economy, a redefinition of wealth from a humanistic perspective, and a sketch of a programme of social reform. Some of the critique rests on misunderstandings or misrepresentations of the ideas of David Ricardo and J. S. Mill, but its main point is that the assumption of 'economic man' is a partial view that omits people's social affections from the science of political economy. Even deductions correctly made from such a partial assumption would be misleading and not applicable to reality.

Ruskin painted a very different picture of what constituted real wealth, personal and national, from that of the political economists of his day. He believed that when the social affections are added to economic interest as a source of human motivation, moral assessment and considerations of justice must enter into the definition of wealth. Ruskin's credo was that 'there is no wealth but Life'. Since production is the flow issuing from the stock of wealth, he also raised the question of what is 'useful production'?

Ruskin denied that certain forms of production commonly accepted as such were indeed useful, and he instanced bayonets and bombs. He coined a term for non-wealth—'illth'—though it is not clear to what exactly he applied this term. He also pointed out that certain things were necessities of life, clean air, light, and clean water, but had no commercial value. His own criterion of useful production was whether production was life-enhancing, and his conclusion was that the welfare implications of a nation's accumulation of wealth, when examined through a moral lens, were ambivalent. Accumulation of wealth could be indicative of national progress, or of its exact opposite.

Ruskin was the champion of honest workmanship and a critic of the division of labour, which he thought destroyed it. His programme of social reform included the establishment of government-regulated factories and workshops for 'the production and sale of every necessity of life', in a bid to stamp out bad workmanship and product adulteration (including of food). He wanted the government to provide free training schools for youth with universal coverage. He advocated government provision of work for the unemployed at a fixed minimum wage, and government support for the sick, the old, and the destitute. None of these reforms occurred in his lifetime, but thanks to Beveridge, Attlee, and others some were incorporated into the British welfare state after his death.

Ruskin was no friend of equality and, and like Carlyle and his 'heroes', believed in the innate superiority of some people to others, not least of men to women. The morally superior people were those who should be appointed, he insisted, to guide and lead a transformation that would make vital satisfaction the basic principle of a reformed economy.

The economist J. A. Hobson agreed that 'there is no wealth but life' was the right motto for a modern movement of social reform, but he saw two objections to Ruskin's elaboration of it. The first was that Ruskin had interpreted vital satisfaction as meaning what producers and consumers *ought to* desire and value, rather than what they *actually did* desire and value. 'This doctrine of the intrinsic value of things, though sound for social ethics,' he complained 'is baffling when suddenly injected into an analysis of current industry and its products' (Hobson 1920: 88). This raised the problem of the source of valuation in a humanized economy.

Hobson's second objection was to Ruskin's neglect of class interests as an impediment to social transformation. 'Somehow or other, the landowners and capitalists are to regard their land and capital and the power it gave them over the lives of the workers as a public trust. . . . How this total change of character and outlook was to come about Ruskin never explained' (Hobson 1920: 93–4). This raised the problem of the politics of achieving a reformed economy. The two problems of source of valuation and politics of reform are obviously linked, and we shall see that they present themselves again to those currently attempting to give a human face to the process of development.

Ruskin's reputation remained high until the First World War and then waned, perhaps because bayonets and bombs were generally seen again as a form of useful production. Most of the first half of the twentieth century was dominated by war and rumours of war. The economic requirements of war planning drove the construction, led by Richard Stone, of national accounts of production, income, and expenditure at the start of the Second World War. The moral assessment of useful production no doubt seemed an unhelpful luxury as long as the struggle for survival lasted. Only when it was over did the question of the welfare implications of national production seem relevant again.

Dudley Seers was a New Zealander with links to the New Zealand Labour Party and had worked as an economic statistician at Oxford University, the newly founded United Nations, and the UK government. He took up Ruskin's campaign to dethrone the use of the gross national product (GNP) as a measure of economic welfare. In a famous speech as President of the Society of International Development in 1969, Seers asked: 'What are we trying to measure?' He doubted that the maximization of production was the correct goal of development, arguing that increasing employment and promoting more equitable income distribution would do more to alleviate poverty. Economies, he argued, could grow even in the presence of 'the obscene inequalities that disfigure the world'. Seers led the International Labour Organization's (ILO) first employment mission to Colombia in 1971, writing a report that discussed ways of promoting employment, and did so without ever mentioning the words 'economic growth'.

Mahbub ul Haq's recantation

In the introduction to *Poverty and Progress* (1879) Henry George wrote: 'So long as all the increased wealth which modern progress brings goes but to build great fortunes, to increase luxury and make sharper the contrast between the House of Have and the House of Want, progress is not real and cannot be permanent.' This insight proved to be highly relevant to mid-twentieth-century Pakistan. It was the Pakistani economist Mahbub ul Haq who became the most determined champion of human development as opposed to economic growth. Born in pre-independence India in 1934, he survived the inter-communal massacres of 1947 and settled in the new state of Pakistan. After graduating from Punjab University he went on to take further economics degrees at elite Western universities—Cambridge and Yale—followed by post-doctoral work at Harvard. In 1957, he returned to government service in Pakistan as Chief Economist at the Planning Commission. At this time his favoured strategy of development was an investment-led path, either capitalist or statist, under a liberal economic regime—outlined in his 1963 book *The Strategy of Economic*

Planning. His experience through the 1960s showed him that, while his favoured strategy was quite consistent with rapid economic growth, it had little effect on the incidence of poverty.

The standard theory of 'trickle-down' prosperity from the upper ranges of the income and wealth distribution to those in the lower ranges did not operate in Pakistan. In 1968 ul Haq publicly identified the impediment. Twenty-two industrial family groups dominated the Pakistani economy, owning the bulk of the industrial, banking, and insurance assets in the country. They built great fortunes and lived in luxury, but this did not generate any real progress or development of the country.

What was worse, this extreme degree of inequality was a factor behind the break-up of Pakistan. The free play of market forces naturally favoured the richer region of the country (West Pakistan) as well as the richer income groups located there. In 1971 East Pakistan, the poorer region, successfully seceded to become the new state of Bangladesh. As a contribution to nation building, the economic strategy of the 1960s was a manifest disaster.

Ul Haq became Policy Planning Director at the World Bank between 1970 and 1982, guiding Robert McNamara's agenda to widen the scope of the bank's project lending beyond large infrastructure projects. In 1976, he published *The Poverty Curtain: Choices for the Third World*, which was in part an auto-critique of his own previous role in Pakistan as a liberal economic planner. He rehearsed the paradox of rising levels of per capita income coexisting with falling industrial wages, growing unemployment, and increased poverty, attributing it to lack of attention to the composition of production and the structure of demand.

Ul Haq was now echoing the concerns that Seers had expressed, but he made a new departure. He advocated the setting of fixed consumption targets that were based on human needs. Consumption planning should not be in financial terms but in physical terms, 'in terms of a minimum bundle of goods and services that must be provided to the common man to eliminate the worst manifestations of poverty: minimum nutritional, educational, health and housing standards, for instance.' Ul Haq roundly declared: 'to weight basic needs by ability to pay is outrageous in a poor society' (ul Haq 1976: 35).

Shortly afterwards, Dharam Ghai at the ILO published a volume entitled *Basic Needs Approach to Development* (Ghai et al. 1977). Paul Streeten, who had joined the World Bank in 1976, persuaded ul Haq that this was an important policy initiative that deserved further exploration in the bank. Javed Burki, Norman Hicks, and Frances Stewart were recruited to do further work with ul Haq and Streeten on the topic. Their conclusions were published in *First Things First: Meeting Basic Human Needs in Developing Countries* (1981).

Originally, the ideas of basic human needs had a foundation in the Aristotelian concept of the full life and included personal autonomy as well as access to material commodities. However, in the World Bank version, it was confined to the provision of goods and services required to achieve adequate standards of nutrition, health, shelter, water and sanitation, education, and other essentials. This was valuable in acknowledging the multiple dimensions of deprivation that accompanied lack of income, but it did not address the dimensions of personal autonomy and agency, except to note euphemistically that the reallocation of public resources 'often requires major changes in the power balance of society'—a polite allusion to the problem of the politics of reform.

Not altogether surprisingly, the basic needs approach came in for a volley of criticism. The greatest objections were that this was another top-down, state-led initiative and that it included only material needs. Dudley Seers captured the spirit of both of these objections when he remarked: 'basic needs are most perfectly met in a well-run zoo' (Jolly 1989: 35, n. 7). The operational feasibility of the approach was also open to doubt if it required 'major changes in the power balance of society'. Although Dudley Seers died in April 1983, his question—What are we trying to measure?—and its twin—What should we be trying to measure? (Seers 1972)—long survived him, and continued to demand a more coherent answer. The best response yet is due to Amartya Sen.

Amartya Sen, functionings and capabilities

Amartya Kumar Sen is an Indian economist, born in what became Bangladesh. After attending Presidency College, Calcutta, he took a degree in economics at Cambridge, where he was a fellow student of Mahbub ul Haq. His initial area of research was the conundrums of the mathematical theory of social choice, but by the 1980s his interests had taken a more practical turn. The analysis of famine and gender bias in food allocation had by this time brought him onto the ground of economic development.

While a Fellow of Trinity College, Cambridge, Sen decided to branch out from economics to study related topics in philosophy, such as epistemology, ethics, and political philosophy. Hence, he was well equipped to engage with the issues that arose from John Rawls's *A Theory of Justice* (2009/1971). Two aspects of Rawls's theory of justice provided the point of departure for Sen's answer to the question of what it is that development economists should be striving to measure.

Rawls provided a critique of, and an alternative to, the utilitarian theory of justice (an elaboration and refinement of Jeremy Bentham's principle of the 'greatest happiness of the greatest number'). Sen sympathized with Rawls's project of displacing the metric of happiness or utility. One of its undesirable features was that it tended to favour allocating more resources to those with expensive tastes—the gourmets and art collectors—because of the large amounts of psychic pleasure that they derived from their consumption. The other side of that coin, one very relevant to poverty and development, was that poor people who had mentally adjusted to their state of deprivation would not register much a of psychic gain if they were given an increased allocation of commodities. Their extra happiness would weigh lightly in the utilitarian scale against the extra happiness derived from luxury consumption.

However, Sen disagreed with Rawls's second principle of justice—that inequality in the distribution of income and wealth should not be permitted unless the departure from equality was to the benefit of all members of society. To evaluate this principle it was necessary to define the least advantaged members of society, and Rawls proposed to do that in terms of access to 'social primary goods', namely things that every rational person is presumed to want, irrespective of his or her particular life plan. Sen objected to this procedure, pointing out that it was insensitive to people with special needs: 'having the same supply of primary goods [as others without special needs] leaves them clearly worse off' (Sen 1984: 280). He did not regard this a trivial case, since old age and chronic illness were hardly rare conditions in human life. So while rejecting measurement in terms of utility, he also rejected measurement in terms of goods or commodities.

This led Sen on to reject the traditional focus of development economics on the expansion of the GNP, aggregate income, and the total supply of particular goods. What really mattered, he argued, were people's entitlements to consumption and the capabilities that their entitlements generated. The ultimate objective of economic development was to expand what people can or cannot do—what he called their functioning and their capabilities to function. How long do people live, how much illness do they have to endure, how well nourished are they, and what skills do they have to participate in economic and cultural life? He quoted with approval Marx's aim of 'replacing the domination of circumstance and chance over individuals by the domination of individuals over chance and circumstances' (Sen 1984: 497). That was the ultimate end, while the growth of GNP, which still obsessed many development economists and politicians, was no more than one possible means towards the achievement of that end.

To some extent, the lessons that Sen drew from criticizing Rawls's theory of justice were convergent with the basic needs approach. Both aimed at creating opportunities for more abundant human lives. Both supported programmes of social reform, such as improved nutrition, health services, sanitation and water, shelter, and education. Yet there were also yawning conceptual differences.

Sen was keen to move beyond envisaging development in terms of the provision of, in Paul Streeten's words, 'particular goods and services required to achieve certain results'. Sen regarded the connections between particular goods and services and the achievement of desired capabilities as too tenuous and too multifaceted to make the former a good proxy for the latter. In his view, 'operating on the commodity space rather than directly on the space of capabilities involves additional problems' (Sen 1984: 514).

Sen also noted that absolute deprivation in terms of capabilities could involve relative deprivation in terms of commodities. In other words, loss of social respect and social exclusion could result not just from what one did or did not possess or consume, but also from one's consumption relative to that of others. Further, the basic needs approach seemed to imply a concern with meeting basic needs only up to a minimum level of capabilities. It represented a truncated version of the capability approach, whereas the latter was of a more general application and could be useful for judging advantage and deprivation in rich countries as well as poor ones.

Finally, and perhaps most important of all, Sen pointed out the passivity implied by the emphasis on people's needs and the distribution of commodities to them to fulfill their needs. While this was appropriate for children or other dependents, it rendered adults as victims rather than as responsible agents. Placing the emphasis on what people are able to do—their capabilities— recognizes the importance of personal agency, which in turn linked to issues of freedom. In Sen's estimation, the basic needs approach had confined itself to an arbitrarily narrow box, from which it could be released if it were seen as no more than one part of his capability approach. It would be liberated thereby from the fetishism of its commodity focus, and would gain a broader relevance to policy formulation.

The dissonance between the basic needs and the capabilities approaches was a clash between Sen's philosophical project of constructing a normative theory of human development, a problem of social ethics, and those trying to work out a practical programme of social reform. As Hobson had noted, the two activities do not necessarily hang together. The latter group was convinced that, for practical purposes, one could match specific inputs with non-income measures of poverty, while Sen could see all the logical objections to doing so. However, he also thought that the two approaches were not ultimately irreconcilable. Although the constructive nature of his criticism made a rapprochement between the two approaches possible, the tension between those with a more practical agenda and those more worried about logical coherence continued to dog the human development project as it gathered momentum.

The Human Development Report

During his time at the Bank, ul Haq refused several offers of Z. A. Bhutto, the prime minister of the day, to return to Pakistan, but he accepted General Zia ul

143

Haq's offer of the Finance Ministry, which he occupied from 1982 to 1988. He promoted some worthwhile income distribution measures, but lacked the power to enforce the integration of production and distribution policies. He drew the conclusion that change came less from office holding than from leading advocacy campaigns that changed ideas.

For that task he was by now very well fitted. Not least among his advantages for this role was the fact that, unlike many of the thinkers discussed in this book, he hailed from a developing country. He had a Western education, but had returned home in a leadership role to do his best for his country. At the same time, he was not an apologist for his country, right or wrong. He had been courageous in criticizing what he saw as its failings—such as the dominance of the twenty-two families. His criticisms of Western policies and of the policies of the South (i.e. the countries of the southern hemisphere) thus had an even-handed quality. This brought him much credibility in international circles. Moreover, his colleagues admired his personal qualities. They regarded him as a powerful animator of teamwork, capable of conveying his intellectual excitement to them and synthesizing their contributions to the project that he was directing.

One of the figures who inspired him was Barbara Ward, the economist, author, and early environmental campaigner. Her credo was 'our visionary perspective is the true realism'. Ul Haq joined the North–South Roundtable of the Society for International Development when she was the Chair. After her death in 1981 when ul Haq succeeded her as Chair, the United Nations Development Programme (UNDP) and the North–South Roundtable organized a series of conferences whose report reviewed country progress of the social sectors and the resulting human resource development. This was a way of keeping alive a countervailing intellectual current in the decade of the 1980s when neo-liberalism became the conventional wisdom and the guide of much development practice. Yet ul Haq saw that more was needed to strengthen and protect an alternative view of development. He found a new but unlikely ally in William Draper III, Administrator of UNDP since 1986.

Draper was an American businessman who had been nominated by Ronald Reagan for the post, who venerated the private sector and who had little respect for old-style UN officials. He had a folksy manner and an endearing habit of misspeaking that that led him to champion 'bottoms-up development'. He guided UNDP from a being a congeries of loosely connected projects into becoming a major source of advocacy, with an overriding goal of human development and a subordinate goal of poverty reduction through grass roots participation. In 1989 he recruited ul Haq to launch the *Human Development Report* (HDR) along the lines of the previous UNDP/SID conference reports. Ul Haq had noted how quickly the World Bank had been able to close down its basic needs work once a new bank president (Tom Clausen) arrived, so he asked for and was given greater institutional protection. This special treatment Draper granted him in the form of a Human Development Report Office that was outside the main structure of the UNDP.

In his autobiographical note for the Nobel Prize Committee, Amartya Sen recalled:

> In 1989 [Mahbub] was put in charge, by the United Nations Development Programme (UNDP), of the newly planned 'Human Development Reports.' Mahbub insisted that I work with him to help develop a broader informational approach to the assessment of development. This I did with great delight, partly because of the exciting nature of the work, but also because of the opportunity of working closely with such an old and wonderful friend. Human Development Reports seem to have received a good deal of attention in international circles, and Mahbub was very successful in broadening the informational basis of the assessment of development.

The Human Development Index

In fact, their collaboration was not quite as straightforward as this glowing account states. An issue between the two old friends was the place of the Human Development Index (HDI) in the new HDR. While ul Haq aimed to attract public attention, Sen was doubtful about the validity and usefulness of the index that had been devised to do so. The inventors of the HDI wanted to dislodge gross domestic product (GDP) per capita as the arbiter of national development, and also to dislodge the companion notion that poverty was simply a matter of lack of per capita income. Neither Charles Booth nor Seebohm Rowntree, the Victorian pioneers of poverty analysis, had regarded poverty as an exclusively economic phenomenon. Nevertheless, twentieth-century economists narrowed the focus of poverty analysis and concentrated on refining just one investigation method, the delineation of a 'poverty line'—the income level below which individuals and households should be counted as among the poor.

Yet lack of income is not the only source of social disadvantage. Disadvantage has many causes—poor health, inadequate education, precarious housing, casual employment, and political exclusion, among many others—as well as by low income. Poverty has multiple dimensions, but poverty was being measured only in the economic dimension. This would not matter if income were aligned with all the other sources of disadvantage. Empirically, however, there is a mismatch between low income and other sources of disadvantage.

The inventors of the HDI wanted to reflect different dimensions of well-being and poverty, but they also believed that they had to come up with a single number. Just one number was needed, they thought, if the interest of a wide public was to be engaged: more than one was a turn-off. 'We need a measure of the same level of vulgarity as GNP—just one number, but a measure that is not as blind to social aspects of human life as GNP is,' ul Haq is said to have told Sen. How could one square this circle? The HDI was constructed as an index that combined a measure of income (GNP per capita) with indicators of life expectancy and literacy. The only way to combine them was to assign each dimension an arbitrary—equal—weight in the overall index number.

The statistical crudeness of such a design was evident. In addition to the arbitrary weighting, the HDI also suffered from false aggregation and incommensurability. Sen initially advised against the inclusion of the HDI in the HDR. Later on he took a more relaxed and pragmatic view and recognized that even methodologies in which 'it is easy enough to pick holes' can attract widespread interest in the subject matter to which they are applied (Sen 1999: 359). Despite its statistical flaws—or perhaps because of them—the HDI had a simple intuitive appeal. It seemed to show something important about the disjunction of economic growth and social achievement, something to which politicians, campaigners, and journalists could readily respond.

Nonetheless Sen's diplomatic compromise on the HDI could hardly disguise the yawning gap between his picture of the richness and abundance of functionings and capabilities that contribute to a good life and the HDI's inclusion of just two—longevity and literacy. Behind this discrepancy lay the problem of the source of valuation. For the purposes of making an index, who was to say what were the capabilities that contribute to a good life?

Sen was unwilling to specify a list of basic or essential capabilities. For him, the valuation of capabilities was a matter for individuals. Yet at the same time it was not entirely a matter for individuals: his desirable capabilities were 'capabilities the individual has reason to value'. This way of putting it implies that if individuals value some capabilities unreasonably, they are not desirable. While stressing that any liberal theory needs to be robust enough to comprehend a vast variety of preferences and contexts, Sen's appeal to the criterion of reasonableness also set a limit to that variety.

Sen does not see it as the responsibility of the philosopher to provide a blueprint of the good life. Rather, while philosophers can provide advice, the limits to be placed on individuals' valuation of capabilities must occur through a process of public reasoning and democratic decision-making. Nevertheless, he remains optimistic that through these procedures a consensus will emerge that some capabilities associated with basic needs are urgent moral and political priorities for the reduction of severe deprivation. At this point it is hard not to conclude that Sen's capability approach has come full circle.

Several disciples of the capability approach certainly seem to have concluded that Sen, in his desire to be comprehensive and open-minded, deliberately left his evaluation framework undertheorized. Various attempts have been made to extend and strengthen the capability idea.

The American philosopher Martha Nussbaum aimed at constructing a 'capability theory of justice'—a theory of ideal institutional arrangements designed to enhance people's basic capabilities (Nussbaum 2011). Sen has argued against this ambition that theories of perfect justice, suitable for evaluating entire societies, are unnecessary for the needs of practical reasoning and the diagnosis of injustice. The plural grounding of claims of injustice on different principles that need not be ranked or reconciled would be sufficient, he argues (Sen 2010).

Nussbaum, however, asked: What activities performed by human beings are so central that they seem definitive of a life that is truly human? She produced a list of ten basic capabilities and constructed around them a partial theory of justice focused on the idea of human dignity. These capabilities, she advocated, should be regarded as human rights and inscribed in every constitution. Critics, however, thought that her list was not sufficiently cross-cultural and universal and too influenced by the perspective of American liberalism. One is reminded of Hobson's comment on Ruskin's doctrine of the intrinsic value of things: 'it can hardly be held that such final interpretations of human ends are of sufficiently general acceptance to respond to precise scientific treatment' (Hobson 1920: 88). She was also criticized for the utopian character of her advocacy: Had any country in the world, critics wondered, ever achieved her standard of social justice?

Sen was right in judging that the HDI would spark interest and provide some simple evaluative information. When the ranking of countries according to GNP per capita was compared to the ranking according to the HDI scores, misalignment was evident. Some countries generally regarded as prosperous, e.g. oil-rich economies in the Middle East, had low human development scores relative to their GNP per capita, while poorer countries sometimes did surprisingly well in HDI terms. This illustrated the fact that some countries were better than others at converting the economic resources at their disposal into desirable social outcomes. From that fact in turn arises the question whether the differences in achievements relative to resources were the result of specific pro-poor policies or other factors.

In 1995 Mahbub ul Haq decided to return to Pakistan to produce a regional Human Development Report for South Asia. Richard Jolly, recently retired from UNICEF, was asked to take over as editor of the main HDR. This was an opportunity to drop the HDI or come up with an improved version. Like Sen, Jolly regarded the HDI as essentially arbitrary, but also like Sen he was swayed by political considerations to retain it. It was not until 2010 that a more sophisticated index of multidimension poverty appeared in the HDR.

The multidimensional poverty index (MPI) uses the language of the capability approach to measure poverty. The selection of three dimensions of well-being measured using ten indicators is in effect the obverse of a list of the capabilities that generate well-being. The three dimensions are health (nutrition and child mortality), education (years of schooling, school attendance), and living standards (cooking fuel, sanitation, water, electricity, floor, assets). The choice is further constrained by the availability of data to achieve the aim of wide international comparison (the database included 108 developing countries by 2014) (Alkire et. al. 2015).

It would be possible to define people as poor (a) if they are lacking in *any* one of the three dimensions or (b) if they are lacking in *all* three dimensions. In developing countries, choice (a) gives the result that most of the population is poor, while choice (b) results in only a minority being poor. If one wants to avoid such a large variation in the estimation of poverty, one must adopt an arbitrary weighting scheme. In practice, a person is classified as MPI poor if deprived in three or more of the ten weighted indicators.

The published results for 2014 showed that 1.6 billion people, some 30 per cent of the 108 countries' total population, were 'multidimensionally poor'. Of these, 52 per cent lived in South Asia and 29 per cent lived in sub-Saharan Africa. A total of 71 per cent lived in middle-income countries and 85 per cent lived in rural areas. The findings of the MPI also take policy makers into new aspects of the incidence of poverty. The main advantage of this index for policy makers is that it can be decomposed by region, by ethnic group, and by dimension. It can reveal that differences also appeared between the types of poverty experienced by different countries and by different subgroups of a country's population. Nevertheless, its choice of indicators and its weighting system for its chosen indicators remains subjective, although it is claimed in its defence that the country rankings are not unduly sensitive to the choice of weights.

Human development: strengths and weaknesses

It seems indisputable that the authors of the human development perspective have consolidated a new vocabulary of development—the vocabulary of functioning and capability and empowerment. This new vocabulary has changed the normative orientation of development, installing the expansion of people's capabilities as the ultimate goal of the intention to develop. By the same token, it has demoted economic growth to be no more than one means to attain the ultimate goal, undoubtedly necessary, but certainly not sufficient.

A good indication that this normative victory has been won is that its opponents are willing to deny that they ever thought anything different. They always knew that economic growth is not sufficient to reduce poverty, they say; their point was only that economic growth could have quite a powerful effect in reducing poverty and had had that effect under certain conditions. By all means look at the deviations from the correlation between economic growth and poverty reduction, but do not ignore the strength of the correlation—that is now their message.

The dispelling of normative confusion and the increase in conceptual clarity has been worthwhile. Much international policy advice and aspirations are now phrased in the human development vocabulary. What difference has it made to the practice of development? One area of public life that became infused with the language of human development was the development goals established through the United Nations. Such goals were by no means new. In 1960, the UN had established a 'development decades' with a target for economic growth. The difference in the 1990s was that the goal of economic growth was replaced, in a series of UN summit meetings, by goals related to specific human development objectives—education, the rights of the child, gender equality, maternal health, and social development, and that national governments signed conventions committing themselves to national actions to support these goals.

The template of specific human development objectives was used again when the international community adopted the Millennium Development Goals (MDG) 2015. The MDGs are not uniform in the way that they are drafted, but they include goals of education, gender equality, reduced child mortality, and improved maternal health alongside more aggregative goals like reducing poverty and ensuring environmental sustainability. When all countries and all the development institutions pledged themselves to further these goals, the human development perspective reached a new and higher level of public exposure. Periodic checks on how far the world had advanced towards the targets succeeded in keeping the objectives in public view.

Yet it is far from clear what practical consequences followed. A more accurate and more visible scoreboard on development progress has been erected, but few believe that erection of a bigger and better scoreboard will have an effect on the performance standards of the sport that it is recording. They are determined in other ways. The MDGs are global targets, and are not broken down into national targets to which the signatory nations have committed themselves. They are targets for which, while everybody is responsible, nobody is responsible. Therefore, signing up to the MDGs is an invitation to a free ride. It is an easy option for every government in the world to sign up to them. A government could say 'no' and become an international pariah, but will more likely choose to say 'yes' in the hope that that will be a passport to extra international aid.

In fact, there is little evidence that national governments have changed their policies because of the adoption of the MDGs, or that donor agencies have changed their aid allocation mechanisms as a result. What we have gained is a new and more precise language of political aspiration. In reality, the most substantial reduction of poverty has occurred in China, especially in rural China, during thirty years of rapid economic growth. Millions of Chinese have been lifted out of poverty and this is the largest single contribution to the attainment of the MDG for world poverty reduction.

Human development?

To have the key to human development is a grand claim, and one cannot help wondering whether the highly individualistic focus of the current version of the human development approach is sufficiently broad to merit the adjective 'human'. To highlight the importance of the freedom of each individual to be and do the things that each has reason to value is all well and good, but human beings are not just individuals, they are social animals. It is essential to them that they share language, culture, ethics and morality, politics, and political institutions. 'Collecting information about individuals' wellbeing only, including their ability to participate in society and collective action, omits a very important aspect of human life, namely that human life is embedded into a complex web of structural relations that do not belong to any individual as such' (Deneulin 2014: 57).

These structural relations are ways of reconciling the freedom of the individual with the freedom of all the other individuals with whom that individual has to live in community. The human development approach has little to say about these macrosocial dimensions of human life, except that there should be public space for public debate and methods of arriving at political consensus. These counsels of perfection are so vague that all the big issues of social development, such as the roles of religion, ethnicity, legal evolution, and legitimate government, are skated over or avoided altogether. This leaves the question of who is responsible for the expansion of capabilities up in the air, adrift from any anchor to political institutions or systems of taxation.

Perhaps not surprisingly in a development perspective that aspires to own the brand label 'human', one can detect large lacunae, areas of incompleteness and clouds of vagueness and ambiguity. Some of this results from calculated philosophical discretion, but the rest derives from the neglect of social questions deemed to be of little interest to champions of freedom of the individual. Much will therefore depend on how the language of capability is extended in future work and the extent to which it can be stretched to address more fully the social affections for which Ruskin, among others, claimed a central place in political economy.

References

Alkire, S., and Santos, M. E. (2010). Acute multidimensional poverty: a new index for developing countries. Oxford Poverty & Human Development Initiative (OPHI) Working Paper 38.

Deneulin, S. (2014). Constructing new policy narratives: the capability approach as normative language, in G. A. Cornia and F. Stewart, eds, *Towards Human Development*, 45–65. Oxford: Oxford University Press.

George, H. (1879). *Progress and Poverty: An Enquiry into the Cause of Industrial Depressions, and of Increase of Want with Increase of Wealth: The Remedy*. London: K. Paul, Trench & Company.

Ghai, D. P., Khan, A. R., Lee, E. L. H., and Alfthan, T. (1977). *The Basic-Needs Approach to Development: Some Issues Regarding Concepts and Methodology*. Geneva: International Labour Organization.

Haq, M. u. (1963). *The Strategy of Economic Planning: A Case Study of Pakistan*. Karachi: Oxford University Press.

Hobson, J. A. (1920). Ruskin as political economist, in *Ruskin the Prophet*. London: George Allen and Unwin.

Jolly, R. (1989). Dudley Seers (1920–1983): his contributions to development perspectives, policy and studies. *IDS Bulletin* 20(3), 31–42.

Nussbaum, M. C. (2011). *Creating Capabilities*. Cambridge, MA: Harvard University Press.

Rawls, J. (2009/1971). *A Theory of Justice*. Cambridge, MA: Harvard University Press.

Ruskin, J. (1906/1862). *Unto This Last*. London: G. Allen.

Seers, D. (1972). What are we trying to measure? *Journal of Development Studies* 8(3), 21–36.

Sen, A. (1984). *Resources, Values and Development*. Oxford: Basil Blackwell.

Sen, A. (1999). The possibility of social choice. *American Economic Review* 89(3), 349–78.

Sen, A. (2010). *The Idea of Justice*. London: Penguin.

Streeten, P., Burki, S. J., ul Haq, M., Hicks, N., and Stewart, F. (1981). *First Things First: Meeting Basic Human Needs in the Developing Countries*. Oxford: Oxford University Press.

Ul Haq, M. (1976). *The Poverty Curtain: Choices for the Third World*. New York: Columbia University Press.

11

Double-edged development, 1767–

There is nothing either a good or bad but thinking makes it so.

—William Shakespeare, *Hamlet*

George du Maurier drew a cartoon that soon became famous. It shows breakfast being served in a bishop's palace. The bishop says to a young curate whom he is entertaining, 'I'm afraid you have got a bad egg, Mr. Jones.' The young curate replies, 'Oh no my lord. I assure you that parts of it are excellent.' The phrase 'the curate's egg' soon became a favourite term to describe something that is bad but has redeeming features. What is a relevance of the curate's egg to the discussion of socioeconomic development?

Most people who think about economic development take an extremely positive view of it. They accentuate the positive, latch onto the affirmative, and eliminate the negative to give it an ideal image. It is an idea of which the appeal can be boosted by placing it on the moral high ground of promoting human betterment, fulfilment, and the enrichment of lives through the expansion of choice. It is also represented as a benign quest for the end of poverty and human degradation through the optimal distribution of wealth and income. If failures and setbacks occur in development programmes, these negatives are eliminated by attributing them to lack of commitment, competence, or political will, and the remedy recommended is to be smarter and try harder.

A minority, however, accentuates the negative and sees economic development in completely opposite terms. Far from being the highly moral enterprise that its advocates claim it to be, the minority believe that it is a rhetorical and practical cover for a system of imposition and oppression, conceived in various forms. This can be as a network for draining physical and financial resources from the areas that the poor inhabit. It can be as camouflage for the suppression of the cultural values of poor indigenous ethnic groups. It can be an excuse for the destruction of the natural environment. It can be as a hegemonic power's way of manipulating weaker states by setting the rules of the international system to suit its national advantage. Whatever the precise description of the hidden agenda attributed to it, development is unmasked as fraudulent in its claims and injurious in its effects (e.g. Escobar 1995). If the occasional development project proves to be beneficial to those affected, that accident hardly redeems the bad faith of the enterprise as a whole.

While these two opposed camps continue to battle it out, they do not occupy the entire field of discourse about development. An even smaller minority see development as a phenomenon that has two aspects, both the positive and the negative. They are the Mister In-betweens of development thinking. In their view, the creation and destruction associated with development are simultaneous and form an essential unity. This can be seen in the everyday examples of replacing an old structure or installing new equipment of a superior technical vintage. Each involves the destruction of what had existed previously, though this negative dimension of the process usually is hidden from view (Cowen and Shenton 1996: viii–ix). In addition to the destruction necessarily involved in redevelopment, however, negative consequences may be lurking in the future consequences of the new investments. The realization of the advantages to be derived from new opportunities can hardly be done without causing adverse side effects, and side effects cannot always be known in advance. Well-intentioned actions for improvement may well run into unanticipated complications. Exponents of a double-edged evaluation of development thus often hold the view expressed in Robert Burns' homily to the mouse whose nest he wrecked while ploughing: 'foresight might be vain; the best-laid schemes of mice and men gang aft agley.'

This chapter explores further the views of some of the relatively few writers who have explained development as double-edged. This line of thinking stretches from the eighteenth century to the present day. There are various ways in which different authors describe how the positive and negative aspects of the process interact, and which effect is said to be the stronger. Their common link is a willingness to make a broader evaluation of the development process instead of being exclusively either an advocate or a critic of it.

The ambivalence of Adam Ferguson

Although the majority of the Scottish savants took a positive view of the emerging commercial society, not all shared the general approbation. Adam Ferguson, in his work *An Essay on the History of Civil Society* (1767), was the most important figure to express scepticism about social progress and to warn of future dangers, notwithstanding all that commercial society had achieved.

Ferguson did not deny the achievements of commercial society, and indeed acknowledged them:

> The productions of ingenuity are brought to the market; and men are willing to pay for whatever has a tendency to inform or amuse. By this means the idle, as well as the busy, contribute to forward the progress of arts, and bestow on polished nations that air of superior ingenuity, under which they appear to have gained the ends [of] knowledge, order and wealth.   (Ferguson 1966/1767: 183–4)

Yet Ferguson painted commercial society in darker hues than his Edinburgh colleagues. He warned about three features of commercial society that he believed contained the seeds of future dangers. First, he saw that 'refinement and plenty foster new desires, while they furnish the means, or practise the methods, to gratify them' (Ferguson 1966/1767: 216–17). The fostering of new desires was significant because it implied that economic activity was no longer a matter of satisfying fixed desires or the ordinary necessities of existence. If novelty itself became desirable and new desires could be fostered, the scope of economic demands could expand without limit and the future would become one of perpetual change. That a stationary state could ever be reached was, in his view, an illusion.

Second, the increasing division of labour undoubtedly raised productivity and improved workers' skills, but it also separated people into different occupations and professions. While some occupations would be monotonous, undemanding, and unrewarding, others would require powers of direction and leadership and hence bring both greater fulfilment and greater rewards. Social and economic inequality, already arising from differences of natural abilities and property ownership, would inevitably thereby increase.

The division of labour would also have an effect on social psychology: 'in its termination and ultimate effects [it] serves in some measure to break the bands of society . . . and to withdraw individuals from the common scene of occupation, on which the sentiments of the heart, and the mind, are most happily employed' (Ferguson 1966/1767: 218). In *The Wealth of Nations*, Adam Smith acknowledged the negative social consequences from increasing the division of labour, but argued that they could be counteracted by state provision of education. Ferguson did not think so.

This was because he also thought the inequality consequent on the increased division of labour would have a negative political effect. It would be difficult to preserve a functioning democracy in conditions of inequality. Thus, to be able to legislate and maintain an education system that would validate Adam Smith's claim was most unlikely (Hill 2007).

Ferguson was a Highlander at heart. Alone of the Edinburgh literati, he was able to speak Gaelic, and he had served as a chaplain with the Black Watch, a Highland regiment, between 1745 and 1754. He did not declare his admiration of the tribal life of the Scottish Highland clans, or his fears that such societies would eventually disappear altogether under the impact of the emerging division of labour, but such fears are easy to detect in code form in his allusions to life in ancient Sparta. Ferguson then was no believer in inevitable and irreversible social progress. Coupled with its economic and social advantages of superior knowledge, order, and wealth, commercial society would, according to Ferguson, be in perpetual motion, growing ever more unequal, divided, and alienated.

His sociological critique of economic progress was linked to a keen appreciation of the so-called 'law of unintended consequences'. Institutions are never the product of the designs of politicians, he asserted. This followed from the proposition that 'men, in general, are sufficiently disposed to occupy themselves in forming projects and schemes: but he who would scheme and project for others, will find an opponent in every person who is disposed to scheme for himself'. In other words, every general plan of improvement is liable to be disrupted as a result of individuals' personal schemes that are in conflict with it. As a result, 'nations stumble upon [their] establishments, which are indeed the result of human action, but not the execution of any human design' (Ferguson 1966/1767: 122).

He cautioned further that the enlightened assume too easily that the less enlightened are anxious to change their situation. 'We imagine, perhaps, that rude nations must have a strong sense of the defects under which they labour, and be so conscious that reformations are requisite in their manners, that they must be ready to adopt, with joy, every plan of improvement, and to receive every plausible proposal with implicit compliance … We mistake, however, the characteristic of simple ages: mankind then appear to feel the fewest defects, and are then least desirous to enter on reformations' (Ferguson 1966/1767: 123–4).

In the work of Ferguson one finds three elements that recur in his successors who view development as double-edged. The first is the sense that the genie of applied technology has escaped from its bottle, and that, whatever happens, cannot be put back. The second is that plans of improvement rarely work out as they are planned, because their consequences cannot be foreseen in advance. The third is that it is easy to overestimate people's enthusiasm for having their future determined by others, however benevolent or altruistic the intentions of those others may be. Later writers who saw development as double-edged often shared these three basic insights.

Ambivalence about industrialization: J. S. Mill

In the nineteenth century, however, Ferguson's work was largely ignored. Marx was aware of it and included a few citations of it in *Das Kapital*. In general, concerns about the great industrial changes occurring in Britain overshadowed debate about the future problems of commercial society. The rapid development of manufacturing industry was a huge step change from the commercial society of eighteenth-century Britain; the onrush of industrialization sparked a new public discussion that tried to weigh the gains and losses arising from it.

This debate about the advantages of modernity was marked by controversy and ambivalent attitudes. Thomas Love Peacock, in his 1816 novel *Headlong Hall*, represented the prevailing ambivalence in the opinions of two of his characters, Mr Foster and Mr Escot. While Mr Foster conceded the existence of some attendant evils, he emphasized the beneficial results of the new forms of manufacture: 'The manufacturing system is not yet purged from some of the evils which necessarily attend it, but which I conceive are greatly overbalanced by their concomitant advantages.' Mr Escot saw some advantages, but questioned the purposes of applied science: 'Profound researches, scientific inventions: to what end?...to disseminate independence, liberty and health? No: to multiply factitious desires...to invent unnatural wants... Complicated machinery: behold its blessings...Wherever this boasted machinery is established, the children of the poor are death-doomed from their cradles' (quoted in Coleman 1992: ix).

The young John Stuart Mill might have had the fictional Mr Foster and Mr Escot in mind when, in his 'Essay on Coleridge' (Mill 1950), he contrasts the views of two 'students of man and society'. One observer is, like Mr Foster, a worshipper of the contemporary enlightened age. He is forcibly struck by 'the multiplication of physical comforts; the advancement and diffusion of knowledge; the decay of superstition; the facilities of mutual intercourse; the softening of manners; the decline of war and personal conflict; the progressive limitation of the tyranny of the strong over the weak: the great works accomplished throughout the globe by the co-operation of multitudes'. The other observer, like Mr Escot, fixes his attention on the accompanying social losses:

> the relaxation of individual energy and courage; the loss of proud and self-relying independence; the slavery of so large a portion of mankind to artificial wants... the demoralizing effect of great inequalities in wealth and social rank; and the sufferings of the great mass of the people in civilized countries, whose wants are scarcely better provided for than those of the savage, while they are bound by a thousand fetters in lieu of the freedom and excitement which are his compensations. (quoted in Coleman 1992)

What does Mill make of these two entirely variant views? He wants to combine them in an ambivalent overall assessment. He thinks that in major controversies in social philosophy both sides are right in what they affirm, though wrong in what they deny. If the adherents of either of the two views could be made to accept their opponents' views in addition to their own, little further would be needed to make their doctrine correct. In the dispute between those who worshipped civilization and those who championed independence, all that is positive in the opinions of either side is true, Mill concludes. The difficulty lies in 'framing, as it is necessary to do, a set of practical maxims which combine both'.

His position is the simultaneous coexistence of its benefits and its costs in a process of civilization—the coincidence, in other words, of both the advantages of civilization and its discontents. Here was another exponent of a double-edged view of development. That view was the basis both for his robust criticism of many contemporary laws and for his campaigns for political reforms—for the removal of discrimination against women and for more inclusive democratic representation in the political system.

The ambivalence of Friedrich Engels and Karl Marx

Although Mill's contemporary Friedrich Engels is often thought of as merely the minor figure in the partnership of Marx and Engels, in fact he had an intellectual trajectory of his own. While working as a clerk in the Manchester branch of his father's cotton business in 1842–4, he acquainted himself not just with the factory system and its workers, but also with the social conditions of the different classes living in the city. The original German version of *The Condition of the Working Class in England* published in Leipzig in 1845 proclaimed 'an industrial revolution, a revolution that altered the whole civil society' caused by 'the invention of the steam engine and machinery for working cotton' in large power-driven factories (Engels 1993/1845: 15).

Engels acknowledged that the Industrial Revolution brought about an increase in the quantity and a fall in the price of manufactured goods, great commercial prosperity, and the accumulation of capital. Yet, there was a price to pay:

> on the other hand, a still more rapid multiplication of the proletariat, the destruction of all property-holding and of all security of employment for the working class, demoralization, political excitement. (Engels 1993/1845: 20)

Engels identified two different types of negative effect. One of the factors by which industrial capitalism was causing poverty was the destruction of the old artisan industry that had made the same products previously. This was the fate of the handloom weavers, who became unemployed or irregularly employed, as their skills lost their market value in the face of the productivity of the power loom. The other type was the negative consequences of the new industry. These included the harsh conditions of factory employment

157

damaging workers' health—the long hours of work, the unhealthy working conditions, and the loss of life and limb in factory accidents; the terrible housing in which the workers lived; and the unsanitary urban conditions brought about by increasing population and the influx of those seeking factory work from more economically stagnant regions of the country. Above all, manufacturing employment separated the worker from the things that previously had cushioned the direst effects of poverty—a parcel of land, access to the commons, help from the extended family, and the relative generosity of outdoor poor relief in rural areas.

Engels' expectation that the new working class had a revolutionary potential was an illusion that was soon exposed. Yet this class did find within itself new powers of self-protective political agency that went beyond the marches and sporadic violence of the pre-industrial poor. The skilled worker trade unionism of mid-Victorian times broadened out towards the end of the century into a more inclusive movement that then financed a political and parliamentary representation of the interests of labour. As a result the Liberal Party pushed through much pro-labour legislation in the years before the First World War (Daunton 2007: 534–5).

Engels himself helped to create the intellectual atmosphere in which such legislation could find political support. The belated translation in 1892 of his work into English as *The Condition of the Working Class in England* was influential in this regard. By then Engels had the benefit of hindsight and acknowledged in the Preface that, as capitalism matures, it is able to overcome some of the difficulties that attended its 'juvenile stages'. He gave credit to the Liberal Party as the political mechanism that had gone some way to reconcile the interests of the workers with those of the manufacturers, who were the party's leaders and financiers. Yet he still maintained that the essential nature of capitalism had not altered since he first wrote. The essence of capitalism— the separation of the wageworker from everything except his labour power, and the growing inequality that this caused between the income and wealth of capitalists and workers—had not changed. His evaluation of the development of capitalism therefore remained double-edged.

Engels' ambivalent judgement derived from evidence that he had gathered from personal observation. Collaborating with Karl Marx, however, he helped to elaborate a theory of the contradictions of capitalism that also was double-edged. The theory concerned the ways in which capitalism would undermine itself and pave the way for a socialist future.

The foundation of the theory was economic, the tendency of the rate of profit to fall. Its fall induces an intensified exploitation of labour and a concentration of capital in the hands of large capitalists, as they absorb small capitalists who can no longer compete under the new conditions. Greater labour exploitation, i.e. the decline in the ratio of variable to constant capital, increases the 'reserve army' of the unemployed at the same time as the volume of capital also increases. Attempts to countervail the falling rate of profit only make the economic situation even more contradictory.

The contradiction results in economic crises of rising destructiveness—for small capitalists, workers, and the unemployed. The shrinking large capitalist class must hire managers, and are distanced from their capital. Their private appropriation of the fruits of labour becomes ever more visible, thereby aggravating class conflict. A further contradiction is that, as labour exploitation and class conflict are intensified, the working class improves its self-organization, having been disciplined by the very mechanism of capitalist production itself (Kolakowski 1978: 297–301).

Then a proletarian revolution then transforms the social scene. When the insistent greed of the bourgeois class has brought about its own downfall, it has also generated sufficient economic surplus to make socialism possible. This will permit the abolition of the division of labour, liberating all the powers of each human being, and will require the social planning of production in order to meet social needs. After all the misery and pain of the capitalist era, mankind will enter a realm of freedom. It will not be complete freedom, as the requirements of physical production will persist. It will be freedom in the sense that compulsions connected with social life will be eliminated, and social life will be a fulfilment of individuality rather than a curb on it. In this way, socialism will be able to reap the harvest of a decadent capitalist system.

Development is double-sided, but in Marxian theory its two sides are not contemporaneous but follow each other. The first is an epoch of oppression and alienation, which creates the conditions for the second—the realization of a new epoch of social freedom.

Joseph Schumpeter and creative destruction

Like Engels, the Austrian economist Joseph Schumpeter published a path-breaking book on economic and social development in German, and it took decades before it was translated into English.[1] Schumpeter saw economic development as a phenomenon that was fundamentally different from the circular flow of economic life, which moved towards a general equilibrium within a fixed set of parameters, in line with the economic theory of the time. For him, development involved large, discontinuous changes that he, like Engels, described as 'revolutionary', and which could not be analysed using the method of economic statics. His prime example of this kind of change was

---

[1] Schumpeter's *Theorie der wirtschaftlichen Entwicklung* (1911) had a subsequent edition translated by Redvers Opie as *The Theory of Economic Development* (1934).

the introduction of railways, of which he wrote: 'add successively as many mail coaches as you please, you will never get a railway thereby' (Schumpeter 1934/1911: 64, .n. 1).

However, he wanted to build a specifically economic theory of development rather than resort to the kind of grand evolutionary theories of historical progress, such as those formulated by Marx and Engels. The mechanism of discontinuous change that he identified was the activity of entrepreneurs, the putting together of new and radically different combinations of the factors of production, financed by credit. Alongside the entrepreneurs, the bankers exercised a supervisory function on entrepreneurial activities through their control of the flow of credit (Cowen and Shenton 1996: 416).

Schumpeter argued that the owners of existing combinations of factors of production do not generally pioneer new combinations of factors, e.g. that the owners of stagecoach businesses do not usually establish railways. So in a competitive economy with private property, the arrival of a new combination involved the elimination of the old combination. Socially, the force of competition between firms caused the rise and decline of family fortunes and families' acquisition and loss of social status, and this meant that, contrary to the view of Marx and Engels, entrepreneurs never coalesced into an enduring social class.

Their activities, however, involved a form of 'creative destruction'. It was a dynamic process capable of destroying existing technologies and equipment, and existing occupations and skills, so that they could be replaced by newly created ones that were, if the entrepreneurs judged it well, more productive and more profitable. In this view, entrepreneurs act to disrupt the tendency to equilibrium, finding their economic opportunities precisely amidst the routine- and habit-driven economic behaviour of others. They animate a process of industrial mutation that incessantly revolutionizes the economic structure from within, incessantly destroying the old one, incessantly creating a new one. 'This process of Creative Destruction is the essential fact about capitalism,' Schumpeter believed (1950/1943: 83).

Schumpeter wanted to know whether the process of economic development inflicted other costs, in addition to the displacement of old and uncompetitive businesses. His answer was that it did. However, he did not chalk up every crisis that occurs during economic development to the account of the process itself. Some crises, he acknowledged, were the result of conditions external to the economic system, such as bad weather or the outbreak of wars. Only one type of crisis was intrinsic to economic development—the boom and bust of business cycles. These cycles became the focus of his research leading to his *Business Cycles* (1939).

Schumpeter argued that new enterprises do not appear independently of each other, in a continuous stream. The appearance of one or a few entrepreneurs opens up opportunities for others, generating a tendency for entrepreneurs to swarm or cluster together. Yet those who join the swarm at a later stage are likely to have less entrepreneurial skill than those who led the way. Initially, the demand for factors of production leads to inflation, but this is followed by deflation when the rush of investment is over and the products of the new enterprises flood the market. Boom then turns to depression, causing the collapse of the businesses of the weaker entrepreneurs. The supervision of credit flows that the bankers undertake is inadequate to suppress this cycle.

While Schumpeter thinks that depressions have a function—to eliminate obsolete firms and firms not adapted for future competition—he acknowledges that they also cause some destruction that is functionless, the elimination of firms that would have been sound and survived if they had not been caught up in the secondary effects of the depression. In principle, government policies could prevent this happening, but the practical task of distinguishing one type of destruction from the other required, he thought, information that is in reality unobtainable.

In his conclusion, Schumpeter wrote of the destruction caused by development as 'the necessary complement of the emergence of new economic and social forms and of continually rising real incomes of all social strata' (Schumpeter 1934/1911: 255). Yet he always tried to maintain his scientific objectivity, rejecting the claim that he was trying to glorify the entrepreneur. At this point, he declined to express any opinion about the comparative merits of the social organization—capitalism—in which the entrepreneur plays his crucial role.

He later relented and tackled that question. In *Capitalism, Socialism, and Democracy* (Schumpeter 1950/1943), he argued that the very success of capitalism as an economic system would end up undermining its own social foundations. He thought that the capitalist social order must be fragile. Unlike Marx and Engels, Schumpeter denied that entrepreneurs formed a social class. Fortunes could be passed onto the next generation, but entrepreneurial skills could not, so their economic and social status was unavoidably precarious.[2] At the same time, the activities of entrepreneurs provoked hostile reactions from the rest of society, and he believed that these reactions would eventually undermine the political support for the continuation of capitalism.

Schumpeter was highly unusual in that he did not, at least in his final years, combine his double-edged view of development with scepticism about large-scale economic planning. No socialist himself, he nonetheless became convinced that socialism was capitalism's heir apparent. He examined all the standard economic arguments for the impossibility of socialism and persuaded

[2] Schumpeter (1934/1911): 67.

himself that they did not hold water. Admitting the large bureaucracy that would be needed to administer the socialist economy, he comforted himself with the thought that capitalism had already become highly bureaucratized and that a socialist bureaucracy would be tolerable if the right administrators could be recruited. Like Max Weber (2009), he saw some type of rational bureaucracy as inevitable. When he looked forward, he saw it coming, but in another sense, he did not look forward to it at all. Although he was an exponent of double-edged development, by the end of his life he had persuaded himself of the efficacy of national economic planning.

Albert Hirschman on the consequences of investment

At the same time as Schumpeter was writing *Capitalism, Socialism, and Democracy*, a similar optimism about the organizational capacity of the state pervaded the pioneering development economics of Paul Rosenstein-Rodan (1943). He argued that, while individual industrial investments in underdeveloped countries were likely to be unprofitable, a big push of complementary industrial investments could be profitable for all. This was because a range of complementary investments would create additional demand for each other's products, so each individual investment would become profitable by benefiting from the pecuniary external economies created by the big investment push. Economic development would occur, if the state could manage to orchestrate this form of balanced growth in the area with which he was especially concerned, which was the East and southeast Europe.

This idea soon spread to other areas. The Canadian economist Lauchlin Currie led a mission to Colombia on behalf of the World Bank (1949–50). This was the World Bank's debut intervention in the field of economic development. Albert Hirschman, a German economist who had immigrated to the USA, was employed on the Colombian Planning Council at the time when Currie's plan of development was being implemented. Hirschman became convinced that Currie's *Development Program for Colombia* was overambitious and unrealistic in its aims and scope.

He expressed his scepticism in a paper written for a conference in 1954 at MIT, where Rosenstein-Rodan was on the faculty. Hirschman was one of the very few people who already had on-the-ground experience of trying to promote development. The opening words of his paper 'Economics and Investment Planning: Reflections Based on Experience in Colombia' gave a stark warning. 'Our abilities will sooner or later invite reactions of the type: "But the Emperor has nothing on!" ' He surmised that economists nursed a desire for power that led them to overstate what they were actually able to achieve. The result was 'an optical illusion that economics as a science can

162

yield detailed blueprints for the development of underdeveloped societies.' This was not a complete rejection of economics, but a claim that economists' overambition set up a negative dynamic in which the foreign expert was believed to be all-powerful, while the local collaborators who had to execute the grand plan of balanced growth were left feeling incompetent and disempowered (Adelman 2013: 322–3).

Yale University gave Hirschman an opportunity to write up his reflections on his Colombian experience. In preparation for writing *The Strategy of Economic Development*, he re-read Burke and Hayek, the former a critic of a politics based on philosophical abstraction and the latter a critic of economic planning because of the inevitable absence of prior agreement on plan goals (see the discussion of Hayek in Chapter 5). With such thoughts in mind, Hirschman disputed the wisdom of the balanced growth strategy. Rather than try to anticipate in advance every detailed requirement of the economy's future path, he argued for a pragmatic approach through the identification of good opportunities for private investment. These investments would create backward and forward linkages to other economic activities and act as incentives to relieve the bottlenecks and shortages that would arise as the process of development unfolded.

Like Schumpeter, his preferred microeconomic strategy of unbalanced growth put entrepreneurship and private investment at the centre of the action. Again like Schumpeter, he saw the dual aspect of development. He was mindful that:

> in general economic development means transformation rather than creation *ex novo*: it brings disruption of traditional ways of living, of producing, of doing things, in the course of which there have always been many losses; old skills become obsolete, old trades are ruined, city slums mushroom, crime and suicide multiply, etc, etc. And to these social costs many others must be added, from air pollution to unemployment. (Hirschman 1958: 56)

Hirschman refers here to both the competitive destruction of old industries and the social ill effects of the new industries, which economists call external *diseconomies*. He argues that the growing capitalist firm tended to be protected from having to internalize the external *diseconomies* that it creates, although periodically and belatedly the state does intervene to force them to bear a portion of these social costs. At the same time, firms were free to merge in order to internalize external economies. From this asymmetric process emerged the relentless trend towards the large capitalist firm, to which Marx and Engels were the first to call attention (Schumpeter 1950/1943: 34 and 48).

Hirschman explained: 'From the point of view of investment incentives, the capitalist system, especially as it existed in the nineteenth century, was hard to beat: there was a minimum of internalization of external diseconomies, and there was no limitation on the internalization of pecuniary external economies through acquisitions, combinations, or mergers with closely interdependent economic activities' (Hirschman 1958: 58). 'It was the peculiar lack of internalization implicit in the private enterprise system—the way in which the institutions of that system "hid" certain costs from the entrepreneurs—that was largely responsible for the dynamic economic changes that took place' (Hirschman 1958: 59). Hirschman thus ascribes rapid development not just to the activities of entrepreneurs, but also to the regulatory framework in which those activities were allowed to take place.

In marked contrast with Schumpeter, Hirschman saw flaws in the idea of socialist economic planning. He pointed out that central planning of investments by the state would internalize external economies and diseconomies alike. In this situation, the planners would have an incentive to avoid investments in new products or new processes that would cause existing capacity to become obsolete prematurely. As he put it:

> In this respect, then, a planned economy is likely to behave much like the guild system; the process of 'creative destruction' is constitutionally alien to it because destruction here means self-destruction rather than the destruction of somebody else. Taking into consideration the interests of existing firms will lead to a tendency to avoid frequent changes in the design and quality of consumer goods or the frequent introduction of substitutes that might gratify the foolish whims of the consuming public but could disrupt production schedules and endanger the value of a portion of the country's human and material assets.   (Hirschman 1958: 59–60)

In short, in those sectors where production is already established, and development means redevelopment, central planning has a conservative tendency that will probably lead to sluggish innovation and loss of technological leadership. In entirely novel sectors, however, this tendency need not apply. Hirschman maintained that the successes (in space technology) and the failures (in consumer goods) of the economy of the former Soviet Union were consistent with this analysis of the limitations of central economic planning.

Hirschman became a highly respected consultant on development and the World Bank commissioned him to visit and evaluate a dozen of their development projects. It was a small sample and the projects were scattered over different economic sectors in different continents, taking Hirschman beyond the Latin American context with which he was familiar. This prevented any rigorous comparison between projects, and the ensuing publication, *Development Projects Observed* (1967), consisted primarily of descriptions and reflections. His reflections, however, emphasized the double-edged nature of development. Many of the sample projects were judged as failures by the standard criteria that the bank used for evaluation—completion to time and budget, fulfilment of original project aims, and generation of sufficient revenue to pay back the loan.

However, Hirschman found that there were other unexpected and unaccounted benefits, despite the apparent failures.

These unintended consequences were highlighted. Originally, he had deployed the idea to raise doubt about the ambition of comprehensive economic planning, which was being advocated by those who favoured balanced growth. He used it to dismiss the idea of the *ex ante* sequencing of investment, which he said was linked to the underlying idea that there was one right way to develop, i.e. that the historical path of Europe had a universal relevance. He denied that poor countries would have to follow the same path and that they could follow it if only the capital constraint were eased.

In *Development Projects Observed*, Hirschman emphasized the different degrees of uncertainty that affected investment projects, but also noted the unplanned consequences—often positive—that accompanied projects that 'failed' according to standard evaluation criteria. They could act as pressure points that stimulated competitive supply activities, once they had revealed the extent of demand, but failed to satisfy it. These narratives of silver linings blurred the apparently hard and fast line between the success and failure of investments, presenting a more ambivalent and double-edged analysis of how development takes place and how it influences growth.

Conclusion

It may seem to be mere common sense to assert that the reality of economic development has many and diverse faces, some positive and some negative. Yet, as previous chapters have shown, most writers on the subject have taken more extreme positions, being absolutely in favour or absolutely opposed. This extremism is difficult to justify, and a minority of writers have taken a broader and more comprehensive view. They have seen development as double-edged, albeit sometimes weighed to the positive side of the scale and sometimes to the negative.

This more even-handed approach serves to remind us how the rhetoric of development has been used to justify and defend policies that violate norms of justice, as well extend them. A common example of policies defended in the name of development is the forced removal of poor people from their ancestral homelands to create clustered villages, as in Tanzania and Ethiopia; or to create dams and irrigation schemes, as in India, Sri Lanka, and China; or to make way for foreign investment in mines or the sale of 'vacant' lands to foreign countries in many places. No doubt there will be beneficiaries from such schemes, at least in the medium term. They are the people who can most profit from electricity, irrigation water, and vehicles, but there will be losers, too.

The losers are usually people who are already poor and who can be most easily pushed around by the strong-arm tactics of governments and corporations.

The creation of winners and losers is why development tends to increase inequality. The hackneyed image repeatedly used on dust jackets of books about economic development is of skyscrapers and motorways surrounded by shantytowns and slums. Ironically, this visual cliché perfectly represents the two faces of the process of double-edged development.

References

Adelman, J. (2013). *Worldly Philosopher: The Odyssey of Albert O. Hirschman.* Princeton, NJ: Princeton University Press.

Coleman, D. C. (1992). *Myth, History and the Industrial Revolution.* London: A&C Black.

Cowen, M. P., and Shenton, R. W. (1996). *Doctrines of Development.* London: Routledge.

Daunton, M. (2007). *Wealth and Welfare: An Economic and Social History of Britain 1851–1951.* Oxford: Oxford University Press.

Engels, F. (1993). *The Condition of the Working Class in England.* New York: Oxford University Press.

Escobar, A. (2011). *Encountering development: The Making and Unmaking of the Third World.* Princeton, NJ: Princeton University Press.

Ferguson, A. (1966/1767). *An Essay on the History of Civil Society.* Edinburgh: Edinburgh University Press.

Hill, L. (2007). Adam Smith, Adam Ferguson and Karl Marx on the division of labour. *Journal of Classical Sociology 7*(3), 339–66.

Hirschman, A. O. (1954). Economics and investment planning: reflections based on experience in Colombia, in *Investment Criteria and Economic Growth*, mimeo. Cambridge, MA: MIT Centre for International Studies.

Hirschman, A. O. (1958). *The Strategy of Economic Development.* New Haven, CT: Yale University Press.

Hirschman, A. O. (1967). *Development Projects Observed.* Washington, DC: Brookings Institution Press.

Kolakowski, L. (1978). *Main Currents of Marxism*, vol. 3. Oxford: Oxford University Press.

Mill, J. S. (1950). *Mill on Bentham and Coleridge*, ed. F. R. Leavis. London: Chatto and Windus.

Rosenstein-Rodan, P. N. (1943). Problems of industrialisation of eastern and south-eastern Europe. *Economic Journal 53*(210/211), 202–11.

Schumpeter, J. A. (1934/1911). *The Theory of Economic Development: An Inquiry into Profits, Capital, Credit, Interest, and the Business Cycle*, vol. 55. Transaction publishers.

Schumpeter, J. A. (1939). *Business Cycles*, vol. 1, pp. 161–74. New York: McGraw-Hill.

Schumpeter, J. A. (1950/1943). *Capitalism, Socialism, and Democracy*, 3rd edn. New York: Harper.

Weber, M. (2009). *From Max Weber: Essays in Sociology.* London: Routledge.

12

Conclusion: The last grand narrative of development, 1938–

> *He who would do good to others must do it in minute particulars. General good is the plea of the scoundrel, hypocrite and flatterer; for art and science cannot exist but in minutely organized particulars.*
>
> —William Blake

The previous chapters have presented and criticized some of the many grand narratives of socioeconomic development. There is no need to recapitulate them here. This concluding chapter has two aims. The first is to explain the origins of neo-liberal ideas of development and their transformation into a neo-conservative doctrine. The second aim is to explain why neo-conservatism will be the final grand narrative of development and will be followed by a mosaic of petty narratives that lack overall coherence.

Political philosophy of neo-liberalism

All political philosophies are based on a particular view of human nature, and the political philosophy of liberalism is no exception. Its basic perception is of society as a set of very diverse individuals, their diversity being the result of genetic inheritance, cultural inheritance, family upbringing, and other forces of socialization. Diversity, combined with individual agency, creates problems of conflict of multiple aspirations and grievances. A liberal political regime therefore pursues no social goals of its own, but creates and maintains institutions that accommodate the widest possible range of behaviour and thereby minimize individuals' conflicts.

When Hayek's *The Road to Serfdom* (1944) was published, it had a big popular reception, especially in the USA. It became the handbook of the neo-liberals and its message that centralized economic planning by the state would inevitably erode the liberty of individuals began to blot out their earlier commitments to state activism. As the neo-liberal network expanded and matured, it underwent significant changes in its political philosophy (Jackson 2010: 138). The proposal to break up large corporations championed by Henry Simons and German Liberals such as Wilhelm Röpke and Alexander Rüstow was quietly dropped. It figured in post-war discussions of the reconstruction of Germany (Wood 1984: 195–7). It was never implemented, but it figured again in Fritz Schumacher's *Small is Beautiful* (1973).

The person who was primarily responsible for deleting this proposal from the neo-liberal policy agenda was Ludwig von Mises (1936/1920). He had written a critique of socialist planning in 1920 based on the impossibility of central planners being able to perform all the necessary economic calculations. When this claim was challenged by exponents of market socialism, von Mises moved onto the threat planning posed to individual liberty and became Hayek's mentor. He was the most right-wing in politics of all the neo-liberals—more so than Hayek, who objected to the indiscriminate use of 'socialism' as a term of abuse. Von Mises used the argument that private monopolies of large corporations were the result of protection and subsidies granted by governments. Therefore, they could be remedied only by reducing the scope of governments' intervention in the economy.

Whereas the early neo-liberals spent time thinking how to distinguish government interventions that are compatible with the operation of the price mechanism from those that are not, the policy thrust of von Mises' argument was the need to return to the 'night watchman' state. Many neo-liberals did not agree, so von Mises told his fellow members of the Mont Pelerin Society: 'You are all a bunch of Socialists!' (Cockett 1994: 114). Von Mises effectively set his face against any modernization of liberalism; he turned neo-liberalism into neo-conservatism.

'Neo-conservatism' is a term most familiar in the realm of foreign policy, connoting policies trying to reassert forms of global power exercised in the past. Neo-conservatism can also be distinguished from neo-liberalism in the economic policy field. The distinguishing characteristic of neo-conservative economic policy is its asymmetrical treatment of capital and labour. While the operations of capital are liberalized and legal protection is extended, the operations of labour are restricted and legal protections are reduced, for freedom of organization, reward bargaining, and cross border movement.

Although Hayek's fears were plausible in a time when Fascism and Communism were rampant, the situation that played out in postcolonial countries was somewhat different. After the rushed decolonizations of the 1960s by Britain and France, the political systems devised by the ex-colonists for the successor states quickly collapsed intro parodies of republicanism— one-party states with presidents for life and jails full of political prisoners.

Many took the Soviet side in the Cold War and adopted the Soviet techniques of economic management that Keynes had described, including a patina of economic planning. By the late 1960s 'the crisis of planning' in developing countries had become a source of comment and concern (Faber and Seers 1972; Stolper 1960; Streeten and Lipton 1968).

Applying welfare economics to international trade

In 1965, Sir John Hicks said of development economics that it is 'a practical subject that draws on any theory that is relevant to it (including sociological theory)'. He added 'if there is any branch of economic theory that is especially relevant to it, it is the theory of international trade' (Hicks 1965: 3–4). This characterization of development economics is important because it supports several of the theses of previous chapters: the need to supplement economics with sociology (Chapter 1); the difference between development economics and growth economics (Chapter 8); and the adverse effect on development of the experimental techniques of controlling international trade, as noted by Keynes (Chapter 5).

In 1967 the Organization for Economic Cooperation and Development (OECD) commissioned case studies of the trade regimes of seven large developing countries (Argentina, Brazil, India, Mexico, Pakistan, The Philippines, and Taiwan). In each case, the economy had been industrialized by protection against imports—using quantitative restrictions or high tariffs. The effects had been to raise the prices of industrial goods and restrict the markets for them. The OECD President claimed that in practice, but in a different form from the USSR, the rural populations have been made to bear the burden of financing industrialization (Little et al. 1970: xviii).

The consequences of this strategy were the same inefficiencies as Keynes had found in Bolshevik Russia—excessive rural–urban migration and urban unemployment; the depression of exports and foreign exchange rationing; growing inequalities of income and wealth; and rule by a small elite group. Calculations of the effective rate of protection (pioneered by Bella Balassa, Max Corden, and others) indicated that the scale of protectionism had been previously underestimated. Anne Krueger extended this critique by arguing that foreign exchange rationing by administrative methods created incentives for unproductive rent seeking and corruption (Krueger 1974). The OECD study covered half of the total population of developing countries and raised the question of how to cope with the inefficiencies that import-controlling trade regimes created.

The OECD had already had a first stab at answering that question when it produced its *Manual of Industrial Project Analysis* (Little and Mirrlees 1968).

This manual provided a method for recalculating the costs and benefits of industrial investments using, instead of actual prices, accounting prices intended to represent scarcities. Explaining why accounting prices were necessary for industrial project appraisal in developing countries, the manual set out a series of government policy practices that prevented actual prices from indicating the relative scarcity of goods and services. They included selective price controls in periods of inflation; long periods of exchange rate over-valuation, causing low demand for exports and rationing of imports; and payment by state-owned industrial enterprises of wages that were too high compared with rural wages and not justified by urban–rural productivity differentials. These instances of price distortion consequences of common policy practices in developing countries provided a catalogue of inefficiencies of their industrialization strategies.

Although much effort was devoted to the refinement and application of social cost–benefit analysis (SCBA) in the 1970s by economists like Partha Dasgupta, Deepak Lal, Ian Little, James Mirrless, David Newbery, Amartya Sen, and Nicholas Stern, the technique had an important practical limitation. Choosing to invest in projects with favourable cost–benefits ratios calculated at accounting prices rather than actual prices ran the risk that they would not return an actual financial surplus, but would require actual fiscal subsidies to meet loan repayments and other recurrent costs. Given that neo-liberals aimed to eliminate fiscal subsidies, the steam soon went out of the application of SCBA. By 1980, it was dawning on neo-liberals that the only good policy was to make actual prices correspond with scarcity prices: hence their slogan 'get the prices right!' (e.g. Lal 1983: 78). An additional problem with SCBA was that it was too complicated, time-consuming for developing country governments to apply to domestic and foreign investments alike; and that its data requirements and assumptions permit a multiplicity of answers that can be manipulated by politically powerful vested interests (Murelius 1981: 9, 13, 93). However, the opportunity to brush second-best welfare economies aside was almost at hand. By 1980, intellectual counter-revolution had gained political power.

The political opportunity of neo-conservatism

Margaret Thatcher was the first of four leaders of conservative parties to gain national political power. As a student at Oxford University in 1945, she read Hayek's *Road to Serfdom*, finding it an impressive anti-socialist tract. In June of that year, Winston Churchill said in an election broadcast that a socialist government would be obliged to fall back on some kind of Gestapo to survive. The Labour Party leader (Clement Attlee) next day simply dismissed 'this theoretical stuff . . . a second hand version of the academic views of an Austrian professor' and went on to win by a landslide (Toye 2013: 199–210). This incident shows why Hayek had so little political traction in Britain. Austrian economics, along with Friedman's monetarism and the Virginia School of public choice, was an import and out of tune with the ad hoc empiricist character of British public life (Desai 1994: 41). As Thatcher pursued her political career for the next three decades after Keynes died in 1946, economic policy was based on an allegedly 'Keynesian' consensus of discretionary counter-cyclical fiscal stimulus. This policy was blamed for causing accelerating inflation and the increasing unruliness of trades unions that plagued Edward Heath's administration 1970–3. In 1974, Hayek was a co-winner of the Nobel Prize for economics and his *Constitution of Liberty* (1960) was recommended to Thatcher by Sir Keith Joseph, who seemed set to succeed Heath as leader of the Conservative Party. In the event, it was Thatcher who supplanted Heath and won the 1979 general election. Her first action was to abolish the foreign exchange controls. This move opened the floodgates to globalization. Capital was now freed to mate with very cheap labour abroad.

Once this had occurred, it was predictable that capitalists in other developed countries would seek similar liberty to move their capital to low-wage economies, manufacture abroad, and export the product worldwide. It was also predictable that the governments of developing countries would begin to compete for foreign direct investment and would do so by lowering tax rates and adopting business-friendly economic policies. The results were the outsourcing of production from developed countries, the stagnation of industrial wages, and productivity. In developing countries, the result was a reversal of economic nationalist policies and a fiscal race to the bottom.

In January 1981, Ronald Reagan took up office as President of the United States. Though sharing Thatcher's conservative instincts, he was not interested in complex ideas. He had difficulty in securing the Republican presidential nomination in 1976 because people had doubts about his economic programme which had three main planks—all old American political favourites—more defence spending, tax cuts, and balanced budget. This was seen as an 'impossible trinity'. Reagan was elected president in 1980 all the same (Brogan 2001: 686).

The analytical tool that was supposed to be able to make Reagan's three economic policy aims consistent was Arthur Laffer's famous diagram relating the average tax rate to tax revenue in a reverse 'C' curve. In the lower half of the diagram, revenue rises with increases in the average rate, but past the inflection point, revenue decreases. If the tax rate is already in the upper half, reduction in the rate will increase revenue through its impact in increasing productivity. At the end of the 1970s, conservative parties in the USA and UK were being urged to reduce tax rates *before* achieving public expenditure cuts

(Wanniski 1978: 16). Alas, poor Laffer! The examples of successful descent of the Laffer curve derive from the ending of wars when reduction of defence spending permits the reduction of prohibitive taxation, and the Laffer effect was too weak empirically to neutralize the expansion of defence spending that was part of Reagan's Cold War strategy. The only way to square that with a balanced budget was to slash non-defence public spending, such as farm subsidies and social security programmes (Stockman 1987: 10–11). They were never on Reagan's agenda.

The final North–South dialogue

The first signs of this change were evident in the reception accorded to the Brandt Report. Willy Brandt, the former Chancellor of West Germany, was invited to head an Independent Commission on International Development Issues. The commission's report, *North–South: A Program for Survival*, was published in February 1980. It was a brave attempt to reenergize the North–South dialogue and to create a consensus on desirable future policies to support global economic development.

Basing himself on the premise of humankind increasingly becoming a single community, the report argued a moral case for wealthy nations shouldering additional responsibilities for alleviating poverty in poor countries. It also argued that from a national perspective to do so would be a matter of self-interest for all, given the dangers of war, poverty, famine, and the exhaustion of resources. The report endorsed the setting up of the Common Fund and called for the swift conclusion of the series of ICAs envisaged at the United Nations Conference on Trade and Development (UNCTAD) V in Manila. On development finance, the report advocated increased transfer of resources to the South, in line with UNCTAD's call for a supplementary finance mechanism. The transfer would be financed by automatic long-term bilateral aid flows and by taxes imposed on the international arms trade and channelled through a new World Development Fund with international membership. The Brandt proposals were well received in the UN General Assembly, but elsewhere there was much less interest and support.

To the Brandt report's proposals, the new conservative leaders were resolutely opposed. Using the most damning description in the new vocabulary of economic liberalism, Brandt was denounced as a purveyor of 'global Keynesianism'. Inflation, not unemployment, was the new public enemy number one, and Western governments were alarmed by the prospective inflationary consequences of the Brandt policies. They thought that the forces of inflation were already dangerously strong and feared that pumping more liquidity into the world economy would only strengthen them further.

Brandt recognized that the report had come at a time when the governments of the industrial countries were deeply anxious about the advent of an
economic recession in the wake of the second oil price shock of 1979. He
thought that the chances of agreement on his proposals would be improved if
they were not discussed in a full-scale international conference, but in a
smaller summit meeting of the leaders of twenty-two countries.

The G-77, being open to all developing countries, was generally unenthusi-
astic about selective participation meetings such as the Conference on International Economic Cooperation (CIEC). Nevertheless, President Lopez Portillo
of Mexico offered to hold informal and unstructured seminar-type discussions
in Cancun for twenty-two leaders, in an attempt to overcome the stalemate in
the North–South dialogue. Margaret Thatcher persuaded Ronald Reagan to
accompany her to the Cancun summit meeting in October 1981. He was
willing to do so once the host assured him that no substantive decisions
would be taken, and that Cuba would not be invited. Mrs Thatcher later
explained their attendance as follows:

> I felt that, whatever our misgivings about the occasion, we should be present, both
> to argue for our positions and to forestall criticism that we were uninterested in the
> developing world. The whole concept of 'North-South' dialogue, which the Brandt
> Commission had made the fashionable talk of the international community, was
> in my view wrong-headed.   (Thatcher 2013)

Thatcher and Reagan went through the motions of expressing concern
about poverty and hunger, but their objective was to resist what they claimed
was pressure to place the International Monetary Fund (IMF) and the World
Bank directly under United Nations control. Other heads of government were
bewildered by this obsession with the 'integrity' of the IMF and the World
Bank, because the Brandt proposal for a World Development Fund was not
meant to replace the Bretton Woods institutions but to supplement them.
Thatcher's riposte was revealing. 'In the end I put the point more bluntly:
I said that there was no way that I was going to put British deposits into a bank
which was totally run by those on overdrafts' (Thatcher 2013: 170).

Structural adjustment and policy-conditioned loans

The Mexican debt repayment moratorium (August 1982) was followed
by similar actions by Argentina, Brazil, Venezuela, and others. This made
New York and London banks (their creditors) very vulnerable and constrained
the World Bank and the IMF to represent the crisis as one of liquidity rather
than solvency. The remedy was thus said to be not debt relief, but restarting
bank lending, and the role of the IMF was to be giver of a 'seal of approval' to

those countries that had adopted 'sensible economic policies' as dictated by supply-side economists (e.g. privatization of state enterprises, trade liberalization, and improving the efficiency of capital markets).

The absence of sensible economic policies in developing countries was only one half of the explanation of the 1980s debt crisis. The ideologically driven and inexperienced economic policies of the new conservative governments in the West were the missing other half of the explanation. Nevertheless, in terms of realpolitik, it was the creditor countries that now held the whip hand. They could impose their partial view of why the debt crisis had happened.

For its first thirty years, the major lending vehicle of the World Bank had been the project loan, supported by technical assistance in formulating and executing development projects. In the 1970s the bank came to the conclusion that the success of their loan projects, measured by their *ex post* rates of return, was being reduced because of a deterioration in the broader economic environment in which they had to operate. Negative trends in the environment included rising oil prices, high inflation, inflexible exchange rates, and import restrictions. In order to address this syndrome, the bank devised a new form of lending called programme lending, in which the vehicle for the loan was not a physical project like a dam or a power station but a programme of economic policy changes to be implemented by the borrower.

At UNCTAD V in Manila (1979), the President of the World Bank, Robert McNamara, announced the launch of this new form of lending, known as structural adjustment loans or sector adjustment loans. These would provide rapidly disbursing foreign exchange on condition that changes in economic policy were made. By the mid-1980s, programme lending—once described by a World Bank president as 'fuzzy loans'—had risen to account for one-third of the bank's new lending. They became the bank's instrument for dealing with the debt crisis, providing rapid disbursement of funds but requiring the privatization of state-owned industries, the ending of state industrial subsidies, the removal of price controls, and the dismantling of restrictions on foreign trade. The application of conditionality was never uniform, but there was an underlying template of economic reforms encapsulated in what John Williamson dubbed 'the Washington Consensus'. In that sense, structural adjustment did have a 'one size fits all' aspect to it.

The search for success stories achieved by this policy template led neo-liberals to celebrate the newly industrializing countries of Asia as examples of the faster growth and improved income distribution that economic liberalization generated. When closer inspection revealed evidence of residual government interventions in trade, industry, and finance, these were dismissed as ineffective or counterproductive, to avoid diluting the purity of the neo-liberal message (Little et al. 1987).

When the World Bank launched its structural adjustment loans in 1979, the senior staff members of the IMF were struggling with the balance of payment problems of developing countries that did not produce or export oil. Given the higher oil prices were likely to be a permanent shock, they needed to adjust to it. In their search for effective methods of adjustment, the staffers investigated supply-side economics as a supplement to their existing adjustment requirements. At this stage, the Reagan administration was more concerned to prevent IMF mission creep and reacted very cautiously to the report.

The cautious approach was dropped during Reagan's second administration. Under the Baker Plan 1985, the microeconomic reforms were to be added to the IMF's traditional macroeconomic adjustment conditions (Kentikelenis and Babb, forthcoming).

The Baker Plan undoubtedly legitimated an expansion of the IMF's responsibilities into the propagation of neo-conservative economics, but it failed to resolve the debt crisis, or ease the implementation of structural adjustment loan conditionality. Growth-oriented adjustment—the justification for expanding the scope of IMF conditionality—turned out to have a very weak impact on actual economic growth. It was estimated econometrically at around an additional one per cent of gross national product (Mosley et al. 1991: I). The debt crisis lingered on until the Brady Plan of 1989 bailed out the private creditor of Latin American countries and the highly indebted poor countries (HIPC) initiatives bailed out the public creditors of sub-Saharan African governments.

The very weak growth effect of structural adjustment loans in the 1980s was due to failure of implementation. Structural reforms are more complex and of more indefinite duration than the macroeconomic conditionality to which the IMF was accustomed, which was simple and strictly quantitative. However, the design of the reform package paid little attention to the problem of reform sequencing and the logic of critical path analysis (Toye 1999, Bliss 2007). In addition, the expansion of the IMF into structural conditionality gave a second agency responsibility for implementation—the IMF now operated alongside the World Bank. This duplication created an opportunity for developing countries to game the system. They could borrow from one agency, renege on its policy conditions, be struck off the eligible list—then borrow from the other agency. Even the introduction of World Bank–IMF cross-conditionality did not entirely solve the coordination problem. The World Bank and IMF could still differ about which countries were creditworthy—as happened over Argentina in 1988 (Boughton 2001). Despite the 1988 World Bank–IMF concordat, disagreements over appropriate reforms were still lively over the Asian financial crisis of 1997–8.

However much controversy structural adjustment lending caused, it is not obvious that it was the only, or even the most effective, method of propagating neo-conservative economic policies in developing countries. The policy-based loans of the World Bank and the IMF gave out an ambiguous signal to entrepreneurs who needed to be convinced to shift their investments from import-substitution activities to export expansion. The sight of policy makers who had previously opposed trade liberalization now embracing it could be reassuring. If such people could change their ways, the toughest opposition had finally been overcome. On the other hand, their *volte face* could be seen as having been bought by the money of foreign creditors. In that case, what would restrain the policy makers from reverting to the old unreformed regime when the World Bank and the IMF retired from the scene (Rodrik 1989: 7)?

The underlying cause was more diffuse and indirect. The world economy was being made more interdependent as neo-conservatives abolished exchange controls and other restrictions on the export and import of capital, improving the prospects for developing countries wishing to attract foreign direct investment. This brought to the fore issues of policy credibility and consistency and how to establish an attractive reputation in a globalizing world. It was not the case that every developing country wanted to stick with a protectionist trade regime. In the 1960s and 1970s at least twenty-two national attempts were made to liberalize trade but, of these, sixteen were reversed within five years. The problem was that governments were unable to make a credible commitment to a liberal regime. This gave an incentive to importers to import in advance of demand and hoard the excess stock. When the next balance of payments crisis struck and the liberal regime was reversed, importers were able to unload their excess stock at exorbitant prices (Michaely et al. 1991, but see also Greenaway 1993). Changes in global trade rules also played their part. Until the start of the General Agreement on Tariffs and Trade (GATT) Uruguay Round in September 1986, developing countries that were former colonies had the status of de facto contracting parties to the GATT, but this was removed from them before the start of the round.

Participation in the new negotiating round was restricted to *de jure* contracting parties, plus countries that committed to becoming *de jure* contracting parties. This put pressure on developing countries to apply for GATT membership, although they had previously rejected GATT as being 'a rich man's club'. Ten were admitted in 1993 and a further nine in 1994. The price of admission was to accept GATT disciplines, which became more stringent with the advent of the World Trade Organization in 1995. After 1986, more and more developing countries set off on the path of liberalizing their trade regimes and their resistance to other neo-conservative policy reforms crumbled. It is a striking fact that 'the most effective institution over the past half century—judged by world economic performance—was the GATT which was not even an international organization' (Krueger 1998: 2017—see also 1983, n. 2).

In 1989, one commentator was able to say: 'the developing world is at present experiencing a wave of trade reform as has never been seen before' (Rodrik 1989:1). An unprecedented wave of privatization was on the horizon, but arrived in full flood only in the 1990s. In that decade privatization revenues totalled US$250 billion in developing countries. Most of the privatizations occurred in Latin America, where foreign investors bought often undervalued assets from telecommunications and power utilities. By contrast, sub-Saharan Africa accounted for only three per cent of developing country privatization proceeds in the 1990s. Overall, the value-added contribution by state-owned enterprise declined as a share of gross domestic product (Parker and Kirkpatrick 2005: 514–15). It fell from 16 per cent in 1980 to 8 per cent in 1996 (Megginson and Netter 2001).

Homo economicus?

By the twenty-first century fundamental questions were being raised about the nature of economic man. While the economics of happiness probed further into people's evaluations of their mental states and found that after a certain threshold, happiness did not increase with increasing income, some behavioural economists devised experiments to test whether people do actually maximize their self-interest. Simple scenarios were set up in which people were given the opportunity to act as self-interested individuals and be financially rewarded for it. Early results indicated that a significant proportion of the participants in these experiments deviated from the behaviour of 'economic man' (which should be 'economic person'), and did so moved by some notion of fairness.

These results were criticized on various grounds. The subjects tended to be North American college students, so not representative of the general population. The contexts of the experiments were highly artificial, and not necessarily representative of motivation in everyday economic exchanges. Participants did not always understand the experimenters' explanation of the rules to be followed . . . and so on. Yet as the experiments were repeated in various contexts, including in developing countries, the results showed a consistency that increased their credibility.

It is easy, however, to misinterpret their significance. Not many economists believed that economic person was a complete description of human beings, or thought that the world was entirely bereft of altruism and public spiritedness. Certainly Alfred Marshall and Leon Walras did not (Pearson 2004: 30–2, 34–7). Most thought of the economic person as a fruitful assumption to make when explaining the everyday processes of economic exchange. It started as an hypothesis, but became a dogma.

Moreover, it is little use to know that people behave irrationally unless there is something predictable about their irrationality. The uncovering of the regularities in irrational behaviour is the achievement of Daniel Kahneman and his collaborator Amos Tversky (Kahneman 2011). They have catalogued many distinct cognitive biases that produce irrational economic behaviour. Their findings include loss aversion—the preference for avoiding a loss over making a gain of an equal amount—and systematic errors in understanding probability and risk. Some of these cognitive biases are subject to manipulation, either to reinforce them or to counteract them, and such manipulations can be useful instruments for aiding development.

Fragmentation

In the twenty-first century we came to the end of the grand narratives of economic development that have been a part of intellectual discourse for the past two hundred and fifty years. What is the reason for this? The break-up of political consensus in favour of globalization is significant, but only part of the explanation. In democracies waves of populism and isolationism, such as the UK's vote to leave the EU and Donald Trump's US election victory come—but also go. Isolationism did not survive Pearl Harbor and McCarthyism did not outlast Senator McCarthy.

No less important than political swings are changing beliefs about how ideas should be translated into practical action. In this regard, there has been a recent revolution in favour of the method of randomized control trials (RCTs). Spurred by the idea that poor people's cognitive biases are a cause of their poverty, Prabhajit Bahnerjee and Esther Duflo published their book *Poor Economics* in 2011. Its title is ambiguous. It can be read both as a rebuke to previous analyses of poverty that proclaimed the economic rationality of poor people and also as an announcement of a new approach based on the contrary premise. The secret of how to reduce poverty is finding ways to correct the cognitive biases of the poor. And the secret of doing that is the persistent application of the RCT method. This perspective thus transforms the nature of development research. The focus shifts from socioeconomic development to poverty reduction. The questions that researchers pose become narrower, more precise, and more small-scaled. Questions like 'Does foreign aid promote economic growth?' are superseded by others such as 'Do specially timed subsidies in district X of a country increase the application rates of fertilizer?'

Development researchers have set themselves up to follow a medical research paradigm while, unlike the big pharmaceutical companies, often lacking the time and resources needed to apply it on a sufficiently large scale. The results are fragmentary—signposts to successful tactics for development in particular places, times, and circumstances. Repeated studies providing what Kaushik Basu has called 'circumstantial causality' cannot be fitted together to provide a grand narrative (Basu 2014: 456).

The past forty years of counter-revolution in development thinking has made it clearer than ever that this is a practical subject with a magpie's approach to social and economic theories. If anything, it has tied the knot to policymaking even tighter by enthusiasts for the RCT method. The special relevance of international trade was emphasized by the repeated attempt to prove that trade liberalization is a cause of economic growth. Looking to the future, admittedly a thankless task, a plausible prediction is the end of grand narratives of development, including the narratives of neo-conservatism, in favour of small stories of 'what works'. It will not be the end of history but it will be the end of a certain venerable strand of the history of political economy.

References

Banerjee, A. V., and Duflo, E. (2011). *Poor Economics: Barefoot Hedge-Fund Managers, DIY Doctors and the Surprising Truth about Life on Less than $1 a Day*. London: Penguin Books.

Basu, K. (2014). Randomisation, causality and the role of reasoned intuition. *Oxford Development Studies* 42, 473–87.

Bliss, C. (2007). *Trade, Growth and Inequality*. Oxford: Oxford University Press.

Boughton, J. (2001). *Silent Revolution: The International Monetary Fund, 1979–1989*. Washington, DC: International Monetary Fund.

Brogan, H. (2001). *The Penguin History of the U.S.A.* London: Penguin Books.

Cockett, R. (1994). *Thinking the Unthinkable: Think- tanks and the Economic Counter-revolution 1931–1983*. London: Harper Collins.

Desai, R. (1994). Second-hand dealers in ideas: think-tanks and Thatcherite hegemony. *New Left Review* 203, 27–64.

Faber, M. L. O., and Seers, D. (1972). *The Crisis in Planning*. London: Chatto & Windus for Sussex University Press.

Greenaway, D. (1993). Liberalising foreign trade through rose-tinted glasses. *The Economic Journal* 103, 208–57.

Hayek, F. (1944). *The Road to Serfdom*. London: Routledge & Kegan Paul.

Hayek, F. (1960). *The Constitution of Liberty*. London: Routledge & Kegan Paul.

Hicks, J. (1965). *Capital and Growth*. Oxford: Oxford University Press.

Independent Commission on International Development Issues. (1980). *North-South: A Program for Survival*. Cambridge, MA: MIT Press.

Jackson, B. (2010). At the origins of neoliberalism: the free economy and the strong state, 1930–1947. *The Historical Journal* 53, 129–51.

Kahneman, D. (2011). *Thinking, Fast and Slow*. London: Allen Lane.

Kentikelenis, A. E., and Babb, S. L. (Forthcoming). Institutional transformation in the world polity: the rise of structural adjustment at the International Monetary Fund. *American Journal of Sociology*.

Krueger, A. O. (1974). The political economy of the rent-seeking society. *American Economic Review* 64, 291–303.

Krueger, A. O. (1998). Whither the World Bank and the IMF. *Journal of Economic Literature* 36, 1983–2020.

Lal, D. (1983). *The Poverty of Development Economics*. London: Institute of Economic Affairs.

Little, I., and Scitovsky, T., and Scott, M. F. (1970). *Industry and Trade in Some Developing Countries*. London: Oxford University Press.

Little, I. M. D., Mazumdar, D., and Page, J. M. (1987). *Small Manufacturing Enterprises: A Comparative Study of India and Other Economies*. Oxford: Oxford University Press.

Little, I. M. D., and Mirrlees, J. A. (1968). *Manual of Industrial Project Analysis*, Vol. 2. Paris: OECD.

Megginson, W., and Netter, J. (2001). From state to market: a survey of empirical studies on privatization. *Journal of Economic Literature* 39, 321–89.

Michaely, M., Papageorgiou, D., and Choksi, A. M. (1991). *Liberalizing Foreign Trade: Lessons of Experience in the Developing World*, Vol. 7. Oxford: Basil Blackwell.

Mosley, P., Harrigan, J., and Toye, J. (1991). *Aid and Power: The World Bank and Policy-Based Lending*, Vol. 1. London: Routledge.

Murelius, O. (1981). *Institutional Approach to Project Analysis in Developing Countries*. Paris: OECD.

Parker, D., and Kirkpatrick, C. (2005). Privatisation in developing countries: a review of the evidence and the policy lessons. *Journal of Development Studies* 41, 513–41.

Pearson, H. (2004). Economics and altruism at the Fin de Siecle, in M. Daunton and F. Trentmann, eds, *Worlds of Political Economy: Knowledge and Power in the Nineteenth and Twentieth Centuries*, pp. 24–46. Basingstoke: Palgrave Macmillan.

Rodrik, D. (1989). The credibility of trade reform: a policy maker's guide. *The World Economy* 12, 1–16.

Schumacher, E. F. (1973). *Small is Beautiful: A Study of Economics as if People Mattered*. London: Blond & Briggs.

Stockman, D. A. (1987). *The Triumph of Politics*. London: Coronet Books, Hodder and Stoughton.

Stolper, W. (1960). *Planning without Facts: Lessons in Resource Allocation from Nigeria's Development*. Cambridge, MA: Harvard University Press.

Streeten, P., and Lipton, M. (1968). *The Crisis of Indian Planning: Economic Planning in The 1960s*. London: Oxford University Press.

Thatcher, M. (2013). *Margaret Thatcher: The Autobiography*. London: Harper Press.

Toye, J. (1999). The sequencing of structural adjustment. Mimeo.

Toye, R. (2013). *The Roar of the Lion: The Untold Story of Churchill's World War II Speeches*. Oxford: Oxford University Press.

von Mises, L. (1936/1920). *Socialism*. London: Jonathan Cape.

Wanniski, J. (1978). Taxes, revenues and the Laffer curve. *Public Interest* 50, 3–16.

Wood, B. (1984). *Alias Papa: A Life of Fritz Schumacher*. London: Jonathan Cape.

Index

Printed and bound by CPI Group (UK) Ltd, Croydon, CR0 4YY